Wines, Beers, and Spirits

Wines, Beers, and Spirits

A Consumer's Sourcebook

Dean Tudor

1985

Libraries Unlimited • Littleton, Colorado

LIBRARIES UNLIMITED, INC.
P.O. Box 263
Littleton, Colorado 80160-0263

3636

Library of Congress Cataloging in Publication Data

Tudor, Dean.
    Wines, beers, and spirits.

    Includes index.
    1. Wine and wine making--Bibliography. 2. Alcoholic beverages--Bibliography. I. Title.
Z7951.T83   1985 [TP548]   016.6412'1   85-5223
ISBN 0-87287-455-9

Libraries Unlimited books are bound with Type II nonwoven material that meets and exceeds National Association of State Textbook Administrators' Type II nonwoven material specifications Class A through E.

Table of Contents

Preface

With over 900 entries, this annotated source guide to information about the wines, beers, and spirits of the world presents carefully written evaluations of books, periodicals, associations and similar trade groups, nonprint materials, museums, and libraries. It is the only current comprehensive guide yet produced for the fast-growing interest in this topic, and it builds on my earlier book, *Wine, Beer and Spirits* (Libraries Unlimited, 1975) with about 95 percent new materials. In addition to the more important reference and general sources, this source guide also covers the geographic distribution, the history, the trade, the techniques, and the evaluative tools used to judge the different styles of wines. There are separate chapters for consumer guides, for cooking with alcoholic beverages, for beers and for spirits, and for the amateur wine maker and home brewer. The text concludes with critical listings of other sources of data, such as regional guides and tourist information, wine charts and ratings, courses and seminars, computer software, games and kits, and secondhand bookstores. A comprehensive author-title-association index provides access to the annotations of each entry described in this all-in-one source guide.

The audience to which this source guide is directed is twofold: the library and its patrons. For the library, this source guide should prove to be an excellent buying guide to the better sources of information in the area of wines, beers, and spirits. For the patrons, it should point the way through the subject literatures, enabling them to find quickly the most appropriate and timely resource tool that answers their need for relevant information. For the library, the guide can pinpoint the most logical source for requested data, while for patrons, the source guide presents informed opinion about which sources to buy for home use or as gifts, especially for those patrons on a tight budget. Thus, for both audiences, this source guide is at once both a buying guide and a subject analysis guide.

This source guide is selective in that only the better and more worthy, less duplicative materials have been chosen for evaluation. Some sources are important simply because they embrace so much more data, are more up-to-date (or are frequently revised), are authoritative and objective in their presentation, are heavily used by experts, and are readily available for purchase. The most important of these books and serials have been starred, and are recommended as a "first look" or as a "first buy." All sources are in print except for maybe a half dozen classics, and all prices are current to the Fall of 1984.

   In certain rare instances, books in foreign languages were chosen because there was nothing comparable in English. This applies especially to written materials about a particular wine region. In those cases, foreign prices have been cited, and these are current in the country of origin. These materials can be ordered through the larger bookstores as any English-language book can be ordered, but the waiting time for their arrival can exceed six months. As editor of a wine publication (*The Grapevine,* for the Toronto Chapter of the International Wine and Food Society), and as owner of my own wine and food consulting firm, I use foreign language materials constantly. Many have reference value and are easily handled with the aid of a translation dictionary, particularly if the information required is only a date, a statistic, an address, a map, or a correct spelling.

   When looking for reading materials on wines, beers, and spirits (either to update this source guide or to search on your own within the indexes or bibliographies mentioned in this source guide), you should keep in mind "library" and "index" forms of subject descriptors. For example, when searching for data about *wine*, you will usually find general material under the heading WINE AND WINE-MAKING, with a geographic breakdown. So information about California wines may be found under WINE AND WINEMAKING—U.S. Data about home wine making can normally be found under WINE AND WINEMAKING—AMATEUR. More specific materials can be found under the name of a country or region, such as BORDEAUX, BURGUNDY, CHAMPAGNE, CHIANTI WINE, CLARET, MADEIRA WINE, MOSELLE WINE, PORT WINE, SAUTERNES, SHERRY, and so forth. Other entries to consider include APERITIFS, FRUIT WINES, HOCK (WINE), and SPARKLING WINES. Terms that will be useful include COOKERY (WINES), GRAPES, VITICULTURE, and the headings WINE IN ART, WINE IN LITERATURE, and WINE IN MUSIC. The "great" wines will have entries under their own names, e.g., CLOS DE VOUGEOT, CHATEAU LATOUR, or BAROLO. For *beers*, appropriate headings are ALE, BREWERIES, CIDER, LAGER, MALT LIQUOR, and PERRY, with additional references under COOKERY (BEER) and MALT or BARLEY. Names are not that important, and it is rare to find anything under such terms as "Pilsner" or "Steam Beer." For *spirits*, general material usually appears under the heading LIQUORS, while more specific data can be located under the type or category of spirit, such as BRANDY, COCKTAILS, GIN, LIQUEURS, RUM, VODKA, WHISKY (BOURBON), WHISKY (CANADIAN), WHISKY (SCOTCH), or WHISKEY (IRISH). Additional material can be found under such terms as DRINKING IN LITERATURE, and HOTELS, TAVERNS, ETC. Specific names are useful, such as COGNAC, ARMAGNAC, BOURBON, and so forth. *Technical data* will be found under such terms as BREWING, DISTILLATION, and FERMENTATION, as well as associated terms for yeast and alcohol conversions.

   This source guide is arranged to flow logically from the general to the specific. The table of contents outlines the scope of wines, beers, and spirits, as found in books, periodicals, audio-visual sources, contacts, and associations, and covers history, trade, techniques, descriptions, evaluations, and related topics. As mentioned above, the more important sources have been asterisked; these tools should be looked at first since they are more comprehensive, more reliable, and more up-to-date than the others. Since the publication of my earlier book, *Wine, Beer and Spirits,* there have been so many changes that 95 percent of the older book had to be discarded.

Introduction

I think wine is to be drunk and nothing aggravates me more than people that collect wine for collecting reasons. The chic thing is not just owning a rare bottle, but to have owned it and have drunk it. You are one up on everyone.

—Eric de Rothschild, Château Lafite-Rothschild
(as quoted in *Wines and Vines,* February 1984, p. 8)

Throughout history man has been attracted to alcoholic beverages for far more reasons than just consumption. To many, wine making is an economic necessity: a job. More than one-fifth of all the agricultural workers in the world depend on the grape. Beer, the easiest alcoholic beverage to make, is vitally needed in areas where the water is usually not safe to drink. And among the other uses of spirits, the results from the discovery of distillation have assuaged more hot tempers than they have created. That many troubles of the world can be attributed to alcoholic beverages cannot be denied. Nevertheless, the benefits can outweigh the negative factors. Prestigious Champagne is thought of as being symbolic of the good life to which we all aspire; the Christian faith equates (or very nearly equates, depending on the sect) red wine with blood. The first French Republic even named a month for the harvest season: Vendémaire. And where would we be without our stockbroker; the word's root is derived from the French *broquier*— a man who tapped or broke a cask to draw wine (he was the only one allowed to do so, for he was the guarantor of the quality demanded by both merchants and growers).

Obviously, this source book stresses the positive benefits of alcoholic consumption. There is nothing here on "alcoholism" or social diseases. The appreciation of wines, beers, and spirits goes beyond knowledge of bottle contents and consumption. These just make up the tip of the prodigious iceberg. An evaluation of alcohol appreciation reveals that it can be a full-time study—and alcohol appreciation contains all the components of a demanding leisure-time activity.

The possibilities are limitless. The cultivation of a personal vineyard can take up all of one's waking hours. Making wines, beers, or liqueurs at home can give immense creative satisfaction. Touring manufacturing plants, châteaux, vineyards, and quiet little towns in search of romatic lore makes a perfect holiday and good travelling both at home and abroad. Building a wine cellar or a wine closet in the home is a constructive task for those who like to work with their hands. The traditional "crafts and collecting" aspects of hobbies are exemplified in the collecting of old bottles or soaked-off wine labels, buying precious stemware and other drinking vessels (or making them from cast-off bottles), collecting toasts, and acquiring beer mats, menus, matches, and serviettes. Laying down a personal wine cellar takes time and money, as well as expertise. Tastings—either with a single wine lover at home, at the vineyard, or with special friends at parties—provide a festive element to the hobby. This leads naturally to cooking with alcoholic beverages, and to entertaining at home, and perhaps to forming a club or society for affiliation with a larger, internationally organized group such as the International Wine and Food Society, headquartered in London, England.

For those of a scholarly bent, there is, of course, just the simple reading of books and articles, perhaps with the possibility of starting one's own library. The historical excursions are endless, and can be supplemented by many locally offered courses through a community college or from an extension department. These are offered in the areas of home entertainment, wining and dining, cookery, wine appreciation, and amateur wine or beer making.

And last, but not least, for those who already have a large interest in the fine arts (e.g., photography, painting, music), there is the possibility of making alcoholic beverages the main theme—tavern drinking songs, a painting of food and wine, or photographs of an Alsatian vineyard.

This sourcebook covers all these and more. It points the way to the best print and nonprint materials covering any themes on wines, beers, and spirits. If you are serious enough to want to learn about these forms of alcoholic beverages, then you should begin by examining and reading the books with asterisks (these are the important ones), subscribing to a few magazines (also with asterisks), and joining a few clubs. This will get you started. Shelf knowledge will tell you what to look for; self-knowledge involves tasting, tasting, tasting, and even more tasting....

That wine, beer, and spirit manufacturers are enjoying their best years cannot be disputed. The public demand for lighter drinks means that a more efficient, higher proofing distillation process can be used, so that spirits can be quickly and cheaply produced in greater quantities. Advances in brewing have produced an acceptable draft-in-the-bottle substitute for those drinkers who prefer an unpasteurized taste. Ale is being brewed once again in the United States; micro-breweries are springing up, with limited runs of beer that is naturally fermented in the bottles. There has been an absolutely phenomenal growth of interest in wine during the past ten years. Domestic wines have dramatically improved, with the greater use of French-type varietals in the blend. The need for white wine, while detrimental to red wine sales, has been an impetus to increased wine consumption and total wine sales overall.

Within the 1962-1982 period, the consumption of wine in the United States quadrupled. (All figures and percentages are derived from the "Annual Statistics Survey" in *Wines and Vines* magazine; this survey is published in each year's July issue, and it covers imports, exports, grapes, country-by-country comparisons, currently and retrospectively, and so forth.) The increase in consumption of spirits during that time rose slightly, levelled off, then dropped, with a pronounced emphasis on the extremes of both lightness (white spirits) and heaviness (cream-based liqueurs). *USA Today* reported on August 20, 1984, that liquor consumption in the United States had dropped 11.6 percent between 1973 and 1983, quoting a report by the Distilled Spirits Council of the United States, Inc. The overall consumption of beer has also decreased, with a declining market for domestic beers (in 1983, the top six breweries controlled 92 percent of American beer production). Interestingly enough, there is now a rising market for imported beer, a "status symbol" like sparkling mineral waters.

In 1982, foreign wines with a value of $781 million were shipped into the United States; this represented about 15 percent of the total wine consumption dollar in the U.S. The value of U.S. wine exports was $38 million. This meant that the trade deficit in wine was $743 million, more than 2 percent of the total American trade deficit. Put another way, 26 percent of the 168 million cases (and equivalents) sold in the United States were foreign imports. In 1973, while I was compiling the earlier version of this book, the figure was 19 percent. Yet most of these imports are virtually needless, for the American domestic industry can quite easily accommodate the "taste" involved; the top ten imports have two-thirds of the total import market, and six of these are Italian (Riunite, Folonari, Zonin). Italian Lambrusco alone led the pack with over 11 million cases sold—more than one-quarter of the total imports. The other top imports are sweet whites and rosés from Spain, Portugal, and Germany.

Domestically, though, things have never appeared brighter. About 90 percent of all American wines produced are from California (principally through E & J Gallo, United Vintners, Almaden, and Heublein), for that state leads in production of volume, types of wine, and quality. At the end of 1983, there were 1,039 bonded wineries in the United States. Of this total, 576 are in California (this figure was 470 in 1980, out of 822 total, and 240 in 1970, out of 435 total). Most such wineries are "boutiques" offering limited bottlings of the great grape varieties at high prices (but this is warranted in terms of the labor, capital, and small production). In 1983, New York had 74 wineries, Ohio 41, Oregon 39, Pennsylvania 35, and Washington 32. The remainder were sprinkled throughout most of the other states.

Needless to say, many urgent problems have resulted from the increased demand for a limited supply of good wine. Two of these have been time and money. It takes time to develop the vine cuttings (at least five to eight years before decent varietal grapes can be crushed), time to make wine (about a year for whites, three years for reds), and time for correct bottle aging to catch a wine at its peak (this may be one to twenty years). Can anyone really afford the layout of capital, for a minimum of ten years, to produce a good wine, from vine cutting to consumption? What about those 100 million or more bottles of Champagne in cave storage in France? And an even larger number in Spain? Already we have seen the lessening of the red Burgundy production and the subsequent worldwide drive to less intensive vinification processes. The "futures" market opens the possibility of a Bordeaux Château selling off its wine while it is still in the barrel, and of course the Beaujolais vignerons are laughing all the way to the bank as their marketable six-week-old *primeur* sells out year after year (this "Beaujolais Nouveau" represents about 85 percent of that area's production). The quick production of white wines and cheap red wines actually shores up a winery's financial reserves so that it can hold onto the greater red wines for a longer period.

Still, with tariff barriers and different wine regulations around the world, the export of *vin ordinaire* from Europe has stalled. There has been a "wine lake" since 1982, with many wines in storage, or being dumped or converted to industrial alcohol. The E.E.C. has already held several emergency meetings over what to do with this so-called "lake." General wine consumption is down in Europe, but consumption of quality goods is up worldwide—quality wines, quality beers, and quality spirits (older rums, Cognacs, single malt Scotches, etc.). People are drinking less, but they have traded up to better quality; they are still spending the same amount of money as before, but they are now drinking the expensive goods (and fewer of them). At the other end of this spectrum, more people than ever before are making their own wines (for a buck a bottle) and beer (for a dime a bottle). All of this tends to drive up the prices of the good wines as the demand exceeds the supply.

Much of this is reflected in the writings about wines, beers, and spirits, whether in the form of a book or as a news item in a magazine or a consumer guide. Wine literature is very well organized, more so than the literature of beers and spirits. The quality of writing is quite high, especially as the literati have taken to producing many lines about wines. Perhaps beer does not appeal to them or to their literary palates. That there are so few materials on spirits is surprising, but perhaps this can be partially explained away by the fact that there is so little romanticism involved—there are no "vineyards" to visit, too many mechanical processes, and so few manufacturers compared to the numbers for wine; also, home production of it is illegal. It is difficult to get excited about something that one cannot produce or touch or see at work. Materials are exceptionally scarce on liqueurs, infusions, and bitters (particularly the latter), probably because of the secrecy of the recipes used to blend and produce them. The fact that spirits are less used in cooking is also a detriment.

Twenty years ago (in 1964), there was only one syndicated newspaper columnist in the United States writing regularly on wines and spirits; now there are several, and just about every newspaper has a weekly column on wines and drinking. John Arlott wrote in *Wine* (Oxford University Press, 1984, p. v): "The increasing publication over the past two decades of books on the subject in English indicates the growing interest—perhaps more self-conscious and literary than in the true wine countries, but nevertheless unmistakable—in traditionally beer and spirit drinking countries."

☐1 *General Reference Books*

This section includes notable *general* consultative sources, statistics, atlases, directories, dictionaries, and encyclopedias. Many of these works are indispensable for the wine enthusiast who wishes to acquire shelf knowledge. In my capacity as a wine writer in Canada, I use them all the time. There are other reference materials that deal solely with wines, tastings, home production, beers or spirits, and the technical and trade areas; these are annotated in their respective chapters. For further information about any kinds of wines, beers, or spirits materials, see the bibliographies listed in chapter 12, beginning on page 205.

1. Berberoglu, Hrayr. **The World of Wines, Spirits and Beers**. Dubuque, Ia.: Kendall/Hunt, 1984. 316p. illus. index. $19.95 paper.

Originally published in 1981 as *Mr. B's Booze Book*, this monograph serves as a general text for hospitality students in "beverage" programs offered at colleges, at universities, and through extension courses. It is not a book on mixology, but rather, a book that comprehensively covers just about all of the wines of the world. Two-thirds of the book deal with still table wines. There is a country-by-country breakdown of the various types of table wines, grapes grown, climatic conditions, and some line sketch maps. Most notable is the thorough section on Italy (perhaps a bit out of proportion in context with the rest of the fine wines of the world), and the specific details given for smaller countries such as Cyprus, Tunisia, Lebanon, New Zealand, Rumania, and the U.S.S.R.

The balance of the book (one-third) discusses aromatized wines (vermouths, bitters), distilled products of spirits, beers, cocktails (with some basic recipes), menus, merchandising of alcoholic products, and bar setups. The appendices contain lists of wine shippers and addresses for various associations. There is also a separate index to the principal grape varieties, allowing tracing of the development of, say, cabernet sauvignon vines throughout the world. The print is small, the book oversized, and the information displayed in two columns. There are no color illustrations, and the maps are sparse. Still, dollar for dollar, this book packs in a lot of detail and is certainly worth purchasing just on that basis alone.

2. Burroughs, David and Norman Bezzant. **Wine Regions of the World**. 2d ed. London: W. Heinemann, 1979; distr. by David & Charles. 313p. illus. maps. index. $14.50 paper.

This is a student's manual, meant for those taking the British Wine Trade examinations that lead to an M. W. appellation. It is a basic text that deals with the study of the vine, its cultivation, the making of wines and spirits, the production of table wines and sparkling wines, fortified wines, liqueurs, beers, ciders, and cocktails. There are many maps, diagrams, and drawings to illustrate the commentaries. What makes this a good book for just about anybody to use to learn the wine business are the running question-and-answer footnotes that test one's skills. The book was published for the Wine and Spirit Education Trust (U.K.).

3.* Doxat, John. **The Indispensable Drinks Book**. New York: Van Nostrand Reinhold, 1981. 224p. illus. bibliog. index. $25.

Doxat's book was conceived, edited, and designed in England; hence, there is a distinct British orientation. The team of five experts covered all types of beverages: not just wines, spirits, liqueurs, cocktails, and aperitifs, but also beers, ciders, mixes, soft drinks, mineral waters, tea, coffee, and cocoa. Each type of drink is described with basic information, historical pictures, and some of the more common product labels for the bottles. It has all been written about before, but not with such panache and certainly not within one set of covers. This is a good book for the beginner, featuring excellent illustrations of the labels and over two hundred cocktail recipes.

4. Doxat, John. **The World of Drinks and Drinking: An International Distillation**. New York: Drake, 1972. 256p. illus. bibliog. index. $9.95.

This is a brief encyclopedia in dictionary form, with appropriate cross-references where needed. Doxat examines the drinking patterns of the major nations around the world, such as the minimum drinking age in Russia. Included are individual entries—"bottles," "closures," "toasts," "customs," "distilling," and "brewing," to name but a few. Anecdotes and quotations make this amusing reading, as in the entry for "vulgarity." Brief histories for all drinks are given. What makes this book valuable are the short corporate histories of wine merchants and distilleries.

5. Fellman, Leonard F. **Merchandising by Design: Developing Effective Menus and Wine Lists**. New York: Lebhar-Friedman Books, 1981. 136p. illus. index. $10 paper.

This is an exceptionally useful little book, one that details how a menu and a wine list are put together. Covered are not only the principles of design for catching customers' eyes, but also the principles of food and wine (which kinds of wines go with which kinds of food). Other material deals with cocktails, carrying spirits in inventory, types of beers, and so forth.

6. Ford, Gene. **Ford's Illustrated Guide to Wines, Brews & Spirits**. Dubuque, Ia.: Wm. C. Brown, 1983. 377p. illus. $18.95 paper.

Ford was once the president of the Society of Wine Educators; he is a syndicated columnist dealing with alcoholic beverages. This book, a rather eclectic package, basically deals with wines. There are 29 chapters, and the material is arranged by type of wine. But Ford also presents literary references, marginal comments, and material on the social aspects of alcohol consumption, as well as over four hundred photographs, charts, and graphs, and some 88 descriptive tables dealing with wines, beers and spirits.

7.* Grossman, Harold J. **Grossman's Guide to Wines, Beers and Spirits**. 7th rev. ed. rev. by Harriet Lembeck. New York: Scribner's, 1983. 638p. illus. maps. bibliog. index. $17.95.

This standard reference work, first published in 1940, is not arranged alphabetically, but by topic. Short introductions deal with definitions and fermentation, and the body of the text swings into the wine-producing countries of Europe. There are 52 pages on America, and there is material on distilled spirits, but only 19 pages on beer. Recipes are also included for cocktails and for food preparations utilizing wine. Although this book has sold well to the general public, it was written for the hotel and food industry. This accounts for its plodding style and the inclusion of material dealing with the wine list, menu making, rules for bartending, hotel and restaurant glassware, inventory, merchandising, and accounting procedures. Numerous appendices include a quick guide to wines and spirits, cost and profit charts, wine classification, a glossary, tables of taxation and duties, various measurement equivalents, a good bibliography, and an extensive index.

8. Hasler, Geoffrey F. **Wine Service in the Restaurant**. 4th ed. London: Wine and Spirit Publications, 1977; distr. by International Publications Service. 84p. illus. $6.50.

The author, a founding member of the Guild of Sommeliers, has written this book primarily for students and trainees in the hotel and restaurant trade. It covers the serving of wine in cocktail lounges and restaurants, catering for restaurant parties and banquets, and other subjects that may contribute to the success of a home dinner party as well.

9.* Hogg, Anthony. **Guide to Visiting Vineyards**. rev. ed. London: Michael Joseph, 1981. 230p. illus. index. $19.50.

Originally published in 1976 by a noted wine writer, this directory now lists over three hundred vineyards, cellars, and distilleries throughout Europe where visitors are made welcome. For each place (arranged by geographic area within each country, beginning with France), Hogg supplies the name, the postal address, the phone number, and the times of availability, as well as travel directions with maps and the proper method of introduction required—which in most cases is by letter of introduction. The Europeans, of course, are the very model of etiquette; they don't want just anybody stepping in off the street. So it is important to get a letter from an agent or merchant before leaving North America. Most principals gladly accept these documents from interested clients.

10.* Johnson, Hugh. **The World Atlas of Wine: A Complete Guide to the Wines and Spirits of the World**. rev. and enl. ed. New York: Simon and Schuster, 1978. 288p. illus. part color. maps. bibliog. index. $35.

Johnson's world atlas is something more than an atlas, since it includes basic information on wine making and choosing wines. At the same time, it is less than what the subtitle promises. The book, lavishly illustrated with color and black-and-white photos, charts, reproductions of about 1,000 wine labels and 143 well-drawn, detailed maps, is divided into seven parts: introduction (history of wine, wine making, etc.); choosing and serving wines (vintage charts are included here); France;

Germany; Southern and Eastern Europe and the Mediterranean; the New World and England and Wales; and spirits. An index and a 7,000-entry gazetteer are appended. France is given almost as much space as the rest of Europe, while all other wine-producing areas (the United States, Australia, South Africa, South America, England, and Wales) are compressed into 29 pages. With this allotment, even France is not covered completely, let alone any other part of the wine world. The 17-page section on spirits is too brief to be of much value and seems out of place. A double page is allotted to each wine region, giving a survey of the region, the grape varieties grown, the major wines produced, and other descriptive matter; photographs of selected labels (tiny reproductions); a locator map, photos of the area, and a detailed map. These maps are the focal point of the work. Instead of showing only political boundaries, they have viticultural detail, indicating contours, elevations, vineyards, and woods. Included in the two introductory sections are some interesting maps of the world's vineyards by countries, in thousands of hectares; graphs depicting world wine consumption (by country) and data on wine-producing areas in the ancient world and the Middle Ages. Among the several informative pieces of miscellany are two double-page drawings of the layout of a château in all of its detail and of a modern winery, and a brief selected bibliography on wine. This "atlas" differs from other wine books in its emphasis on viticultural and economic detail rather than on the simple geographical location of châteaux. It is a useful supplement to *Alexis Lichine's New Encyclopedia of Wines & Spirits*, but certainly in its next edition Johnson should pay attention to American wines.

11.   **Lexique de la vigne et du vin**. Paris: Office International de la Vigne et du Vin, 1972. 700p. maps. index. 200 French francs.

This is a translation/terminology dictionary for wines, like Elsevier's similar work for beer. The seven languages are English, French, Italian, Spanish, German, Portuguese, and Russian. A great number of specialists worked on this project for many years, and the resulting dictionary is in four parts: 1) 2,000 terms and definitions (510 pages); 2) 7 alphabetical indexes (1 per language) plus a special section for Latin terms cited in the book; 3) exhaustive units of measures, both past and present, and tables of equivalencies; and 4) 17 maps and drawings. This is an essential work for the serious student of wines.

12.*   Lichine, Alexis. **Alexis Lichine's New Encyclopedia of Wines & Spirits**. 4th ed. New York: Knopf, 1984. 736p. illus. maps. bibliog. index. $35.

Wine producer and wine merchant Lichine has produced the definitive basic reference-information tool about wines, beers, and spirits. His superb and well-written introductory material covers history; wine, food, and health; wine cellars; vinification processes; viticulture; and spirit making. The main body is alphabetical in arrangement and is self-indexing with appropriate cross-references. Lichine covers geographic areas with the types of vines, types of wines, spirits, beers, aperitifs, and locally applied technical terms. Sketch maps are of all locations. Most entries are long, especially for French and German wine-growing areas, but at least the reader does not have to hunt around for châteaux names or areas (such as Côtes du Rhône); for these, while mentioned under the country (in this case, France), are *also* given their *own* alphabetical entries. The "great wine area" entries have lists of *crus*; an important feature here is the large number of Bordeaux châteaux and Burgundy vineyards described in the text under their own entry. Appendices include: classifications of Médoc wines, as well as Pomerol, Graves, Saint-Emilion, Bourg, Blaye, and German wines; container information; tables of spirit strengths, conversion elements, and vintages; a pronouncing glossary; and a good historical bibliography. There is little on beer, but the spirits seem to be well represented. A nicely organized book that is very enjoyable to read (unlike many reference sources), it needs revision and updating occasionally for areas such as the vintage production figures and tasting notes for new vintages. This deficiency is, of course, unavoidable. Otherwise, a first-rate book.

13.   Marrison, L. W. **Wines and Spirits**. 3d ed. Baltimore: Penguin Books, 1973. 335p. illus. photos. maps. bibliog. index. $2.95 paper.

Marrison's guide to wines and spirits was first published in 1957 and had undergone several reprintings and some revisions. Part One covers an introduction to the quality of wines, wine countries, the history of wine, four chapters on the making of wine and the kinds of wine, vineyards of the world, and how to drink wine. Part Two covers spirits: brandy, whisky (including whiskey), rum, gin, and other spirits. Additional information at the end covers wine production in England, tables and measures, maps, and a classified bibliography. A reading of Marrison's section on pests and wine diseases proves that more information is packed into less space than in any other wine guide encountered (save for the teeny tiny so-called "pocket guides"). He is exceptionally good on wine chemistry. This book contains dense data, and Marrison leaps right into his points with few preliminaries. Thus, he may be a little difficult to read sometimes, as his book is more for study than for perusal. One of the best books on the topic at its price level.

14.   Simon, André L. **Dictionary of Wines, Spirits, and Liqueurs**. 2d ed. London: Hutchinson, 1983. 166p. £ 5.95. paper.

This older book by Simon, still useful, has been made even more useful by its reissuance and updating by Lynne McFarland. It was first issued in 1958. Most of the material that has been extended concerns the "New World," such as the wines and beers of Australia, South Africa, and the United States. Twenty-five thousand terms are identified and briefly defined. The work is good for an overview of the entire alcoholic beverage subject area.

15.   Waugh, Alec. **Wines and Spirits**. New York: Time-Life Books (Foods of the World), 1968. 208p. illus. maps. index. $16.95.

This particular book is very much a continuation of Waugh's earlier effort, *In Praise of Wine*. His personal style, almost like a diary, recounts the brief history of wines and spirits. Still, it reads like any other basic introductory text. There are superb photographs by Arie de Zanger, and the book is worth buying for these alone: they are among the best to be found, and they are particularly valuable for their illustration of techniques. Appendix material covers vintage years, vineyards of France, glasses, bottles, labels, wine and food, wine-tasting parties, and starting a wine cellar (with suggestions for three levels of spending). This is the only book in the Time-Life "Foods of the World" series without recipes in the text. The accompanying recipe book (included in the total price) is spiral bound with washable covers, and a fourth of its 96 pages are devoted to hors d'oeuvres and canapés. There are explanatory recipes for distilled spirits, wines, punches, and hot drinks, and a concluding section on a basic equipment list.

16.   **Wines and Spirits of the World.** ed. by Alec H. Gold. 2d ed. fully rev. Chicago: Follett, 1972. 753p. illus. $29.95.

This posh British book, distributed in the United States, is geared to hotels and restaurants. Each chapter was written by a specialist (e.g., "Germany" by S. Hallgarten, "U.S.A." by Gold). Part One, "Wines," occupies 550 pages. The arrangement is geographical, so one must know a wine's provenance before using the book. France, of course, gets half of the space allotted for Part One, followed by Germany. In the first British edition (1968), North America was represented by two pages for wines of the United States. This second edition has 45 more pages, and all of this coverage goes for the United States and Canada. Sherry, port, Madeira, and vermouth are also in this first section. Part Two is concerned with spirits—brandies, whiskies, vodka, gin, rum, liqueurs, cocktails, cider, and beer. The section on aperitifs appears to be weak, and in the liqueur section, no differences are noted among similar types (e.g., Tia Maria, Kahlua, Zarankaffee). There are special sections on serving, storing, tasting, drinking glasses (British), and label information. Generally, the allocation of space for country of origin is equal to the types and quantities of alcoholic beverage available in Britain. The style and nature of the book are far too salutary when describing sweet wines, and there is a lot of white space and huge print on each page. The thirty-five two-color maps give the basic details, but the two dozen color plates and other photographs complement both the text and the two hundred line drawings. The book can be found on the remainder tables of many bookstores, and consequently it may be a bargain purchase.

⊡ Books on Wines

GENERAL BOOKS

Books in this section deal with the general subject of wines—what they are, how they are consumed, and why some are better than others. However, there is a vast amount of duplication of coverage, and only the "best" books have asterisks. Many of the general books (and even quite a few of the country-oriented books) include very few tasting and evaluative notes, for the publishers feel that this sort of information will tend to date the book. More such information on evaluations will be found in wine magazines and newsletters (see Chapter 9) and in consumer guides (see Chapter 5). Even when superseded, none of the wine-tasting commentaries should ever be pitched out; one day they will be of fine historical value, or of assistance in tracing the changes in one vineyard's vintage years as its wine reaches its peak and then declines. Over the past decade, since the first edition of this wine sourcebook, much information has been filled in. Corporate histories have been published (more are still needed), details on vineyards and smaller areas have been released, vintage charts and notes are much more clear, statistics are more readily accessible, and there are now lots of written descriptions about wine not yet available in the United States.

Basic wine literature tends to be rewritten for new generations. It began with Constable's "Wine Library" of the 1930s, and continued with the McGraw-Hill and George Rainbird series in the 1960s, the Hastings House "Drinking for Pleasure" series of the 1970s, and the Faber and Faber "Library of Wine" series of the late 1970s and early 1980s. A newer contribution is the series of book packages from Mitchell Beazley in London such as the Hugh Johnson books (his atlas, his encyclopedia, his pocket guide for Simon and Schuster) and the Hubrecht Duijker books on France for Crescent/Crown. These books are useful for their uniformity of style and standards.

17.*   Adams, Leon D. **Leon D. Adams' Commonsense Book of Wine**. 3d ed.
        Boston: Houghton Mifflin, 1983. 228p. illus. index. $5.95 paper.
Adams, sometimes known as the Dean of American Wine Writers, first published this book in 1958. Since that time it has assumed the awesome character of a "classic," much like a *grand crus* wine from France. It has worn well, and with updating through the early 1980s it is still a good book for the wine beginner.

Its refreshing style engagingly presents cogent, needed information: how wines taste, their chemistry, an explanation of labels, medical aspects, hobbies, and wine snobberies. Three hundred sixty-two common wines are discussed (one for almost every day of the year?), with commentary on color, flavor, alcoholic strength, and tasting notes. In addition to many charts, there are also some wine recommendations that can be useful for the novice.

18.   Asher, Gerald. **On Wine**. New York: Random House, 1982. 320p. $15.95.
This is a collection of Asher's articles for *Gourmet* magazine. As such, they are brief introductions to various and diverse themes in the wine world, not only commenting on tastings and vintages of wines from various nations and regions, but also discussing bottle shapes, people in the trade, corkscrews, and so forth. His material covers most of the wine-producing nations of the world. Asher is a good writer, but with eclectic tastes, as he constantly searches for new topics for his regular columns.

19.   Bespaloff, Alexis. **The New Signet Book of Wine; A Complete Introduction**. New York: New American Library, 1980. 232p. $3.50 paper.
This was originally published in 1971 as *The First Book of Wine*. It has been revised for its reissuance under a new title. The information includes general data, descriptions of wines and countries, a short pronouncing guide, and material on Champagne, fortified wines, and Cognac. There is consumer information on wine cellars, vintages, and how to serve wine, and a selection of the lower-priced wines.

20.   Burger, Robert. **The Jug Wine Book**. New York: Stein & Day, 1979. 153p. illus. index. $9.95; $4.95 paper.
The material in Burger's book is mainly about bulk wines: the common, everyday materials that suffice for ordinary drinking, parties, cocktails, and coolers. The most endearing characteristic about these "jug" wines is that they are vinous, that is, they do taste of wine, though they lack the sophisticated character. Burger covers both imports (such as Spanish and Italian, and some French) and the domestic market, which is mainly New York and California jugs. Ratings are given.

21.   Churchill, Creighton. **The World of Wines**. 2d rev. ed. New York: Collier Macmillan, 1980. 384p. map. bibliog. $6.95 paper.
Some of these essays first appeared in *Harper's* and *Gourmet*. They cover what wine is, France (one-third of the book), Germany, Italy, Portugal, and Spain, Champagne, fortified wines, and brandies. Each chapter is summarized and followed by a list of principal wines. Vintages are evaluated through 1978, but country wines are stressed. Since its first edition in 1963, lots has happened in the wine business, and Churchill's updating reflects this. There is material on the European Economic Community legislation, the new Italian and German wine laws, the worldwide shortages of quality Bordeaux and Burgundy wines, and the growth of California wines. The book tries to examine the reasons why more people are drinking wine in North America today but does not really go into the question of why less wine is being consumed in Europe today. He concludes the book with advice on wine selections, storage, and serving.

22.   Cooper, Rosalind. **The Wine Book**. Tucson, Ariz.: HP Books, 1981. 128p. illus. $6.95 paper.

An excellently illustrated but reasonably priced guide to current trends in wine consumption. Cooper has also written a similar book for the same publisher on cocktails and spirits. This wine book covers much the same ground as other wine books do, but the pictures are rewarding. All the important countries are discussed, as well as data on what to look for in buying wine, what labels mean, how food and wines match up, storage, serving, and selections for the wine cellar. Very few actual tasting notes, and there is a strong bias towards domestic (California) wines.

23.*   De Blij, Harm. **Wine: A Geographic Appreciation**. Totowa, N.J.: Littlefield Adams and Co., 1983. 254p. illus. maps. bibliog. index. $18.95.

If you are really interested in the wine "trade" (not wine making nor the technology of wine production), then you should look at Harm de Blij's geographical approach. Each country has the vine and the resulting wine, but of course both quality and quantity will vary. Since geography is a spatial discipline of relationships, de Blij concentrates on the more scientific aspects of wine productivity to try to show why certain vines are better than others, and why certain countries are more productive (climate, soils, etc.). There is some detail on the impact of wine legislation (and some material on "wine wars" too) as it ties into the cultural makeup of the people of a nation or language group. Several sections are devoted to the economic characteristics of trade. With the forty maps and charts and the academic tone of writing (de Blij is a teacher at the University of Florida), this book is good reading for the serious student of wine.

24.   Dubuigne, Gerard. **Larousse Dictionary of Wines of the World**. New York: Larousse, 1976. 272p. illus. maps. $14.95.

This book was originally published in France in 1970; thus, it has a decidedly French bias when it comes to accounting for the success of French wines in the world today. The section on German and Italian wines are both short and without maps. Acknowledging its skewed data, the book does cover the major wines, geographic areas, technological processes, and diseases in an alphabetical, dictionary-style arrangement. It has had no updating since 1970; consequently it appears a little tired, with few data on Canada and the United States. Cross-references are indicated by asterisks, and this replaces the index. There are superb color photographs (primarily French): vineyards, grape varieties, the chais, pastoral scenery, wine labels. A second edition was published in France in 1980, in French.

25.   Edita Lausanne. **The Great Book of Wine**. New York: World, 1970. 459p. illus. maps. $50.

This book was expensive when it first came out, but it is now sometimes available on sale or as a remainder. It is a coffee-table book that describes sixty-five hundred different wines, but with only fifty-four labels reproduced in color (grouped by country of origin) and explained. The gorgeous forty-four maps and tipped-in illustrations, however, are not quite enough to compensate for the lack of an overall index (only wine names are indexed). Other information here: storage and serving and tasting, nicely illustrated.

26.   Escritt, L. B. **The Wine Cellar.** 2d ed. London: Jenkins, 1972; distr. by
        International Publications Service. 79p. illus. $5 paper.
This is a detailed account of how to make and stock a home wine cellar, with
advice on serving, tasting, and drinking wine. Other chapters cover a history of
cooperage and casks, bottles, glasses, and wine making. A short but impressive
book.

27.*   Fluchère, Henri. **Wines.** 2d ed. New York: Golden Press, 1974. 160p. illus.
        maps. bibliog. index. $2.95 paper.
While it is very general, this book is also very comprehensive, giving adequate coverage to wine making (good notes and pictures on grape varieties), various countries'
wines, including Russia and Japan, and descriptive information on California
wineries, and how to read labels. The balance of the book is devoted to enjoying
wines: shopping, storing, serving, wine-tasting parties, wining and dining out, wine
and weddings (e.g. Champagnes), wine and food (including what usually goes
together), and how to visit wineries and museums (worldwide, including Spain
and Italy). The color illustrations by the author, an accredited heraldic artist,
appear on every page. Lots of labels are shown, with data on how to read them;
there are seven excellent pointers on what to look for when shopping for wines;
there is an illustrated description of an apartment wine "cellar," a detailed description on how to construct wine racks, and a concluding glossary.

28.   **Gateway to Wine.** By the editors of *Wine Tidings.* Montreal, Canada:
        Kylix International, 1981. 233p. illus. maps. index. $7.95 paper.
This is a diverse collection of writings from the Canadian magazine *Wine Tidings,*
which started out as the voice of the Opimian Society, a wine-buying club in
Canada. There are some original pieces, as well as some updating of the original
articles. The topics include: France, Italy, California, Germany, Spain, Portugal
(all with appropriate sketch maps), technicalities of wine production, and consumer guides for storage, serving, tasting, wine and food, and vintages. There is
some Canadian material here, too, dealing with the evolution of the Canadian
liquor laws and the grape varieties as found in Canada. There is a glossary, along
with an index (unusual for an anthology).

29.   Henriques, Frank. **The Signet Encyclopedia of Wine.** rev. ed. New York:
        New American Library, 1984. 520p. $4.95 paper.
Originally published in 1975, this paperback has now been extensively revised,
in the words of the publisher, with almost 90 percent of the text rewritten. All
aspects are covered in a relatively inexpensive format that is useful for private and
personal purchase, or for libraries' paperback collections. The highlight of the book
is the rating of over six thousand wines (from one to five stars of excellence),
with special notations for vintage years. The alphabetical arrangement is based on
the name of the wine (from the label), thus allowing direct access to the data without having to go through the countries or the regions concerned. There are explanations for various types of wines, such as when it is ready to be served and how to
serve it, as well as general material about all the wine-producing countries.

30. Ivens, Dorothy and William M. Massee. **Just Tell Me What I Want to Know about Wine.** New York: Grosset & Dunlap, 1981. 164p. $7.95 paper.

This engaging little book presents about ninety questions and their answers, framed as a good beginning point for those novices who want to know about what to serve, prices and values, the combination of food and wine, and so forth. The emphasis is on inexpensive, commonly available wines. Massee is a well-known wine writer; Ivens is his wife.

31. Johnson, Frank E. **The Professional Wine Reference.** New York: Harper & Row, 1983. 401p. $9.95 paper.

Johnson's book was first published in 1977 as a trade-oriented tool by the magazine *Beverage Media.* With Harper & Row it now has a consumer appearance, and the data has been updated and extended. It has a basic dictionary-arranged A-to-Z format for about 950 short articles, cross-referenced by the use of small capital letters. Each entry has a pronunciation guide, which is needed by every consumer who orders wine in a restaurant, bar, or shop. Subjects covered include wine terminology and tasting, the geographic areas, and the more important wineries and châteaus. Material on Ontario, British Columbia, and New York State, while short, is concise and up-to-date. Other material presented in this book includes information on the varietal wine grapes and wine characteristics, and it is accessed by country and grape variety (e.g., Sancerre-France, Loire-sauvignon blanc-light-bodied, dry). This last section is very good when determining wine and food matchups.

32.* Johnson, Hugh. **Hugh Johnson's Modern Encyclopedia of Wine.** New York: Simon and Schuster, 1983. 544p. illus. index. $29.95.

This is the latest in the eponymous books bearing the name of the author in the title. It has updated coverage of some seven thousand wine producers in thirty countries. Each wine is described, by region and style of wine, under country name. Information given includes address, size of property, indication of worth, who the current winemaker is, what the production is, whether the winery is open or not, etc. For example, the section on New York State within the American chapter describes the general growing characteristics of the area, seventeen major wineries, eight lesser ones, and a description of "East Coast wine varieties." Accompanying all of these producers' profiles are some sketch drawings, some biographies, and some general material on wine (types, character, how to make, how to store, how to taste, and related topics). Johnson's newest book begs the inevitable comparison to his *The World Atlas of Wine* and to his *Pocket Encyclopedia of Wine*, both published by Simon and Schuster. In the former, the reader has detailed maps, albeit a decade old by now, while in the latter the reader has vintage indications in a book that is regularly revised. *Hugh Johnson's Modern Encyclopedia of Wine* lies midway between the two, but over the years to come it may not be as regularly revised as his *Pocket* one is. Canadians still have a right to get mad at Johnson (he described Canadian wines as something like soap; this was over ten years ago). In his current book, he provides a paltry and inept three inches on the Canadian wine industry.

33.   Johnson, Hugh. **Wine**. rev. ed. New York: Simon and Schuster, 1975.
       264p. illus. maps. index. $17.95.

This is a short, basic introduction to wines, originally written in 1966. The traditional pattern of description is followed: how wines are made and served, their history, wine selection, and matching wines with food, subdivided by "Aperitifs," "White and Red Table Wines," and "After Dinner Wines." The better wines and vineyards of the world are also covered. Color maps and plates.

34.   Kressman, Edward. **The Wonder of Wine**. New York: Hastings House,
       1968. 227p. $6.95.

As a manager of a family firm of excellent wine producers, Kressman has access to inside information that is presented in this good book of memoirs, a sort of "my life in wine" adventure. Some of the material was previously published in *Wine* magazine, but the personal accounts were not. There is good explanatory material for the layman on the first steps in fermentation and racking. He takes an extensive approach to the wine bottle and to its pedigree, which includes the label, shape, cork, date, grape variety, price, and decanting.

35.   Massee, William Edman. **Massee's Wine Almanac**. Englewood Cliffs, N.J.:
       Prentice-Hall, 1980. 216p. illus. index. $12.95; $6.95 paper.

Massee's "almanac," first published in 1961 as a handbook, offers some help to the newcomer to wine buying. The book covers kinds of wine, how to read labels, red wines, white wines, pink wines, Champagne, aromatic wines, and fortified wines. There is no attempt to be comprehensive; only major wines are introduced and described. The purpose of the book is to provide some assistance to a bewildered buyer. Most of the book was written in chart form. Price ranges and vintage charts are updated through 1979, with a scale for 1980-1990 durability. Miscellaneous topics deal with jug wines, tips on retail store purchases and how to order in restaurants, how to stock a wine cellar, and different categories of wines for different events (everyday drinking, wines to drink before dinner, wines for touring, sailing, and picnics, and wines for tasting). There is a four-language glossary and a guide to wine festivals.

36.   Matthews, Patrick, ed. **Christie's Wine Companions, 1 and 2**. London:
       Christie's Wine Publications, 1981-1983. 2 vols. (192p.; 208p.) illus.
       $21.

Both of these books are collections of essays written by over twenty different authors, such as Pamela Vandyke Price, Hugh Johnson, Julian Jeffs, Len Evans, Michael Broadbent, Noel Cossart, Edmund Penning-Rowsell, Harry Waugh, and Harry Yoxall—a veritable who's who of the British wine-writing fraternity. All of the major wine areas are covered, and each book has about 124 line drawings and halftone illustrations. Topics include: anecdotes, historical notes (corporate histories, biographies), visits to wineries (from Australia to California, moving as the sun does), and some material on foods such as the truffle hunt in Quercy. Definitely a book to buy when you already have the basics.

37.   Millon, Marc and Kim Millon. **The Wine and Food of Europe: An Illus-
        trated Guide**. Secaucus, N.J.: Chartwell, 1982. 224p. illus. index. $19.95.
The Millons are a husband-and-wife team; together they have written and photographed many articles for such British magazines as *Wine Bar Review*. This is their
first book, and it is a comprehensive, but not thorough, guide to eighteen major
wine regions. The Millons decided on six areas in France, four in Italy, several in
Central Europe (only one from Germany) and the Balkans, and the Iberian
Peninsula. Each area covered presents an overview, some commentary on the types
of wines available, a few names and addresses, and the types of food that one con-
sumes. This is a do-it-yourself guide for wine travellers, with route suggestions
(maps, producers, where to stay, what to see, where to eat) and local wine festivals
noted.

38.   Millon, Marc and Kim Millon. **The Wine Roads of Europe**. New York:
        Simon and Schuster, 1984. 285p. illus. maps. $9.95 paper.
In this book, narrative prose has been kept to a minimum. It is a highly useful,
excellently compiled tourist guide and directory to France, Germany, Italy,
Austria, Spain, and Portugal, all the areas that most people are likely to visit, at
least on their first few trips to Europe. Each country has a subarrangement by a
number of regions. For France, this includes Alsace, Bordeaux, Burgundy, Champagne, Loire, and Rhône; in Germany, it is the Rhine and Mosel. Italy has the
Piedmont, Tuscany, Venice, and the Central Region, while Spain has the Rioja
and sherry. Of course, the best wines are produced from grapes grown on the
slopes that surround rivers (or in the valleys); consequently, the major wine routes
follow the paths of rivers and streams. This is also picturesque. For each area within
a country, the Millons have provided a description of the food and wine, how to
get to the region, car rental data, sketch maps and itineraries, a directory of wine
producers and how to access them, wine festivals, wine courses, wine museums,
restaurants, lodgings, and where to get additional information.

39.   Overstreet, Dennis and Ava Overstreet. **Wine Secrets**. New York: Grosset
        & Dunlap, 1980. 181p. illus. maps. index. $26.95.
Overstreet is a national wine consultant for Sotheby Parke Bernet, and he has
opened The Wine Merchant store in Los Angeles. This book is eclectic, but it is
also sophisticated, and useful for the wine person who aspires to more shelf
information. The material includes different wine vintages, wine buffs' vacations,
wine tastings, and wine cellars. There is also a directory of associations and a
glossary of wine terms. The meat of the book, though, is a series of interviews to
obtain the "wine secrets." There are profiles and write-ups about great French
wine makers, such as Louis Latour, Alexis Lichine, Peter Sichel, and Baron de
Rothschild (both of them). From California there are interviews with Robert
Mondavi and Jack Davies. Other industry people and writers have also been
consulted.

40.   Paterson, John. **The Hamlyn Pocket Dictionary of Wines**. New York:
        Larousse, 1980. 256p. illus. $3.95 paper.
This book has a British bias; it covers those wines fairly readily available in the
United Kingdom. The first 70 pages concern general introductory matters, a
glossary, and the French wine classifications. The second part of the book is an

alphabetically arranged series of short descriptions of various types of wines, along with the appropriate cross-references. Vintage charts are included for 1949 through 1978.

41. Pratt, James Norwood. **The Wine Bibbers Bible.** 2d rev. ed. San Francisco: 101 Productions, 1981. 192p. illus. index. $6.95 paper.

This is a glamorous "production number" for those readers who require an artsy-craftsy-type book to explain the mystique of wine. Commonly available information on wine knowledge and wine lore is expressed, with added value being derived from the translated Baudelaire essay and the Raffetto drawings. For the person who has everything, but wants more.

42. Prial, Frank J. **Wine Talk.** New York: Times Books, 1978. 264p. illus. $12.50.

This is a collection of Prial's columns for the New York *Times*, drawn from the 1975-1978 period, and there is no collective index. The material is well-written and concise, if a bit contemporary to the times. The wide range of topics includes: storage, wine cellars, vintages, restaurants visited, biographies, profiles of people and wineries, tasting notes, wine societies, wine areas (especially California), and wine-related products such as port, sherry, and Cognac.

43. Price, Pamela Vandyke. **The Penguin Wine Book.** New York: Allen Lane, 1984. 208p. illus. $24.95.

Price's entry into the general wine book sweepstakes does a good job, in a nontechnical sense, of explaining the complex processes involved in winemaking. She goes on to explore how people can get the most value for their money in purchasing wine, and how to travel wisely when venturing forth into the wine regions of the world. Twenty black-and-white photos accompany the text.

44. Rainbird, George M. **The Subtle Alchemist: A Book of Wine.** London: Michael Joseph, 1973. 206p. illus. bibliog. $10.95.

Originally published in 1964 as *The Wine Handbook*, this time around the practical and realistic Rainbird is assisted by Ronald Searle's hilarious cartoons, as well as more data on country wines of the world. This is another basic, introductory text.

45. Ray, Cyril. **Cyril Ray's Book of Wine.** New York: Morrow, 1978. 125p. illus. $12.95.

This is a good beginning text, written by an exceptionally literate wine writer who has been at it for many decades. Topics include wine with food, the wine regions of the world, how to choose wine, and how to serve wine. There are also many pictures, maps, and reproductions of labels (in color).

46. Robards, Terry. **Terry Robards' New Book of Wine.** New York: G. P. Putnam's Sons, 1984. 512p. illus. index. $19.95.

Robards' book has the engaging subtitle "the ultimate guide to wines throughout the world, illustrated with charts, tables, and black-and-white photographs." Well, that may be, but Robards also states in his introduction (p. 8) "I consider my audience so broad that it encompasses all people who can read, and I have written this book with that concept uppermost." Here, then, are the basics of the grape varieties, making wine, viticulture, wine tasting, best buys, storage, serving, stemware, and related materials. The rest of the book is alphabetically arranged in dictionary fashion, with about a thousand entries, covering specific wines areas and types. This book was originally issued in 1976 as *The New York Times Book of Wine*. Since that time, and in the context of this book, he has found more than two hundred additional California wineries worthy of notice, about a hundred more Italian wines, and a few more from each other wine producing country. He no longer writes for the New York *Times*; he is writing on wines for the New York *Post*. Revision and updating is good through mid-1983. At the end of each entry for a wine type, Robards appends his ratings for aging potential and dollar value. This book is not a bad introduction, except that he fails to adequately differentiate between "aroma" and "bouquet."

47.   Robinson, Jancis. **The Great Wine Book**. New York: Morrow, 1982. 240p. illus. index. $29.95.

All of the best, most famous names in the wine business are described in Robinson's oversized book. It concentrates on the most posh wines from six countries. Needless to say, France leads with twenty-one producers (including the five great Bordeaux reds, Champagne, Burgundy, et al.), and there are five from Germany, three from Spain (including the Torres family), three from Australia, four from California (Mondavi, St. Jean, Phelps, and Ridge), and only one from Italy. The preface states that the book's mission is: "to present the very best the world's vineyards have to offer." Each producer has several pages of illustrations, a topographic colored map, details on production (or, why each thinks that his wine is the best because of his vinification practices, but I don't think that any secrets are given out here), and details on climate and geographic situation. There are tables of comparison for statistical data, selling prices, such as Château Petrus 1961 selling for $306 a bottle in 1982, and so forth.

48.   Schoonmaker, Frank. **Frank Schoonmaker's Encyclopedia of Wine**. rev. and expanded by Julius Wile. 7th ed. New York: Hastings House, 1978. 473p. illus. $14.95.

The first edition of this book, written by the late Frank Schoonmaker, appeared in 1964. Since then it has had regular revisions. Two thousand terms are described and defined, with well over a hundred maps and illustrations of wine labels. In addition there are tasting notes for vintages from around the world, as well as current statistics. Lots of new material has been added by Wile: changing terminology, charts of the largest one hundred U.S. wineries, a table of vineyard temperatures for grape cultivation, and lists of grape varieties with notes on how well they perform in different parts of the world.

49.   Seldon, Philip. **The Vintage Magazine Consumer Guide to Wine**. Garden City, N.Y.: Doubleday, 1983. 402p. illus. index. $12.95 paper.

Basically, Seldon's book is for novices. He moves easily through history of the vine, the types of grapes and wines, how wine is made, the grape varieties employed, the wine regions, maps and wine laws, table wines, sparkling wines, fortified wines, what vintages are, labels, tastings, buying, food-and-wine matchups, and book knowledge. The approach is one of common sense, based on his own *Vintage* magazine efforts (he is Publisher and Editor of *Vintage*). Yet Seldon is largely negative towards other wine writers and magazines in the trade (you should read what he has to say about Terry Robards and Eunice Fried). This is not a consumer's guide to wine so much as it is an insider's guide to the American wine market and writers—what we call "shelf knowledge," not "self knowledge."

50.   Sichel, Allan. **The Penguin Book of Wines.** 2d ed. rev. by Peter A. Sichel. Baltimore: Penguin Books, 1971. 304p. maps. bibliog. index. $3.95 paper.
Originally published in 1965, this book successfully achieves its goal of serving as an introduction to the whole subject of wine. The four parts are well organized. They cover general information (tasting, wine names, storing wine); vineyards, soil, wine making, growers, shippers, and merchants; European wines by country, followed by short descriptions of non-European wines; and a vintage list, a well-selected bibliography (briefly annotated), a glossary, nine maps, and an index. The information is aimed at the British reader, and the maps at the back of the book are too distant from the related text.

51.   Simon, André L. **The International Wine and Food Society's Encyclopedia of Wines.** New York: Quadrangle, 1973. 312p. maps. $17.95.
This is a legacy left behind by André Simon, who died in 1970. It has been developed from a number of his previous books, such as *A Dictionary of Wines, Spirits and Liqueurs,* his *Dictionary of Wine* (1935), and his 1970 edition of *A Wine Primer* (often revised). This book opens with a brief 50-page description of wines of the world, followed by a 200-page "gazetteer" with 40 pages of maps. The seven thousand entries are either vineyard names or place names that correspond to types of wine; hence, great wines and *vins ordinaire* are given equal prominence. Entries are in alphabetical order with adequate cross-references. Each entry on the double-column pages describes in about three lines of concise identification: 1) the corresponding map number; 2) its correct designation in terms of its country's laws and regulations, for example, France's A.O.C. "Pomerol"; 3) its location in terms of its largest neighbor; 4) its quality in a half-dozen words or so (e.g., "ordinary to fair light white dessert wine"); and 5) the country of origin. Its main value then lies in the quick distinction one can make of one wine from others with similar name. There are no illustrations, and as such it is more of a dictionary than an encyclopedia, but the book does provide keys to identification of people, places, and things.

52.   Simon, André L., ed. **Wines of the World.** rev. ed. New York: McGraw-Hill, 1972. 719p. illus. maps. bibliog. out of print.
This is a well-illustrated collection of articles, originally issued in 1967. Specialists contributed chapters that were contemporary for the time: S. F. Hallgarten on Germany, Simon on France, Cyril Ray on Italy, George Rainbird on sherry, and others. The information is compact, and there is a glossary. André Simon died in 1970; in 1981, McGraw-Hill issued a totally new book, *André Simon's Wines of the World,* edited by Serena Sutcliffe (see below). But this first book is still of value.

53.   Spurrier, Steven and Michael Dovaz. **The Académie du Vin Complete Wine Course.** New York: G. P. Putnam's Sons, 1983. 223p. illus. bibliog. index. $19.95.

The subtitle for this book is "a comprehensive course in wine appreciation, tasting and study." It has been copublished in England by Christie's Wine Publications, which also owns part of the Académie du Vin's operations in the New York and London branches (the headquarters are in Paris, and the Academie was founded by Spurrier in 1972). The book is structured like a textbook. Obviously it is also meant to be sold to students at the Académie du Vin. There are four parts. The first ("Foundations") covers the mechanics of tasting, the vines, the vintages, buying, and storing. The second ("Intermediate") concerns grape varieties and wines from around the world. Part Three ("Advanced") approaches wines by type, ranging from bone-dry whites through to full-bodied reds, with horizontal and vertical tastings. Vintages are specified, but this will tend to date the book after awhile. The fourth part ("Special Studies") is a bit of ad hoc-ery with materials on foods, service, oakiness in flavors, tasting, vintages, and related subjects. This is an extremely useful book that people—either alone or in groups—can use to approach wine appreciation in a step-by-step educative manner, at their own speed, and with no tests!

54.*   Sutcliffe, Serena. **André Simon's Wines of the World.** New York: McGraw-Hill, 1981. 639p. bibliog. index. $35.

Sutcliffe was asked by McGraw-Hill to revise André Simon's 1972 book, *Wines of the World* (see above); she found the work difficult and decided to completely redo the book. Thus, there is nothing here that relates to the previous book except for the publisher, the title, and the concept. The sections have been ably coordinated by Sutcliffe (one of the few women to possess the Master of Wine designation in England), and they are arranged by importance, with Europe first, but covering the gamut of the wine-producing areas of the world. Important writers and their specialties include Ian Jamieson on Germany, Sutcliffe on France, Philip Dallas on Italy, and Jullian Jeffs on sherry. California, of course, is included in a much-expanded section, as are the wines of South America. But there is nothing much for Canada. With detail on the top wines, estates, and producers, this book has excellent reference value. The twenty-nine new maps are perhaps too sketchy and need some fleshing out with more details, but the fifty or so color plates are engrossing. The bibliography has been thoroughly recast through 1980, and should prove a good shopping list in terms of the wines explored.

55.*   Sutcliffe, Serena. **Great Vineyards and Winemakers.** Toronto: Prentice-Hall Canada, 1982. 256p. illus. index. $25.

This is an oversized coffee-table book written and presented in nontechnical language. The wine making processes at sixty-seven vineyards have been described, along with photographs and maps of the estates. From France, here are thirty-four owners including Bordeaux (Châteaux Margaux, Lafite, Latour, Mouton, Haut Brion, D'Yquem, Pétrus, and Palmer); Burgundy (Latour); Alsace (Hugel); Rhône (Jaboulet); and the Loire. From Germany, twelve estates are discussed. Italy apparently has four great vineyards, while Australia has six and California has eleven (most "boutiques"). Each country has a general introduction to the style and character of that area, with two to four pages each being devoted to the grounds, the owner, maps, and statistics for the estates. There is much detail on all of the vintages (since 1945 in the case of France, and 1970 for the others). The vineyards have been well chosen to provide a wide range of wine and wine making techniques.

56.　　**Vintage, 1983-** . Annual, from *Vintage* magazine, $20.
The first annual in this new series, really a collection of articles from the magazine, runs to 352 pages. Material covered includes wines, personalities, wine history, reports on vintages, wine news, and so forth, all delivered in nontechnical prose, along with photographs and drawings.

57.　　Wagenwoord, James. **The Doubleday 1983 Wine Companion**. Garden City, N.Y.: Doubleday, 1983. 176p. illus. maps. bibliog. index. $10.95.
This eclectic book takes in the wine year of 1982 and some of 1983. It is a look at wine trends, prices, harvests, and other data. It is also a short history of Mouton-Rothschild (with illustrations of some of the labels). It covers laws and labels of the world, a little haphazardly with illustrations and examples. It has material on storing, serving, and tasting wines, in a practical sense, as well as a section on corks. He covers wine auctions (how they operate, names, and addresses) and wine tours (mainly for the U.S., and arbitrarily at that). There are chapters on Ports and sherries. There are profiles of California and European vineyards, as well as New York vineyards, and he tells what they produce. Wagenwoord also comes up with wine cellar suggestions from thirty-two wine merchants.

58.　　Wasserman, Pauline W. and Sheldon Wasserman. **A Guide to Fortified Wines**. New York: Marlborough Press, 1983. 200p. illus. index. $9.95 paper.
The material in this book has been limited to a discussion of some of the great fortified wines of the world: Port, Montilla-Moriles, sherry, Madeira, and Marsala. Descriptions include how the wines are made, how they are aged and fortified, their anecdotal history, and plenty of tasting notes. Charts abound, such as the one for vintage Port—1811 through 1980—which tells which houses shipped vintage Port in each year. There is also a checklist of the various shippers and the vintages declared, as well as explanations of the differences between the dry and sweet ends of the spectrum for each type of fortified wine.

59.　　Wasserman, Sheldon and Pauline W. Wasserman. **White Wines of the World**. New York: Stein & Day, 1978. 236p. illus. index. $5.95 paper.
The Wasserman writing team sure came up with a winner here, since the topic has deliberately been restricted to "white" table wines. By the mid-1970s, this style of wine was just about everybody's favorite quaffer, in occasions ranging from cocktail parties and happy hours right through to dessert courses. Over three-fourths of the wine sold in North America is white, and by limiting the scope of the writing to just that one kind, the Wassermans have given ample identification to many kinds of white wine of value to those sippers who only like that one type. The format is dictionary style, and all countries are covered, with a preponderance of material on country wines.

EUROPE

In this section are single books (monographs) about the wines of individual countries or various regions of countries in Europe. The countries are arranged in alphabetical order, beginning with France. Many books, though, are not written in English, and while there are translations available occasionally, much information still exists in the original languages. Most of these books are *not* included here unless absolutely necessary; they—and more of them—can be found through the wine bibliographies listed in Chapter 12. I have given associations and societies, magazines, food, tasting guides, museums and libraries their own chapters with their own internal arrangements.

France

Most of what is written about wines is about the products from France— and this often includes up to 85 percent of a general wine book that is supposed to cover other areas as well. Personal accounts also dwell on French wines. But it must be recognized that the best of the French wines are also the best of the world's wines. Because it is a well-defined and important industry, the wine trade and viticulture in France has been the subject of many specialized studies, which are not applied to other countries. The most important French-language documents are listed in this section, along with the English-language books. More can be found through the wine bibliographies in Chapter 12. In the section below, wine books on specific areas in France are described, preceded by general books on all of France's regions.

General

60.   Adam, André. **Dictionnaire illustré des vins de France**. Bruxelles, Belgium: Rossel Edition, 1975. 231p. illus. maps. price not available. paper.
In a dictionary-like format, this tool briefly identifies the regions and the types of wines produced in that region. For example, under Haut-Poitou, it mentions the V.D.Q.S. quality of the wines (reds, whites and rosés) and mentions Vienne as being one of the regional capitals. Twenty-five hundred *crus repertories* are mentioned, and there are ten maps and six photographs in color. There is also material on wine and food, the glasses used in the various regions, serving temperatures, and wine classifications, and a glossary of terms.

61.*   **Atlas de la France vinicole**. Paris: L. Larmat, 1941- . Series, different paginations.
This Larmat atlas provides the definitive series of maps for the French vineyards (it is the one always used when maps are reproduced in books dealing with French wines). The invaluable details have been skillfully prepared under L'Institut National des Appellations d'Origine and published as a part work, in French, that covers the five basic grape-growing and wine-production areas as well as the origins of the important spirits: *Les vins de Bordeaux* (1949); *Les vins de Bourgogne* (1955); *Champagne* (1944); *Les vins des Côtes du Rhône* (1943); *Les vins des Coteaux de la Loire* (1958); and *Les eaux-de-vie de France: le Cognac* (1941).

62.   Comité National des Vins de France. **Annuaire des caveaux, celliers, chais, et autres centres de dégustation des vins de France.** Paris, 1971- .

This annual is a listing of all groups involved with wines in France (growers, châteaux, cooperatives, merchants, shippers, cellars, special wine-tasting spots), divided by wine-producing areas and further subdivided by department and then by town within. Names, addresses, telephone numbers, opening hours, and some indication of tastings available are given. In addition to wines, brandies and eaux-de-vie are also covered; hence there is data here on Cognac and Armagnac. An essential possession for the traveller in France.

63.   Dion, Roger. **Histoire de la vigne et du vin en France des origines au 19e siècle.** Paris: Editions Dion, 1959. 768p. illus. maps. index. price not available.

This French epic is a comprehensive treatise on French wines and vines. Because of its full details on the vineyards and the major wine-producing areas, and its historical perspective, tables, maps, and excellent illustrations, this is one of the most authoritative reference volumes on the history of French wines before the twentieth century.

64.   **French Wines and Spirits.** ed. by Moira MacFarlane. Paris: Leader International Press, 1979. 138p. illus. 40 French francs.

This is a special issue of *Revue Vinicole Internationale*, on how to appreciate French wines. It gives a region-by-region breakdown on French wines for eleven areas (Alsace, Bordeaux, Burgundy, Champagne, Languedoc-Roussillon, Loire, Provence, Corsica, the Southwest, the Savoie, the Rhône). For each it gives a description, maps, types of varieties and grapes, the producers, statistics of production, foods in the area, and the economics of the harvest. There is also material on twelve types of fortified wines and spirits (aniseed, Armagnac, Calvados, Cognac, marcs, liqueurs, Pineau des Charantes, vermouths, etc.). For both the wines and the higher-strength alcoholic beverages there is an analysis of export figures and market promotions.

65.   Jacquelin, Louis and René Poulain. **Vignes et vins de France.** 2d ed. Paris: Flammarion, 1970. 483p. illus. index. 150 French francs.

Originally published in 1960 (and brought out in an English edition by Putnam in 1962), this valuable tool is a collection of the names of all the vineyards in France, as well as of all the I.N.A.O. allowable wine grape varieties. Both authors were skilled oenologists. Introductory material includes a brief history of grape origins, followed by an outline of modern methods of wine growing and wine making with an emphasis on soil and climate. Histories of all the major vineyards are given, and the laws governing them. Geographic coverage also includes Corsica and Algeria. Over five thousand vineyards are listed, and for each is given: the nature of the soil, the grape varieties planted, the yield of the wine, the official classifications of quality for each district, and up-to-date vintage guides. Miscellaneous information includes wine labels, measures, storage and service, wines and food matching, and a wine glossary. There are seventy-six black-and-white photographs and seventeen maps. Absolutely indispensable, and readable by anyone with a meager knowledge of French.

66.*   Lichine, Alexis. **Alexis Lichine's Guide to the Wines and Vineyards of France**. rev. ed. New York: Knopf, 1984. 483p. illus. maps. index. $19.95; $9.95 paper.

This book first came out in 1979; at that time it was a totally recast version of a 1951 book entitled *The Wines of France*. In addition to updating the 1979 version, Lichine has also presented in a new format fourteen wine tour itineraries and maps, and more graded restaurants and hotels at which to eat and to stay. In other words, he has made the book more appealing to the tourist, but at the same time he has dated the book more than ever before. His systematic coverage includes Bordeaux, Burgundy, Rhône, Loire, Alsace, Champagne, Cognac, Provence, and even the Midi (also the French cantons of Switzerland, particularly for restaurants). He presents data on the individual châteaux and domaine owners, as well as what to look for in determining what sets each type of wine apart from its neighbors. The illustrations include black-and-white reproductions of wine bottle labels. Material here also includes information on the French wine vintages through 1983, various statistics, notes on tasting, and the complementary nature of wine and food.

67.*   Price, Pamela Vandyke. **Eating and Drinking in France Today**. London: Tom Stacey, 1972. 324p. illus. maps. bibliog. index. £ 6.

This is mainly a travel book for the tourist, but it also evokes strong memories for the armchair traveler. Part One details how the French eat; how to cope with French hotels; how to interpret a menu; and a general guide to food, wines and aperitifs, including mineral waters, beers, and hot drinks. Other information includes manners and etiquette for the visitor and the preparations involved in picnics. Many of the drinks and much of the food are simply not available domestically, and a trip to France is a necessity for the gourmet. This part of the book is a good introduction to the French social and cultural graces. Part Two is the regional breakdown, with details about visiting the wine areas (from Alsace through the Savoie, arranged alphabetically). Subsections include specialties and dishes, cheese, local wines, things to see and to do (for gourmet tastes; for example, museums dealing with food), wine and life-styles, wine cellars, objets d'art to do with food and drink, and a list of hotels and restaurants personally recommended by Price (this section is now dated). Throughout, there are glossaries and translation dictionaries after each chapter. There are no recipes, but the bibliography does include cookbooks, travel books and guides, and wine books listed through to 1972. A good book for examining a country before you visit it.

68.*   Spurrier, Steven. **The Académie du Vin Concise Guide to French Country Wines**. New York: Perigee/Putnam, 1983. 176p. illus., part color. bibliog. index. $5.95 paper.

The regional wines of France have been described by Spurrier as any wine consumed by the locals and tourists as an everyday wine. Generally, these wines sell for $10 and under in North America. Thus, a Bordeaux A.O.C. red generic will be here in the book, but not the *crus bourgeois,* nor of course, Château Lafite-Rothschild, nor any great wine. All of the wines described here do have some vinous character, above the level of ordinary table wine, but they will not have the sophistication that one associates with the truly great French wines. The text is arranged by broad geographic region and subarranged by type of standard, with the higher ones first: the Appellation Contrôlée areas are followed by the V.D.Q.S.

(Vin Délimité de Qualité Supérieure) areas and the Vin de Pâys areas. (*Vins de table* in France are not regional wines). There is also an index to each named wine. Thus, one can approach the book in one of two ways: he can find the good wines of an area by looking under the name of that area, or he can find the position of a named good wine by checking the index for a page reference. Under each category there is a description of the grape varieties, the geographic area of production (with maps), tasting notes, an indication of the potential for aging, and one of six price ranges— $3.75 to $10 or so. Other material includes a good chapter on French wines in the 1980s (and France's relationship with the E.E.C. in this regard), an explanation of the wine law system (including the new Vin de Pâys regulations from 1979), how to read a label—along with many reproductions in color—and a glossary, wine and food service charts, and vintage charts. There is excellent material here not otherwise available in English.

69.   Spurrier, Steven. **The Académie du Vin Concise Guide to French Fine Wines**. New York: Perigee/Putnam, 1984. 180p. illus., part color. bibliog. index. $8.95 paper.
This is the companion volume to Spurrier's practical survey of French country wines (see the entry immediately above). The main section of the book is devoted to descriptions and information about the major wines. The wines are rated and commented on. There are also chapters on the producers and purchase of fine wines, and vintage charts for each of the fine wine regions of France. A useful book, but the data is available elsewhere (which is not the case with his *French Country Wines* book).

70.   **The Taste of France: A Dictionary of French Food and Wine**. Boston: Houghton Mifflin, 1982. 320p. illus. $10.95.
This highly useful book identifies some four thousand or so terms that are used in the French food and wine industry. The book was originally published in England where they normally do a good job of classifying French information, and the material was put together by three experts. As with all dictionaries, the data are arranged alphabetically by French term, followed by a few lines of description. There are even line drawings to look at, in order to make the definitions more clear. At the back there are textual commentaries on food and wine styles for the various regions of France.

71.   Wildman, Frederick. **A Wine Tour of France**. rev. ed. New York: Random House, 1976. 335p. illus. maps. index. $4.95 paper.
The author, a wine importer, has written a guide to be used for visiting France and the vineyards. He suggests a three-week excursion, and provides a detailed itinerary with recommended routes, lodgings, restaurants, mileage, telephone numbers, and names of proprietors. Four twenty-one-day motor trips are given through Champagne and Alsace; Burgundy and the Rhône; Armagnac, Bordeaux, and Cognac; and the Loire Valley, Normandy and Calvados. Each day has a separate map. Other information provided is the summary of vintages from 1959 through 1975 by region (with charts and ratings), plus material on selection, serving, storing, and drinking wines.

72.   Woon, Basil. **The Big Little Wines of France, Volumes One and Two.**
        London: Wine and Spirits Publications, 1972 and 1976; distr. by Inter-
        national Publications Services. $26 set.
This is a collection of "reports" from the eleven major wine districts of France,
together with a glossary of wine terms ("Language of Wine") and a pronunciation
guide to wines and vineyards. The "reports" have been expanded from their original appearance in *Wine* magazine (1970 to 1975).

73.   Woutaz, Fernand. **Dictionnaire des appellations.** Paris: Editions Librairies
        Techniques, 1982. 351p. illus. maps. 92 French francs paper.
This handy little book covers all the areas of France dealing with four categories
of alcoholic beverages: the A.O.C. wines, the V.D.Q.S. wines, the V.D.N. wines
(Vins doux naturels: sweet wines with their own set of legislation and regulatory
rules, little seen here in North America), and the eaux-de-vie beverages (Cognac,
Armagnac, Calvados, marcs, etc.). Each of the alphabetically arranged entries
describe the wine and the legal requirements, and give the production figures for
1980 (the latest available at the time of publication), the types of grapes used,
and some rating as to the quality of the wine (one to five stars). A useful book,
albeit in French, but easy to read.

Bordeaux

74.*   Benson, Jeffrey and Alastair Mackenzie. **Sauternes: A Study of the Great
        Sweet Wines of Bordeaux.** London: Sotheby Parke Bernet, 1979. 186p.
        illus. maps. index. $24.95.
This is the first book in English about the sweet wines of Bordeaux. All of the
important châteaux are here, with both historical and contemporary information,
as well as wine making data and some wines from Cérons and Loupiac. Each entry
gives the proportions of the grape varieties used, the methods of production, the
quantity produced, and so forth. Vintages are rated, 1890 through 1978, and there
are four useful maps of the area.

75.*   Benson, Jeffrey and Alastair Mackenzie. **The Wines of Saint-Emilion and
        Pomerol.** London: Sotheby Parke Bernet, 1983. 278p. illus. maps. index.
        £ 19.95.
This detailed work covers all of the vineyards and the wines, both great and small
(*Grands Crus* are described as well as the satellite communes), along with tasting
notes from 1900 to 1981. Each entry has material on the proportions of grape
varieties used, the methods of production, the quantity produced, and general
wine making techniques. Every aspect of a single area is covered: history, climate,
geology (including the variations in Saint-Emilion's soils, the distinction between
"côtes" and "graves"). Five major areas are described, and an intensive analysis
is made for well-known properties such as Ausone, Canon, Pavie, Figeac, Cheval-
Blanc, and Pétrus. Ownership records and property sizes are also covered in this
invaluable resource tool. The maps are excellent.

76.   Coates, Clive. **Claret.** London: Century Publishing, 1982. 432p. bibliog.
        maps. index. $32.

These are reprints of articles that originally appeared in *Decanter* magazine, written by a leading figure in the British wine trade. They are assessments of the forty-eight leading properties, together with comprehensive tasting notes of recent vintages (1961-1981), and a few notes on the rarer older wines. There is also material about the Bordeaux scene in general, a glossary of terms, and maps. Within each report there are vertical assessments for each château's wine, while at the back of the book there are horizontal assessments in the vintage section.

77.* **Decanter Magazine Guide to Médoc and Graves, 1983.** London: Decanter Magazine, 1983. 134p. illus. maps. $5 magazine size, soft covers.

78.* **Decanter Magazine Guide to St. Emilion and Pomerol, 1984.** London: Decanter Magazine, 1984. 134p. illus. maps. $5 magazine size, soft covers.
Each of these are short listings of some 250 vineyards and cooperatives, in a profile format: name, address, phone numbers, appellations, proprietor's name, other wines produced, vineyard area, vine varieties, average yield, 1982 vintage production, a statement of the wine-making techniques, the characteristics of the wine, visiting hours, and vintages for sale at the vineyard or property itself. There are notes on the recommended vintages from 1966 through 1982, and articles by Edmund Penning-Rowsell and David Peppercorn. There are advertisements, maps, listings of materials for sale or for purchase within the trade, and reproductions of labels (some in color). A lot of data has been crammed into these two tools; they are extremely useful.

79. Dovaz, Michael. **Encyclopedia of the Great Wines of Bordeaux: The Classified Growths.** Paris: René Julliard, 1981. 255p. illus. maps. $62.
This publication, available in a large-size format, covers the 1855 Classification of Médoc. Each of the important châteaux noted here is given two pages that cover recent vintages (and their ratings), detailed maps, labels, history, land, cultivation, vinification, wines made, and technical details (production, fermentation, percentage composition, aging, etc.). No Pomerols are listed except Château Pétrus. There are lots of color photographs here, in what is essentially a Médoc book.

80. Duijker, Hubrecht. **The Good Wines of Bordeaux and the Great Wines of Sauternes.** New York: Crescent Books, 1983. 200p. illus. maps. index. $19.95.
This book nicely complements the Dovaz book (and indeed there are other Duijker books on Burgundy and Loire and Alsatian wines; see below). The author examines here the *crus bourgeois* of Médoc, Saint-Emilion, Pomerol, and the better wines of Sauternes. It is profusely illustrated with color and black-and-white photographs, maps, and very tiny reproductions of labels. There are very few technical facts here, but the book is useful for atmosphere and background. Material is meant for the traveller, and as such it nicely completes Johnson's *Wine Atlas* for this part of the world. Given the amount of data that already exists on this area, the book is not as important as others Duijker has put together (most notably the one on Champagne and Alsace).

81.   Duijker, Hubrecht. **The Great Wine Châteaux of Bordeaux.** New York: Times Books, 1975. 199p. illus. maps. index. $39.95.

In a large format, with reproductions of labels and 350 color photographs, black-and-white pictures, and maps, Duijker's book records the activities of the wines, châteaux, and people in Bordeaux. He gives profiles of the great red wine estates (history, style of wine, cépage, vintages), but little material on wine assessments and evaluations (see also above).

82.   Enjalbert, Henri. **Les grands vins de Saint Émilion, Pomerol et Fronsac.** Paris: Editions Bardi, 1983. 634p. illus. maps. index. 400 French francs.

Quite similar to the Benson and Mackenzie book on this area, but of course the late Enjalbert's book is in French. It deals with the geology, culture, and history of the communes, with 28 maps and 72 pages of color photographs. It traces the development of the wine estates, with good examples. Enjalbert also breaks the climate down, developing a scheme for four half seasons in eight months. Material, very technical (more so than in Benson and Mackenzie), dwells on soils, grape varieties, water cycles, and drainage. There is a big index of châteaux and estates. A very worthwhile book.

83.   Faith, Nicholas. **Château Margaux.** London: Christie's Wine Publications, 1983. 120p. illus. $11 paper.

This short book details a corporate history of the structure of Château Margaux, one of the leading Médoc wines. It is a story of the vineyard, the château building and grounds itself, and the variety of owners over the years. Material and commentary also includes data on how the wines are made and blended, but reveal few secrets not already known by the knowledgeable oenophile.

84.   Faith, Nicholas. **Victorian Vineyard: Château Loudenne and the Gilbeys.** London: Christie's Wine Publications, 1983. 156p. illus. £ 9.95.

This is the story of two English brothers—the Gilbeys—who purchased the château in 1875 and established it as the oldest wholly English-owned château in Bordeaux. As with so many other corporate history books in the wine trade, the story concentrates on the financial dealings, the vineyards, the plantings, the château building and the grounds itself, and how the wines are made and blended.

85.   Faith, Nicholas. **The Winemakers.** New York: Harper & Row, 1978. 328p. illus. index. $12.95.

Faith examines the Bordeaux wine market, its history, the families, the businessmen, and the politics of the area. He also examines its economic structure (the booms and scandals), concluding with material about what has been called "winegate" (the switching of non-A.O.C. wine for cheap A.O.C. wines and the gross cover-ups). Interesting textual commentary.

86.*   Féret, Edouard. **Bordeaux et ses vins: classés par ordre de mérite dans chaque commune.** rev. and enlarged by Charles Féret. 13th ed. Bordeaux: Editions Féret et Fils, 1982; distr. by French and Europe. 1887p. illus. maps. $125.

The first edition of this monumental work was issued in 1867 by Charles Cocks; for years it was known as "Cocks et Féret," as M. Féret was added to do revisions.

Apparently, all trace of Mr. Cocks has disappeared by now, for "Féret" is the only name on the title page. This is the key reference book to Bordeaux. Part One, in 400 pages, has useful chapters on viticulture, vinification, and the wine trade in Bordeaux. Each region's A.O.C. is detailed, and the different classifications of the châteaux are given. There are many statistics here, all of them useful. While the book is in French, there is a universality in numbers so long as they are arabic numerals. Anyone with a modicum of French should be able to understand this book. Part Two is given over to describing the three thousand or so "châteaux," with data furnished by the owners. They are listed by commune and then in *cru* order (with editorial notes indicating that some wines are better than their listing would indicate). Space is also given over to the cooperatives in the region; these produce about one-third of the wines.

87. Littlewood, Joan and Edmund Penning-Rowsell. **Mouton-Baronne Philippe**. London: Christie's Wine Publications, 1982. 50p. illus. $8 paper.
Littlewood describes and discusses the château, while Penning-Rowsell provides the tasting notes of vintages from 1945 to 1978 (except for 1947, 1954, and 1968, because there were none of these available at the chateau itself). Color illustrations of the current proprietors and historical reproductions of labels and other items complete the information.

88.* Penning-Rowsell, Edmund. **The International Wine and Food Society's Guide to the Wines of Bordeaux**. 4th ed. New York: Scribner's, 1981. 704p. illus. maps. bibliog. index. $14.95 paper.
This is a magnificent work. Part One is a historical survey of the development of Bordeaux, with a history of the wine merchants and a history of the Médoc classifications. The author examines the importance of Bordeaux and its trade to England. Part Two describes the vines growing in each district and the vinification processes. Supplementary material details the opening wine prices for Bordeaux since 1831, the vintages since 1890, and the annual rainfall. Scattered throughout, there is much commentary on individual châteaux.

89.* Peppercorn, David. **Bordeaux**. London: Faber and Faber, 1982. 428p. illus. index. $24.95; $10.95 paper.
Peppercorn had a difficult subject to write about, since it is hard to find anything new to say about Bordeaux that hasn't already been said before (except, of course, for current information). However, he does so admirably by concentrating on the "trade" aspect, discussing the merchants and châteaux through a vast array of statistics, the appellation contrôlée regulations, the various I.N.A.O. Bordeaux châteaux classifications, and detail on climate, soils, quantities, and prices. Of course, most space is devoted to the Médoc, Graves, Saint-Émilion and Pomerol areas, with a fleeting look at the rest of Bordeaux (perhaps he is a bit too short with the Sauternes and the barsac areas). Individual châteaux and their owners are nicely profiled.

90. Pijassou, René. **Le Médoc: Un grand vignoble de qualité**. Paris: Editions Jules Tallandier, 1980. 2 vols. 1473p. illus. maps. bibliog. index. 280 French francs. ($75) paper, slipcased.

This is a good historical sourcebook, very serious (it was a 1978 thesis presented to the University of Bordeaux). With photographs, it has become a critically acclaimed work on the wines, vineyards, and châteaux of the Médoc area. The detailed history, the quality factors, the geographic influence and scope, the vinification processes, the descriptions of all the communes—they are here. He also comments on the quality of specific wines, both then and now (with vintages indicated). The work concludes with an extensive bibliography.

91.   Ray, Cyril. **Fide et Fortitudine: The Story of a Vineyard.** London: Pergamon Press, 1972. 111p. illus. £ 3.50.

This corporate history was written to commemorate the 150th anniversary of Barton's acquisition of Château Langoa and Leoville. The work gives much historical background and the story of the Barton family (plus some material on Guestier, the other half of "B & G"). There is also detail here on the Burgundy and Rhône acquisitions of the B & G group through natural expansion.

92.   Ray, Cyril. **Lafite: The Story of Château Lafite-Rothschild.** 2d ed. London: Christie's Wine Review, 1979. 162p. illus. bibliog. index. $16.

Ray, the author of many other corporate histories, has produced this memoir of Lafite's first hundred years. At the time, it was the first English book ever to be devoted to a single vineyard and its wine. Lafite is probably the most famous wine in all the world, and this fame contributes to the Second Empire nature of the Lafite vineyard. There are comparative prices of the first growths and Lafite auction prices, from the 1806 to 1970 vintages, vintage notes of 1847 to 1977 (with dates of picking, yields, quality, and production), and a postscript by Edmund Penning-Rowsell. A well-written account brimming with biographical detail and social history.

93.   Ray, Cyril. **Mouton-Rothschild.** London: Christie's Wine Publications, 1982. 96p. illus. $11 paper.

A good solid history of a château and family, including the grounds, the vineyards, the art of wine making and blending, and the on-site wine museum. There are also 32 pages of illustrations, tasting notes, and auction prices from 1858.

Burgundy

94.   Arlott, John and Christopher Fielden. **Burgundy: Vines and Wines.** rev. ed. London: Quartet Books. 1978. 250 p. illus. maps. index. £ 3.95 paper.

A good, reliable standard history and account of the production of the red and white wines of Burgundy. Individual chapters carefully detail the area with respect to geography, production, *Appellation Controllée* laws, histories of vineyards, and statistics of production.

95.   Duijker, Hubrecht. **The Great Wines of Burgundy.** New York: Crescent Books, 1983. 199p. illus. maps. index. $19.95.

Half of this book is devoted to colorful pictures in a standard format, which Duijker uses for the Bordeaux, Burgundy, Alsace, Champagne, and Loire areas.

The layout includes small reproductions of the labels and small print in general, but there is atmosphere and useful background information here. There is nothing really technical (and many of the wines are not really assessed nor rated), but there are facts of value for the traveller. The emphasis is on the individual grower and the estates and their wines.

96.   Gadille, Rolande. **Le Vignoble de la côte bourguignonne.** Paris: Les Belles Lettres, 1967. 688p. maps. tables. bibliog. index. 150 French francs.

97.   Grivot, Françoise. **Le Commerce des vins de bourgogne.** Paris: Sabri, 1964. 224p. illus. maps. bibliog. index. out of print.

These two books, both in French, do a comprehensive job of covering the basic material dealing with Burgundy. Gadille's book deals with climates, microclimates, morphological and topological structures, soils, erosion, rainfall, sunshine, plant life and vegetation, and the evolution and history of the vine. He attempts to determine what factors create the best wine. The wide fluctuations of soil and climate are examined, and comparative investigations are made into the years of best- and mediocre-quality wines. Also covered are the influences of modern techniques and the human elements. By examining the physical and human foundations of a high-quality viticulture, the author tries to answer the question, "what makes Burgundy wine so fantastic and so perfect?" The Grivot book deals with commerce: the impact of Burgundy wine on the economy of France. He examines the wine industry's structure, the roles played by the grower, the broker and the shipper, the merchant and the relevant associations, and discusses the A.O.C. laws and the annual auctions at the Hospices de Beaune.

98.*   Hanson, Anthony. **Burgundy.** London: Faber and Faber, 1982. 378p. illus. bibliog. maps. index. $30.

Hanson is a British professional M.W. active in the wine trade. His book clearly shows the fragmentation of the holdings of vineyards in the French Burgundy area, by way of lists, maps, and cogent explanations. Other material in this comprehensive survey includes a history of wine making in the region, the influences of soil, climate, vines, and methods on the finished product, wine laws, tasting notes, and specific details on the "trade," which is the complicated system involving the growers, brokers, merchants, and consumers. Of course, all the major estates are covered, and there are twenty-one line sketch maps to show locations. Appendices include vintages, statistics, and a glossary of terms.

99.   Orizet, Louis. **Mon Beaujolais.** Macon: Editions de la Grisière, 1976. 139p. illus. maps. price not available. paper.

Although in French, this book is relatively easy to follow since it is a lighthearted approach to a lighthearted wine: Beaujolais. He discusses the gamay grape, the vignerons, the vineyards, and the wine itself as he visits the cellars and quaffs in his travels the wines of Chénas, Côte de Brouilly, Fleurie, Juliénas, Morgon, Moulin-à-Vent, Saint-Amour, and so forth. Drawings are by the author.

100.   Poupin, Pierre and Pierre Forget. **Les vins de Bourgogne.** 4th ed. Paris: Les Presses Universitaires de France, 1977. 221p. illus. maps. bibliog. index. 50 French francs.

The third edition of this work, from 1964, has been translated into English from French and published by the Presses Universitaires de France. For more up-to-date information, the fourth edition is available in French, with topographic maps and material on the vines, the climate, and how wine is made. An area-by-area survey of both red and white wines is given. Material is also given for eaux-de-vie and sparkling wines, the wine trade, wine cellars, vinous festivities, and facts and figures. This is a very authoritative and highly useful book on the wines of Burgundy, their appellations, and the comparative rankings from Chablis to the Beaujolais.

101.   Rodier, Camille. **Les Clos de Vougeot.** Dijon: L. Damidot, 1959. 173p. illus. maps. index. out of print.

This is a reprint of a 1931 classic that gave a solid history of one of the Côte d'Or's oldest and most celebrated vineyards. Many anecdotes and much wine lore abound in the text, which is liberally sprinkled with prints, maps, and drawings.

102.   **Le Vin de Bourgogne.** Paris: Editions Montalba, 1976. 234p. illus. maps. price not available.

Six authors were involved in producing this book for the armchair traveller. Each vineyard of significance is given a short history, and there are tables of statistics dealing with production and consumption. Raymond Dumay presents details on history, the classification of wines, tasting notes, and food matches (along with a chapter on the gastronomic association la Confrérie des Chevaliers du Tastevin), while Pierre Poupon writes on the *vignerons* and on Clos de Vougeot. Other writers comment on the economy and the trade, although politely. Useful and easy to read in French.

103.*   Yoxall, Harry Waldo. **The International Wine and Food Society's Guide to the Wine of Burgundy.** 2d ed. New York: Stein & Day, 1979. 192p. illus. maps. bibliog. $10.

Originally published in 1970. Yoxall's book also covers marc and sparkling wines from the region (and some rosés). He visits the domaines, the auctions of the Hospices de Beaune, and the tastings, and he also eats the classic meals. His liberal (at least, legal) definition also includes Chablis and Beaujolais; consequently these wines are also included here. In this context he deals with "fake" Burgundy wines. Also, there is a discussion about prolonged vinification versus short vinification. Several appendices cover vintage charts, classifications, listings (by *"grand"* and *"premier"* *crus*) plus material on the A.O.C. minimum and maximum quantities in the vinification processes. His recommendations for tastings and his notes are very appropriate.

Champagne

104.   Arlott, John. **Krug—House of Champagne**. London: Davis-Poynter, 1976.
224p. illus. bibliog. index. £ 10.

This is a history of the Champagne firm, with lots of illustrations, historical photographs and scenery, reproductions of older labels, and other good artwork. There are facsimiles of cellar holdings, genealogical tables, and portraits, as well as a glossary and a two-page bibliography for further readings about the Krug firm and Champagne in general.

105.*   Campbell, Dennis, ed. **Champagne: The Anytime Wine**. London: Faber
and Faber, 1983. 176p. illus. $7.95 paper.

This is a basic history of Champagne, complete with many photographs and drawings illustrating the good life. The general book shows how Champagne is made, the types of grapes involved, the procedures for the secondary fermentation (and the Dom Pérignon legend), and the many social uses of Champagne. There is also some material on the assessment of the various vintages.

106.   Cronin, Isaac and Rafael Pallais. **Champagne!** New York: Pocket Books,
1984. 97p. illus. bibliog. index. $5.95 paper.

Cronin's book covers more than just French Champagne; it also delves into any kind of sparkling wines: the German *sekt*, the Italian *asti*, the Spanish *cava*, even the American bubbly (as well as other forms of French sparkling wines, principally from the Loire area). A lot of ground is covered in a summary mode, since the book gives a good once-over to the Champagne industry. There are lists of producers and material on their house styles; there are quick definitions to the technical processes. Topics also include a history of French Champagnes, the development of other countries' knock-offs, a guide to labelling requirements, how to taste champagne, some recipes for mixed drinks (mainly all the traditional drinks, starting with Kir Royal and Mimosa), and some food recipes that are rich and elegant, as befits the Champagne style.

107.   Dovaz, Michael. **L'Encyclopedie des vins de Champagne**. Paris: René
Julliard, 1983. 255p. illus. maps. $60.

This publication, available in a large-size format and only in French at the moment, is quite similar to his *Encyclopedia of the Great Wines of the Bordeaux*. All of the important companies are here, with a minimum of two pages each that cover: recent vintages, detailed maps, labels, history, land, cultivation, vinification methods, the styles of wines that are made, and technical details of the blending processes, production, fermentation, percentages of composition, aging, and so forth. There are many color photographs here. The listings of the houses of Champagnes have information about the cuvées produced.

108.   Forbes, Patrick. **Champagne: The Wine, the Land, and the People**. rev.
ed. London: Victor Gollancz, 1982. 492p. illus. maps. tables. bibliog.
index. $25.

Forbes presents a unity of subject matter: Champagne refers to the province, the wine field within, and the wine itself. Hence, in this epic, which is the result of nine years' work (plus eleven years between the first and revised editions), Mr. Forbes deals with wine, countryside, soil, geological features, history, and people. He opens his book with a travelogue, then a history (Champagne was the crossroads of Europe), followed by a discussion of sparkling Champagne and its modern history. Part Two is more technical, dealing with how the wine develops (how it is planted and tended, the annual cycle of work) and a description of the harvesting and vinification. There are also the obligatory tips on drinking, anecdotes, people and food, material on the bottle construction and corks (very important), and chapters on the fifteen great champagne makers in a sort of corporate history style of writing. The book concludes with a useful 6-page bibliography.

109.   Ray, Cyril. **Bollinger: The Story of Champagne.** London: Peter Davies, 1971. 179p. illus. maps. index. £5.
This is a corporate history of a Champagne manufacturer, by an author who is skilled in such writing (see entry 92 in the section on Bordeaux wines). Apart from the Bollinger firm itself, the highlight here is the fine detail that Ray presents, such as his description of the story of the 1811 Champagne riots.

110.   Simon, André. **The History of Champagne.** London: Octopus Books, 1971. 192p. illus. maps. bibliog. index. $9.50.
This is a reprint of the 1962 Ebury Press version, itself an update of Simon's 1905 epic, *The History of the Champagne Trade in England.* Simon, an exceptionally acute and learned wine writer, here presents several interesting topics of value: the social aspects of drinking Champagne, the growth of an industry (from its origins to 1960), the story of the cork and Dom Pérignon, the idea of *chaptalisation* (adding sugar to the must, developed by M. Chaptal), what vintages mean, the special kinds of bottles and corks and glasses, and the legislation behind the protection of the word "Champagne" (as in "Spanish Champagne," now a "no-no" phrase). Simon began his wine career in the Champagne importing business (for Pommery); he knew his material. Illustrative sections here are very useful: there are color photographs, tables of statistics (sales and shipping), maps, and many historical quotations.

Other Regions

111.*   Blanchet, Suzanne. **Les vins du val de Loire.** Saumur: Editions JEMA S.A., 1982. 734p. illus. maps. 300 French francs.
This exhaustive book is extremely useful. Although written in French, it is structured much the same as Féret's book on Bordeaux wines; it is a directory-listing of the vineyards and the wines, and anyone with a French-English dictionary could certainly use this book. Most of it is in tabular form, and there is some English written in it (but scattered throughout). In scope it covers the Pays Nantais, the Anjou-Saumur, and the Touraine regions of the Loire. It lists every vineyard over two hectares, arranged by commune. There is one page per entry, with the population of the area, hectares of the area and hectares under vine, the number of vineyards, the soils and climates, the wines produced and their appellations, reproductions of the various labels, and a listing of the vignerons and viticulturers, along

with their addresses and production figures. At the beginning of this magnificent tool, there is a superb section that clearly outlines the organization and administration of the Loire area, with maps and material about the government.

112.   Brunel, Gaston. **A Guide to the Vineyards of the Côtes du Rhône.** New
        York: St. Martin's, 1984. 254p. illus. $30.
This is a fairly complete guide to the wines available from the Côtes du Rhône area. It was first published in Paris by Ed. J. C. Lattes in 1980.

113.*   Duijker, Hubrecht. **The Wines of the Loire, Alsace and Champagne.**
        New York: Crescent Books, 1983. 200p. illus. maps. index. $19.95.
In common with the other books by Duijker, this oversized picture book presents basic data on the wines of the three regions (Alsace, Loire, and Champagne), along with colorful maps, tiny reproductions of the wine labels, and text about the major producers. Actually, this is one of the better books in the series, since there is little information about these areas in English, apart from the general survey books. Of course, the stress here is on white wines. The wines of Alsace have always been underrated, and there are great bargains to be had from both the Loire and Champagne districts.

114.*   Hallgarten, S. F. **Alsace and Its Wine Gardens, Cellars, and Cuisine.** rev.
        ed. London: Wines and Spirits Publications, 1978. 240p. illus. index.
        $11.95.
This is an indispensable guide to the many varietal wines of Alsace, including a detailed journey along the "route de vin." Covered are the history, the geography, the language, and the character of the area. All the wines are discussed, and the author points out that most people are either Riesling or Gewurztraminer lovers.

115.*   Livingstone-Learmouth, John and Melvyn C. H. Master. **Wines of the
        Rhône.** 2d ed. London: Faber and Faber, 1983. 383p. illus. maps. index.
        $24.95; $10.95 paper.
This book was originally issued in 1978; the second edition is about 50 percent larger. The arrangement is by appellation, e.g., Cornas, Hermitage, Crozes-Hermitage, and so forth; but while there is some detail on the rarely seen light Côtes du Ventoux (almost like a Beaujolais), there is nothing here about the Côtes du Rhône "primeur" wine, which is like Beaujolais nouveau and has been made at least since 1979. The appendices include the A.O.C. laws, vineyard figures, crop figures, and exports. There is a calendar of wine fairs, a listing of the wine cellars open to the public, and a glossary, but no bibliography. Like several of the other Faber books on wine, the authors here tend to be a little critical of the wine trade in the area.

116.   **Les Vins du Roussillon.** Paris: Editions Montalba, 1980. 127p. illus. price
        not available.
Although in French, this book is quite easy to understand with the aid of a French-English dictionary. It is highly useful, because there is little information around on the Roussillon wines from the Southwest of France. Six writers were involved,

as well as quite a few photographers, for this series of photo-essays. They cover travel, history of the vine, traditions of the wine, technical trade data and quality of the product (with the usual laws and regulations), and the matching of food and wines.

117. Wasserman, Sheldon and Pauline Wasserman. **The Wines of the Côtes du Rhône.** New York: Stein & Day, 1977. 230p. index. $15.

This basic book covers the history of the area, the producers, the various vintages, and the cuisines of the Rhône River. A good book for the data on the start of the vines that go back to Roman times, on the story of the Popes, and on the strong character of the wines, both red and white.

118.* Weston, J. M. **Wine from Where the Mistral Blows.** London: Wine and Spirits Publications, 1981. unpaged. maps. photos. £ 4.95.

A highly useful book dealing with the Languedoc-Roussillon area, especially noted for its political unrest and overproduction of wines. The history here concerns the V.D.Q.S. wines, the loss of the North African colonies (and their export markets), and the attempts at recovery—still in progress. The wines here are the Minervois, Corbières, Fitou, Côtes du Roussillon, and the Blanquette de Limous: all are heavy and grapey in feel and in taste. The book covers the land, the people, and the gastronomy. There are six double-page maps in color, as well as black-and-white photographs. There are also technical appendices of facts and figures of wine production and exports.

119. Yapp, Robin and Judith Yapp. **Vineyards and Vignerons.** Shaftesbury, Dorset: Blackmore, 1979. 128p. illus. £ 7.95.

The Yapps are involved in designs and drawings; there are seventy-six such illustrations here of the wines and artisans and vignerons of the Loire and Rhône valleys. The text describes the countryside, the wine-growers, and the wines, with good sections on the sauvignon blanc grape and the varieties needed in the Rhône area. Covered are Pouilly-Fumé, Sancerre, Hermitage, and Côte Rotie.

Germany

120. Ambrosi, Hans. **Where the Great German Wines Grow: A Guide to the Leading Vineyards.** New York: Hastings House, 1976. 240p. illus. index. $12.95.

Ambrosi is a prolific wine author in Germany. This current book is basically a directory of addresses and phone numbers, with a description of some ninety estates that have a vineyard area of more than fifty acres. He is only concerned here with wines that have been produced since 1971, when the new laws took effect. He provides descriptive histories, and notes on the mansions and cellars, soils, grape varieties, and labels and vineyards' marketing all over the world. Tourist data is indicated, such as routes of travel, visiting hours, and tasting facilities. The illustrations are basically line drawings of maps and wine labels (and there is an in-depth explanation of how to read a German wine label). There are lists of important societies and information centers as well as their addresses; and there is also a very useful German-English dictionary of both the appreciative and the technical terms used in the German wine industry.

121.   **German Wine Atlas and Vineyard Register.** rev. English edition, translated by Nadia Fowler. New York: Hastings House, 1979. 90p. illus. maps. $9.95.

This atlas was originally published in West Germany in 1974; there are 66 color-coded maps and 101 color photos. It greatly expands and complements Johnson's *The World Atlas of Wine,* especially since it has positional maps to show the relationship of the eleven major areas to each other. Other useful maps include road routes for travellers, colorful key maps that show the general and individual sites of properties and vineyards, and a geographical arrangement by region with a text of historical details. There are photographs of scenery, artifacts, buildings, and grape varieties. Sidebars include data on geography, microclimates, wine cultivation, and historical points of nonwine interest. The atlas concludes with useful addresses and a listing of wine festivals.

122.*   Hallgarten, S. F. **German Wines: A Journey through the Wine Districts of Western Germany.** 5th ed. rev. and enlarged. London: Faber and Faber, 1981. 397p. illus. maps. bibliog. index. $19.95.

This is a classic book that was originally published in 1951. It contains superb black-and-white photos and decent maps, and many personal accounts. The extensive bibliography makes reference to numerous German works. The first third of the contents covers the history of German viticulture, the grape harvest, sweetening, fermentation, filtering, blending, the 1971 German nomenclature, diseases of the vines, judging and tastings, and when to drink German wines. The next third concentrates on touring each of the eleven major areas—Rheinhessen, Nahe, Rheingau, Mittelheim, Mosel, Franken, etc.—along with descriptions of German "Sekt" (sparkling wines), wine festivals, and local cuisines. The last third of the book has appendices dealing with German wine-growing centers, vineyards, class names and districts, tasting notes, glossaries, and wine classifications.

123.   Loeb, O. W. and Terence Prittie. **Moselle.** London: Faber and Faber, 1972. 221p. illus. maps. bibliog. index. £ 6.

When my sourcebook first came out in 1974, this book by Loeb and Prittie was hailed as "the only modern wine book in English that deals with one particular section of German wines." It was the newest book in my chapter on German wines, but now, ten years later, it is the oldest. Still, it *is* still the only book in English devoted to a particular region of Germany. It is a complete book, with maps and photographs that present concise information on all the vineyards in the Mosel Valley. Covered are the principal vineyards of the Upper Mosel, Saar, Ruhr, and the Middle and Lower Mosel Valleys. Both authors draw on personal experience and the historical record. Loeb was a wine merchant born in the Mosel area, and Prittie was an experienced wine journalist.

124. Meinhard, Heinrich. **The International Wine and Food Society's Guide to the Wines of Germany.** New York: Stein & Day, 1976. 276p. illus. index. $15.

Meinhard had originally written a 102-page book in 1971; this is the revised and expanded version, in English. He begins with a short history that goes back to the second century A.D., discussing the "Romanized" Celtic wine growers. He continues with little side trips into various legends and lores of the grape and the wine, including the effects that Christianity had. Then he presents a tour of the vineyards in eleven areas, along with sketch maps. He states the characteristics of each area, listing over seventeen grape varieties and wines, how they are grown, and their relative measures of sweetness. The 1971 wine laws are discussed, modernization is commented on, and much advice is given on selecting from a German wine list. A useful book.

125. Pieroth, Kuno. **The Great German Wine Book.** New York: Sterling Press, 1983. 208p. illus. index. $22.50.

Originally published in German in 1980, this book serves as a general survey of German wines with chapters on history, art, and literature, the eleven wine districts and their characteristics, the German style of wine making, the uses of wine, the German wine laws of 1971 and their subsequent revisions, German wine vintages through 1981, the combination of food and wine, and a wine-tasting glossary of both English and German terms. Pieroth is well qualified to write this book, for he is a managing director of a Nahe district wine maker that has been established for almost three hundred years. The book comes with many large color illustrations and reproductions of both a historical and a contemporary nature. The typeface is overly large.

126. Raelson, Jeffrey E. **Getting to Know German Wines.** Miami, Fla.: Banyan Books, 1979. 80p. illus. maps. index. $4.95 paper.

This is a consumer-geared, slight book on the straightforward characteristics of the German wines available in the United States. It has easy-to-read maps and a good guide to the wine label. Raelson also attempts an evaluation of the vintages since 1900.

127.* Ray, Cyril. **The Wines of Germany.** New York: Penguin Books, 1979. 224p. illus. maps. bibliog. index. $3.95 paper.

Prolific writer Ray here turns his skills to the world of German wines. In a breezy, chatty style he covers the history, the grape varieties, the wine laws, and the regional characteristics of the eleven districts. Then, as he did with his Italian wine book (see entry 138, under Italy), he gives a detailed listing of the major vineyards and their wines, always with his interesting comments and production figures. An interesting book to read.

128.* Sichel, Peter M. F. **The Wines of Germany: Frank Schoonmaker's Classic.** rev. ed. New York: Hastings House, 1980. 223p. illus. bibliog. index. $10.95.

Schoonmaker probably knew more about German wines than any other English-speaking individual. His classic study was originally published in 1956 and was comprised mainly of reprints of his articles from *Gourmet* magazine. Subsequent updatings have only been applied to changes of ownership of the various vineyards and of the vintage years. Sichel has totally recast the book (and indeed it is now his own) to be a short but reliable guide to the laws and the labels of the German wines. The early material dealing with geography and wine types and the description of the four major growing areas—Mosel, Rheingau, Rheinhessen and Palatinate—are still Schoonmaker's. Sketch maps are included, as well as a discussion of growers and vintages (this latter is by Sichel). Concluding material deals with how to buy and store German wines, and how to serve and taste them. Quite properly there is limited material on red wines and on "Sekt." Appended is a "brief list of German wine-tasting terms."

Italy

129.*   Anderson, Burton. **Burton Anderson's Guide to Italian Wines**. New York: Simon and Schuster, 1984. 160p. illus. maps. bibliog. index. $8.95.

Twenty regions are covered in this by now well-established format of pocket guides to wines and foods. The alphabetical range is from Abruzzi to Veneto, with descriptions of hundreds of wines: where they came from, the grapes used, the percentage of the blends, how the wines taste, when to drink, the leading producers, and a star rating system on drinkability and value. Each region has a vintage chart-commentary, travel tips, maps, regional food specialties (with accompanying wines being suggested), and recommended restaurants in the area. Only this latter is highly restrictive and immaterial if you don't intend to travel to Italy. The introductory matter has a glossary of terms, temperature charts, listings of the important grapes, some information on the laws and labels, and details on the present state of the industry in Italy. The index is complete, with a mention of every single wine commented on in the regions concerned.

130.   Anderson, Burton. **Vino: The Wines and Wine Makers of Italy**. Boston: Atlantic-Little, Brown, 1980. 416p. illus. index. $19.95.

Anderson, who now lives in Tuscany and writes about Italian wines for the major magazines, has visited all of the major wineries of Italy. His book is arranged by the twenty regions, and within each is presented a series of interviews with Italian wine makers. The work is largely biographical, with material on how to make wine rather than what the wine tastes like. Photographs are included, as well as specific vintage charts for dozens of wines.

131.*   Dallas, Philip. **Italian Wines**. 2d ed. London: Faber and Faber, 1983. 309p. maps. illus. index. $24.95; $11.95 paper.

Dallas' book was first published in 1974, in North America by Doubleday. Of course, in the past ten years there have been immense changes in the Italian wine industry. For wine connoisseurs, these changes are mainly in the newly designated D.O.C.G. laws for certain wines that will be available in 1984 and 1985, for barolo, barburesis, vino nobile di Montepulicano, and brunello di Montalcino. The structure of the Italian wine markets is related to the commercial change of the North

American consumer; that is, the public perception of Italian wines has been heightened because of a good marketing campaign, while wines in other countries have been overtaxed or made scarce (thereby forcing many drinkers to change to Italian wines for value). Dallas' book discusses all this, but at the moment (with the soft franc and the aggressive marketing of the French food and wine associations in mid-1984), there has been a resurgence of French wine imports into North America. Dallas' book describes the various types of wine available, region by region, with appropriate indexes to the names of the wines.

132.   **Discovering Italian Wines: An Authoritative Compendium of Wines, Food and Travel through the Nineteen Producing Regions of Italy.** Los Angeles: Ward Ritchie Press, 1971. 136p. illus. index. $7.95 paper.

After a foreword by Robert Balzer and five pages devoted to the "history and legends" of wine, the book consists of two main sections: "The Controlled Wines of Italy, by Region" and "The Foods of Italy." The wines are described in about a paragraph, and their properties and characteristics are defined (color, taste, and alcoholic content). In the second section, regional recipes are presented with some commentary by the late Mike Roy. Good, lively color photographs make this an attractive book, and useful despite its apparent ancestry within the Italian National Wine Committee.

133.   Flower, Raymond. **Chianti: The Land, the People, and the Wine.** New York: Universe Books, 1979. 305p. illus. bibliog. index. $17.50.

Flower has been a twenty-year resident and wine grower in the Chianti area of Tuscany. This is a basic descriptive book, told with anecdotes and biographic profiles of some of the wine makers, owners, and colorful residents of the countryside. There are several useful appendices: places of interest, a list of the major producers, and notes from local archives.

134.*   Hazan, Victor. **Italian Wine.** New York: Random House, 1982. 337p. illus. bibliog. index. $17.95.

Hazan is husband of Marcella Hazan, who has written the definitive cookbooks about Italian food. Here he presents his information in a chatty style, but unlike most other books on Italian wine that list the grape products in a geographical arrangement, Hazan prefers to arrange his material by character. Thus, first up are the big red wines (barolo, chianti, brunello, rubesco, amarone, and others, some minor), followed by the medium-red wines (e.g. barbera), and then the light reds (e.g., valpolicella). His second section lists the white wines, again in three categories: light and crisp, full and fruity, and sweet. There is, of course, an index so that you can go straight to the description of the wine. If you like one style of wine, then you might want to browse through the surrounding pages in order to learn more about other, similar wines. This is an effective book, mainly for its arrangement by type of wine. Other useful material here includes the sections on the wine laws and production zones (with maps), chapters on how to serve and when to serve wines, and a glossary.

135.   Ortolani, Vinicio. **Wines of Italy and Italian Wines Imported into Canada.**
         2d ed. Ottawa: Runge Press, 1976. 127p. illus. index. $10.
Ortolani's book is in four parts. The first concerns general wine data (origins,
storing, serving, tasting, glasses). The second is an overview of Italy's wine regions,
with maps, pictures, the names of wines, and an explanation of the D.O.C. wine
laws. Part Three is a name, with descriptions for each as to grape varieties, aging,
coloration, taste, food accompaniment, alcoholic content, and acidity. For
example, Elba is listed "light gold (11%), cold–hors d'oeuvres and fish–better
young." Part Four is a listing of specific labels available in the various provinces
of Canada. A useful book, with brief, snappy comments.

136.   Pelluci, Emanuele. **Antinori Vintners in Florence.** Firenze: Vallecchi
         Editore, 1981. 113p. illus. price not available.
This English translation of a corporate history of a chianti wine company comes
with a series of black-and-white photographs. Antinori is a very well-known name in
the region. Along the way the author also manages to describe the history and
development of chianti wine and the Tuscany province. As a history of the Antinori
family, there is much detail on their estates, the character of the family, their
business acumen, and so forth. Near the end of the book, Pelluci gives an assessment of the wines and the vines and their styles.

137.   Pelluci, Emanuele. **Brunello di Montalcino.** Firenze: Vallecchi Editore,
         1981. 132p. illus. maps. $20 paper.
This, too, is an English translation of an Italian work. Pelluci here looks at the other
great Tuscan wine: brunello. This is Italy's most celebrated, longest-lasting wine,
and the story is incredibly rich in detail: history, folklore, vineyards, and producers
and their styles. There are about a hundred photos, in both color and black and
white, as well as maps indicating the lines of demarcation for the various estates.

138.*   Ray, Cyril. **The New Book of Italian Wines.** rev. ed. London: Sidgwick
         and Jackson, 1982. 158p. bibliog. index. $19.95.
This is an index to the principal wines of Italy. Arrangement is by region from
north to south (with preliminary material for a general discussion of each area),
followed by the types of wines found locally. This dictionary form results in over
six hundred entries; each entry has a description of the grape varieties used, the
percentage of alcohol allowed, and tasting notes. The introductory matter outlines
the history of Italian wines. First published in 1966, it was immediately translated
into Italian and it won a Bologna Trophy in 1967. New material includes a discussion of the newer D.O.C. and D.O.C.G. wine laws, the new E.E.C. wine legislation, and the unprecedented growth of the wine cooperative movement in Italy.
This is a very useful book, despite the fact that no more than a couple of dozen
of the wines are available in either Britain or the United States. Most good Italian
wines stay at home, but they are learning that marketing the good wines will pull
along the sales of their more inexpensive wines.

139.   Ray, Cyril. **Ruffino: The Story of a Chianti.** Florence: Ruffino, 1978.
         153p. illus. $38.

Ray by now is master of the vinuous corporate history; he has written about a half dozen of these types of books. All are interesting and insightful into the work of the vintner's art. This particular book is more a glossy paean to Ruffino (note the publisher), and there are many double-page color plates. Here, then, are details about the wine, the countryside, and the house of Ruffino, a well-known and respected wine producer in the region.

140.   Roncarati, Bruno. **Viva Vino: D.O.C. Wines of Italy**. London: Wines and Spirits Publications, 1976. 189p. illus. maps. index. £ 10.
This is a detailed description of quality Italian wines, with particular reference to the new laws on controlled denomination of origin. Roncarati explains all the new regulations since 1963 and the amendments. This is an exceptionally well-detailed, well-written account covering the main geographic areas.

141.   Sarles, John D. **ABC's of Italian Wines: An Encyclopedia**. San Marco, California: Wine Books, 1981. 221p. illus. maps. index. $12.95.
Sarles is a wine merchant. In this book he presents brief historical sketches of the wine of Italy, tracing their development to the modern day and including a pronunciation guide. Each of the alphabetically arranged entries that comprise the main bulk of the book are concisely written and informative as to types of grapes used, where the wine is made, and its main characteristics. Twenty-three maps and 325 labels serve as illustrations, and there is an index to the wines and the regions in alphabetical order.

142.   Wasserman, Sheldon. **The Wines of Italy: A Consumer's Guide**. New York: Stein & Day, 1976. 227p. illus. bibliog. maps. index. $10.
Wasserman presents the basics in an easy-to-read, flowing manner. The description is regional and proceeds from north to south. He rates the labels by price categories and vintages, but there are no outright assessments on the tasting qualities. Along the way there are many statistics, wine law listings, and descriptions of Italian wines of value for under $5, and a concluding glossary of terms.

Portugal

143.*   Bradford, Sarah. **The Story of Port: The Englishman's Wine**. 2d ed. London: Christie's Wine Review, 1978. 160p. illus. bibliog. $10.50 paper.
A solid, historical work (it goes back to the Douro in 137 B.C. for the founding of Oporto), this book is really the history of an area and its trade rather than the story of a wine. There is a detailed description of the port trade today, including how port is made, important information about individual shippers and their practices, and an explanation of how "vintage" port is determined and the difference between Oporto-bottled and foreign-bottled port. Appendices describe the vintage years from the eighteenth century, and the British Port Houses (importers and merchants); these supplement Charles Sellers' *Oporto Old and New* (London, 1899), which described the geneaology of the "portocracy." Throughout the text there are extensive quotations from historical correspondence; the work concludes with a bibliography and a glossary of port terms (two pages each).

144.   Delaforce, John. **The Factory House of Oporto.** London: Christie's Wine
        Review, 1979. 108p. illus. $10 paper.
This well-researched volume on the Factory House in Oporto deals with the trade,
customs, and notable personalities of the "portocracy." The Factory House is an
elegant Regency mansion in the heart of the old city where the British "factors"
or merchants assembled to discuss the port wine market and to socialize. They still
meet there for business and social purposes. A very interesting history.

145.   Fletcher, Wyndham. **Port: An Introduction to its History and Delights.**
        London: Sotheby Parke Bernet, 1978. 124p. illus. index. $22.50.
This is an engaging discourse on the techniques and history of port. Along with
basic data on the Douro region, Fletcher presents a series of corporate histories
of the various shippers and the tables of notes on vintage ports since 1870. There
are many useful color photographs here. Fletcher, at the time of writing, was a
director of Cockburn's and Harvey's; hence, there is lots of information here on
Cockburn.

146.*   Howkins, Ben. **Rich, Rare & Red: The International Wine and Food
        Society's Guide to Port.** London: W. Heinemann, 1982. distr. by David
        & Charles. 169p. illus. bibliog. index. $18.95.
The Bradford, Fletcher, and Robertson (see entries 143, 145, and 149) books on
port were all issued or brought up to date through 1978; Howkins here extends
the time frame to 1982 through the updated statistics and vintage charts. Apart
from that, this is a basic primer with details on history, types of vineyards, matura-
tion schedules, and the trade, with good material on how to visit the producers,
how to taste fortified drinks, and a description of the varieties of white port, ruby
port, tawny port, late bottled vintage port, and vintage port. Also, there is some
interesting material on the port knockoffs from around the world, principally
the United States, Australia, and South Africa.

147.   Knox, Oliver. **Croft: A Journey of Confidence, 1578-1978.** London:
        Collins, 1978. 32p. illus. £4.50.
This is a very short history of the Croft company and its activities in Portugal,
particularly with port, in celebration of its four hundred years in business. Good
color illustrations.

148.*   Read, Jan. **The Wines of Portugal.** London: Faber and Faber, 1982. 190p.
        illus. maps. bibliog. index. $15.
This book was originally written in 1973 as *The Wines of Spain and Portugal*;
the author and the publisher have now wisely split the book's topic into two and
have produced a revision. This book is far more comprehensive than that of a
decade before, primarily because of the increased availability of data and a new
awareness of these wines as "good buys" in these inflationary times. The inclusion
of photographs, the appendices on production, exports, estate names and qualifications, the short chapters on spirits, the glossaries of Portuguese technical wine
terms, and the sketch maps of the wine-producing regions—all of these enhance the
value of this member of the Faber series of wine books. The wines are described

according to region, with some emphasis on soils, climate, grape varieties, vinification practices and tasting notes. Port, of course, has its own short chapter, and there is already a book in the Faber series on port—Robertson's (see entry 149). Also of some interest here is the chapter on cork, especially since Portugal produces 52 percent of the world's cork. The bibliography is excellent for further reading, albeit mostly for Portuguese-language documents.

149.   Robertson, George. **Port**. London: Faber and Faber, 1978. 192p. illus. bibliog. index. $12.95; $7.95 paper.
Robertson has been a leading figure in the Portuguese wine and port trade. His book in the Faber wine series covers the regions, history, land, soil, climate, and production, with chapters on selecting, serving, and keeping a cellar. This is largely a technical work, but it thereby becomes an excellent reference book, made even better by the updating provided by Howkins (see entry 146).

150.   Stanislawski, Dan. **Landscapes of Bacchus: The Vine in Portugal**. Austin, Texas: University of Texas Press, 1970. 210p. illus. maps. bibliog. index. $14.50.
With eighty-one illustrations and a series of folding maps, this is a very readable account of the spread of viticulture in Portugal. It is mostly historical, with some technical aspects discussed. The effect of the vine and the grape on the character of the economy of Portugal is clearly shown. The author examines the prime growing areas and tries to account for the role played by wine in the emerging agricultural economy. Much statistical information is used.

Spain

151.   Casas, Penelope. **The Foods and Wines of Spain**. New York: Knopf, 1982. 457p. illus. index. $17.95.
Casas' book does a good job in describing the regional cuisines in about four hundred recipes. She also presents interesting data on mixed drinks, with a variety of sangrias and hot beverages as well. There is a concluding section on Spanish wines and sherries. This has many charts of evaluation to distinguish one type of wine from another, indicating vintage years and good buys, plus details on the unique wine-making process so vital to the sherry industry. This book also has an extensive section on "tapas," the Spanish appetizers; the 50 pages here describe some delicious preparations suitable for home entertaining with a sherry party. Maybe "tapas and sherry" will replace "wine and cheese"?

152.   **Decanter Magazine Wine Guide to Spain**. London: Decanter Magazine, 1983. 72p. illus. maps. magazine size, soft covers $5.
Decanter magazine, one of the world's leading wine publications, has issued this exciting guide to the good wines of Spain. There are reports from all of the regions (sherry, Montilla, Penedès, Valdepeñas, Rioja, and so forth), as well as the *cava* wines (Spanish "Champagne," made through the Champagne method of secondary fermentation in the bottle) and profiles of forty-one Rioja bodegas. Each of the latter have been assessed through the various vintages of the past decade. John Reeder contributes a chapter on new trends in Spanish wine making. There is also a chapter on Spanish olives, but this seems out of place. Advertisements complete the package of surveys.

153.   Gordon, Manuel Gonzalez. **Sherry: The Noble Wine.** New York: A. S.
         Barnes, 1972. 237p. illus. maps. index. $15.

This classic study was originally published in Spanish in 1948, and is here translated
by Floyd M. Dixon. Gordon was active for fifty years in the family firm of
Gonzalez Byass. Everything that an enthusiastic wine amateur would want to know
is contained between these two covers: vineyards, grapes, flor, soleras, two centuries of sherry trade, and detailed information about the town of Jerez. Extensively illustrated with 32 pages of illustrations, 18 line drawings and 2 maps.

154.   Huetz de Lemps, Alain. **Vignobles et vins du nor-ouest de l'Espagne.**
         Bordeaux: Les Impressions Bellnef, 1967. 2 vol. illus. maps. bibliog.
         index. price not available.

This is a useful Ph.D. dissertation, unfortunately only available in French. It is a
concentrated study of twelve years of research into an area responsible for one-
fifth of Spanish wine production but almost 100 percent of her quality wines:
Rioja and parts of Navarre. This exhaustive study of a microclimate deals with the
types of grapes, the history of the vineyards since the Roman times, and the influence of the vintners who fled to the area away from the phylloxera louse that was
invading Bordeaux in the late nineteenth century (this is why the Rioja wines have
a Bordeaux style about them). There is much detail—and statistics, which are
universal to read—on the production of the vineyards, the business of marketing,
the production of special wines and eaux-de-vie, and the development of the
bodegas and the cooperatives.

155.*   Jeffs, Julian. **Sherry.** 3d ed. London: Faber and Faber, 1982. 314p.
         illus. maps. bibliog. index. $19.95.

Jeffs is the general editor of the Faber series on wines (he has one other book here
on European wines). That there is much material available in Spanish about sherry
is demonstrated by Jeffs' lengthy bibliography. The first part of the text here is
historical, based on original sources in both Spanish and English, and emphasizing
the wine trade and politics of the two countries. Some descriptions are given of
important wine merchants through history. Part Two is descriptive of techniques,
the importance of flor, and the solera system. Other scattered material deals with
Manzanilla, blending, choosing a sherry (from fino to cream in sweetness range),
statistical data on exports, the Guy-Lussac scales, and other bits of information
that have never been published before. The book was originally published in 1952,
and it immediately won an award from the O.I.V. It was last revised in 1970, and
the changes in the sherry trade over the past decade are all cogently explained.
This includes the economic slump, the high labor costs, the mergers of firms, and
new technologies (most of which became applicable only after the death of
Franco). The appendices include a list of Spanish trade names, cask making notes,
further statistics, and a glossary of terms.

156.   Layton, T. A. **Wines and Castles of Spain.** New York: White Lion Pub-
         lishers, 1974. 254p. illus. index. $10.

This is a tour book, useful for its regional approach to the wines of Spain. Nothing
too technical here, and the writing is first-class, since Layton has had experience
with this type of book before and really knows his wines. Of course, many of the

castles are now "paradores" that travellers can stay at, much like country inns (see entry 160).

157.   Millner, Cork. **Sherry ... the Golden Wine of Spain.** White Hall, Va.: Betterway Publications, Inc., 1984. 168p. illus. index. $18.95.

This interesting book is meant for the general reader; it has neither the depth nor the substance of the Jeffs book (see entry 155). It does have some interesting material on American producers of sherry (Almaden, Paul Masson, Taylor, Gallo, and Christian Brothers) and how they fit into the overall context of sherry making around the world. There are also lists of Spanish bodegas (producers of sherry) and some commentary on the myths and legends that have sprung up around the sherry process, particularly the solera system. There is also material on Spanish sherry labels. Recipes include three dozen for food (paella, gazpacho, and the like) and two dozen for mixed drinks using sherries (both dry and sweet varieties). The book concludes with a glossary.

158.*   Read, Jan. **The Simon and Schuster Pocket Guide to Spanish Wines.** New York: Simon and Schuster, 1983. 144p. illus. maps. index. $6.95.

The pocket-guide format was pioneered by book packager Mitchell Beazley, with Hugh Johnson's *Pocket Encyclopedia of Wines.* The format is useful (slim), but the contents are awkwardly expressed: rudimentary and small maps, and teeny-weeny print, difficult to read in a dim light. Covered here are all of Spain's reds, whites, rosés, sparkling wines, aperitifs, dessert wines, sherries, brandies, and liqueurs. Read organizes his book by the twelve major regions, subarranged by producer, and with a one-to-four-star rating on quality, with vintage data. There are lists of regional food specialties and restaurants, but the latter are only useful if you are personally visiting the area. The introductory matter contains valuable material on the wine laws and the grape varieties. Spanish wines, of course, have always been underrated and underpriced, so it is good to have this book as a guide.

159.*   Read, Jan. **The Wines of Spain.** London: Faber and Faber, 1982. 267p. illus. maps. bibliog. index. $15.

This book was originally written in 1973 as part of his *The Wines of Spain and Portugal;* in revising and updating the material, the author and publisher have sensibly issued two books to replace it. This book has much more information than its predecessor, primarily because of the increased availability of data and a new appreciation of these wines as "good buys"—particularly in the long-lived Rioja reds. The value of this discourse on Spanish wines is further enhanced by the inclusion of photographs, the appendices on production, exports, estate names and qualifications for the areas, the short chapters on spirits, the glossaries of Spanish technical wine terms, and the sketch maps of the wine-producing regions. The main body is a description of the wines according to region, with some emphasis on soils, climate, grape varieties, vinification practices, and tasting notes. Sherry has its own short chapter, and there is already a book in this Faber series on wines for sherry (see entry 155). The bibliography is excellent for further reading, albeit mostly for Spanish-language documents.

160.   Read, Jan and Maite Manjon. **Paradores of Spain: Their History, Cooking and Wines.** New York: Mason/Charter, 1977. 224p. illus. maps. index. $14.95.

Paradores are state-sponsored renovated castles, monasteries, and large houses in Spain, catering to the tourist trade as a sort of very elegant bed-and-breakfast. Twenty-eight of them are described here, with about 150 photographs and maps. Each description has a section on the local foods, the local wines, customs, and about two food recipes from each.

161.   Reay-Smith, John. **Discovering Spanish Wines.** London: Robert Hale, 1976. 159p. illus. maps. index. £ 3.50.

Reay-Smith notes the improvement in Spanish wines over the past decade (much of this can be attributed to their exporting better wines and doing more marketing). He describes the care and skills required in the production of a quality wine, and profiles many wine makers and their families. The prestige areas are covered, such as Rioja and Jerez, the wine families are introduced, such as the Torres group, and the important wines are covered in the areas of sparklers, brandy, or Chartreuse. The illustrative matter includes photographs, diagrams, and maps. The appendices list many quality sherries, table wines, brandies, and the names of exporters and their firms.

162.   Torres, Miguel. **Wines and Vineyards of Spain.** Barcelona: Editorial Blume, 1982. distr. by Wine Appreciation Guild. 176p. illus. $19.95.

Bodega Torres is in the Penedès region of Spain. They use extremely modern and French methods for their wine production. This book, by a member of the firm's family, covers wine history, vineyard cultivation, wine making, and consumers, with many references to Spain and to its wine laws and regulations. Included in the book is a listing of bodegas of the Rioja area, and there are contributions by Jan Read on Spanish table wines in general. Additional information includes an evaluation of Spanish aperitifs, sparkling wines, brandies, and liqueurs.

Other European Countries

163.   Barty-King, Hugh. **A Tradition of English Wine.** Oxford: Oxford Illustrated Press, 1977. 250p. illus. bibliog. index. $24.

This is a readable survey of the history of English wine making, and a study of the recent revival in English viticulture. There are numerous historical illustrations of the Roman Era to the present. Useful, but not technical.

164.   Churchill, Creighton. **The Great Wine Rivers of Europe.** New York: Macmillan, 1971. 256p. illus. index. $9.95 paper.

This motorist's guide is useful for its approach: it follows the rivers of Europe. Thus are covered the major wine districts that are found in the Mosel Valley, the Rhine, the Rhône, the Loire, and the Gironde. Detailed descriptions are given for each country, the vineyards, the grapes, and the characteristics of the wine produced in each region. Churchill and his wife make travel suggestions: roads, hotels, restaurants, and wine-tasting spots.

165.   Duttweiler, Georges, ed. **Les vins suisses.** Genève: Editions Générales, 1968.·311p. illus. bibliog. index. 46.5 Swiss francs.
These 16 chapters in French run through general material on wine making, but there is specific data on wine producers (by canton) and regional gastronomic specialties, institutions and associations in Switzerland, legislation on wines and protection of the consumer, and the role of wine and grapes in the economy, with relevant statistics. The book ends with a listing of all the wine types available in Switzerland.

166.   Gunyon, R. E. H. **The Wines of Central and South-Eastern Europe.** New York: Hippocrene Books, 1972. 132p. illus. index. $9.95.
There is much obscure information about the wines from the Asia Minor area, and from behind the Iron Curtain. This book rectifies the previous lack of information from these neglected areas. Countries covered include Austria, Czechoslovakia, Hungary, Yugoslavia, Bulgaria, and Russia, as well as some of the Balkan states (Albania, Romania, Greece). A useful book for rapid identification of wines that are still considered "curiosities" or novelties, although they are well made.

167.   Halasz,, Zoltan. **The Book of Hungarian Wines.** Budapest: Corvina Press; distr. in London by Clematis Press, 1981. 212p. illus. bibliog. $20.
This is a historical text, with an extensive Hungarian bibliography but no index. Each district is discussed, including the major ones of Eger, Balaton, Tokay, and Szekszárd. There are chapters on food and wine, medicinal use of wines, instructions for making vermouth, folklore, taverns and inns, and the wine exporting firm of Monimpex (a state monopoly). The concluding section describes the scientific basis of wine production in Hungary today, along with simple illustrations. Naturally Egri Bikaver ("Bull's Blood") is the pride of Hungary, and there are many pages devoted to its delights.

168.   Hallgarten, S. F. and F. L. Hallgarten. **The Wine and Wine Gardens of Austria.** London: Argus Books, 1979; distr. by International Publications Service. 339p. illus. maps. index. $17.50.
This book by the Hallgartens, experts on Germanic wines such as those from Germany and Alsace, provides a full description of the Austrian varieties, as well as providing some good social and historic background. This is the first book in English on Austrian wines.

169.   Jeffs, Julian. **The Wines of Europe.** London: Faber and Faber, 1971. 524p. maps. index. $19.95.
As noted on page 13, "this book does not pretend to be an encyclopedia listing all European wines." Detailed information is still best found in some of the larger reference sources, such as Lichine's or Johnson's books. Still, there is much here of note, particularly for obscure areas. Jeffs' book presents interesting historical information on pressing and fermentation, followed by details of soils, climate, vineyards, and wines in famous regions of France, Germany, Italy, Spain, and Portugal. The text is well footnoted, but there is no bibliography. There is an index to wines and the regions. Sixteen maps indicating wine-growing areas are included.

170.   Ordish, George. **Vineyards in England and Wales.** London: Faber and
        Faber, 1978. 186p. illus. maps. index. $17.95.
This well-researched history and detailed guide presents interesting and informative
information about a valuable viticultural lesson: the activities of wine growers
battling against a harsh climate. The English Viticultural Association reports that
as of 1983 there were 850 members in the Association—that is a lot of growers
for such an inhospitable climate!

171.   Pogrmilovic, Boris, ed. **Wines and Wine-Growing Districts of Yugoslavia.**
        Zagreb: Zadruzna Stampa, 1969. 98p. illus, part color. maps, part color.
        price not available.
This slim book is mostly filled with illustrations and maps, but each wine district
is carefully examined in view of the potential for tourists and the quality of the
wine. Good sections on merlot and Lujute wines.

172.   Smith, Joanna. **The New English Vineyard.** London: Sidgwick and Jack-
        son, 1979. 241p. illus. index. £ 8.95.
Another useful and informative book on the British wine industry. This is a practical guide to growing vines, and it covers the United Kingdom and Eire. It contains
a gazetteer of British vineyards and their wines.

NORTH AMERICA

United States

General

173.   Abel, Dominick. **Guide to the Wines of the United States.** New York:
        Simon and Schuster, 1979. 160p. map. bibliog. index. $3.95 paper.
Here is some good general background on the wines of California, the Pacific
Northwest, and New York. It also includes a short review of sparkling wines,
fortified wines, and brandy.

174.*   Adams, Leon D. **The Wines of America.** 3d ed. New York: McGraw-Hill,
        1984. 597p. illus. maps. index. $19.95.
Adams has spent over half a century travelling and tasting wines. Upset by wine
merchants who wrote books favoring their European wine imports over the domestic variety, he first produced this historical and descriptive book in 1973. Since the
last edition in 1978, there have been about four hundred fifty new bonded wineries
created in North America; Adams looks into many of these, as well as updating his
book in general with new figures and facts. Starting from the Scuppernong country
where wine has been made for four hundred years, he travels through the mid-
Atlantic states, the Midwest, the Finger Lakes, New England, and then California,
the Pacific Northwest, Canada, and Mexico. Other material here includes data
about the rise of the boutique wine makers and kosher wine makers. Each winery
visited has some details presented on tours, hours of opening, and wines tasted.
Some of the concluding chapters deal with the impact of French hybrids and a
chronology of wine history in North America. And the book is up-to-date through
the end of 1983. There are twelve small distribution maps.

175.	Better Homes and Gardens. **Favorite American Wines and How to Enjoy Them.** Des Moines, Ia.: Meredith, 1979. 96p. illus. index. $4.95.

Besides the general data on making, buying, and storing wine, there is also a collection of some forty-five food recipes here that use wine. The bulk of the book, though, is an alphabetical arrangement by common or varietal name for fifty-eight wines. Under each entry are given guides to pronunciation, some tasting notes, serving notes, price ranges on a national basis, some national producers, and other data. Photos of wine labels are also included. A useful book for the price.

176.	De Groot, Roy Andries. **The Wines of California, the Pacific Northwest and New York.** New York: Summit Books, 1982. 463p. index. $19.95.

The main point of this book is food writer De Groot's attempt to classify the top two hundred wineries in America, along European principles. He claims that this is the "first" classification in North America. He examines the varietals used in the production of U.S. wines and the styles made by the wineries in different regions, and he discusses the important wineries and wine makers. There are maps of the wine districts as well as four indexes (general, grape varieties, vineyards and wineries, and wine maker indexes), and a directory of the names and addresses of the major vineyards and the wineries. The exercise of classification is instructive to follow, but it doesn't succeed.

177.*	Fegan, Patrick. **Vineyards and Wineries of America: A Traveler's Guide.** Brattleboro, Vt.: Stephen Greene Press, 1982. 314p. illus. $9.95 paper.

In pocket format, this book gives maps and addresses for more than 930 wineries. Typical data also include the phone number, visiting and tasting information (if applicable), and eating facilities. All U.S. bonded wineries are covered, and they are geographically arranged by state or within state for ease of travel planning. His practical advice is also included: plan ahead, know your wines, don't visit more than four wineries a day (two before lunch and two after lunch tops), and keep a research log/diary. Other material here has a listing and brief description of the types of grapes grown in North America, and some details on approved and soon-to-be-approved place names for wine label listings.

178.	Hazelton, Nika. **American Wines.** New York: Grosset & Dunlap, 1976. 96p. illus. index. $4.95.

Another color book, one of a series dealing with foods and food preparations. This book also contains some fifty-seven recipes for cooking with wines. It gives a brief overview of wines and wine making, focussing on the attributes and types of American wines, such as the California varietals, the Southeast scuppernong, and the New York concord. A basic text, with good illustrations.

178a.	Kaufman, William I. **The Traveler's Guide to the Vineyards of North America.** New York: Penguin Books, 1980. 203p. illus. index. $5.95 paper.

Professional writer Kaufman has assembled a package of some 800 wineries and vineyards, all arranged by area beginning with California (and occupying 75 pages), then moving to the Pacific Northwest and the Great Lakes, and then to other places. The data for each is basically the same: name of the vineyard or winery, name of the vineyard or winery, address, name of person to contact, visiting hours, schedules of tours, lists of types of grapes grown, wines produced, wine-tasting availability and facilities, retail sales on the premises, and capsule histories. There are also recommendations for local foods and restaurants, places to stay, and things to do (points of historic, cultural, and scenic interest). While Canadian materials are listed, they are largely incomplete.

179.   Massee, William E. **Joyous Anarchy: The Search for Great American Wines**. New York: G. P. Putnam's Sons, 1978. 311p. illus. maps. index. $10.95.

This is a tour of the great vineyards of the United States, with lists of recommended wines from jug varieties to boutiques. The book also includes general primer items as well, since it covers wines and wine makers from all over the United States, with brief chapters on sparkling, fortified, and aromatic wines, with an appendix (glossary, maps). An uncomplicated introduction to basic information, largely on California wineries.

180.*   Meisel, Anthony and Sheila Rosenweig. **American Wine**. New York: Simon and Schuster, 1983. 192p. illus. index. $14.95.

A good book for the armchair traveller, since it is full of general data about American wines expressed within a coffee-table format with gorgeous full-color photographs of the wine making process, several American wine makers, wineries, and other "on location" scenes. The first 30 pages cover the usual general terms about wines and foods and service and tasting. The balance of the book has a listing of 225 vineyards grouped in order through 1 of the 4 regions: California, New York, the Pacific Northwest, and other states. These wineries are about half of the most active ones. For each, the authors furnish a description about the history, the philosophy, and the different types of wines produced—all in sixty words or so. There are recent labels in black and white (sometimes in color) as well as some action shots. The big firms are here, e.g., Gallo, Masson, and Inglenook, as well as the better-known boutiques. But there are no ratings nor evaluations of the wines.

181.   Misch, Robert Jay. **Quick Guide to the Wines of the Americas**. New York: Doubleday, 1977. 128p. illus. index. $4.95.

Misch pioneered the "quick guide" concept. In his last book (pocket sized but hardcover) he covers the California vineyards in about 80 pages, gives 20 pages to New York, 11 to others in the United States, 8 to Latin American wines, but *none* to Canada. There are short discussions of the individual producers, as well as material on buying, serving, and storing wines. Good, crisp style.

182.   Quimme, Peter. **The Signet Book of American Wine**. 3d ed. rev. New York: New American Library, 1980. 324p. bibliog. illus. index. $2.50 paper.

First issued in 1975, this typical survey book covers all the basics of labels, regions, wineries, wine tasting, and so forth, with a glossary of tasting terms. There is not much here on jug wines, which is a major shortfall of an otherwise informative and inexpensive book.

183.*   Tartt, Gene. **The Vineyard Almanac and Wine Gazetteer.** 6th ed. Saratoga,
         Calif.: Tartt, 1984. 159p. illus. maps. $3.95 paper.
This is a listing of all of the eight hundred or so wineries in the United States that
are *open* to visitors: where to go, how to go, and what to find. There are vintage
reports on over fifty-eight districts and states producing wines, as well as general
news and views and recipes (truly an "almanac" of hodgepodge detail). There is
an explanation of the new labeling regulations and place names, and advice on what
to drink with different foods (most of them weird, such as elk, buffalo, hush
puppies), as well as a historical chronology of dates, and space to jot down your own
tasting notes. Maps have been added for this edition, and there is also a dictionary
of three hundred wine terms. Also new this time is a wine newsletter directory of
American wineries that publish information about themselves (free or otherwise).
This book is an inexpensive source that is useful because it is regularly revised.

California

184.   Balzer, Robert Lawrence. **The Los Angeles Book of California Wines.** ed.
        by Darlene Geis. New York: Abrams, 1984. 271p. illus. maps. index.
        $35.
First published in 1978, this book presents a colorful synopsis of the California
wine industry. Five wine regions are discussed: the North Coast Counties, the Bay
Area and Central Coast Counties, the South Central Coast Counties, the Central
Valley, and Southern California. For each, 128 (in total) individual wineries were
identified, arranged alphabetically, and described with a short history and details
on the physical layout and equipment, philosophy of wine making, and tasting
notes. Tours of each region are given, as well as recommendations (nonevaluative)
for wines to try. Introductory material includes a general history of California
wines, along with an overview of the industry and a description of the grape types.
Maps are given for each area, and there are about 169 photographs, many in excellent color.

185.*   Benson, Robert and Andre Tchelistcheff. **Great Winemakers of California.**
         Santa Barbara, Calif.: Capra Press, 1977. 303p. illus. $15.
This book explores the myths and methodologies of making fine wines. Twenty-
eight wine makers are explored here in this series of biographical conversations, and
each one has a different way and manner of making his wine—which is as it should
be. Most wine makers here disagree with each other, such as on the matter of cold
fermentation principles, on the type of oak to use, when the vintage is to begin,
and the effect of soil and climate. Excellent reading.

186.   Blumberg, Robert and Host Hannum. **The Fine Wines of California.**
        Garden City, N.Y.: Doubleday, 1971. 311p. illus. index. $9.95.
The authors' purpose in this book is to provide the consumer with a way of
differentiating among the many similarly priced wines available from California.
They concentrate on "fairly detailed descriptions of well over 250 wines produced
by the major California premium wineries" (p. 81). The database has been drawn
from visits to twenty-four major wineries and twenty small ones. The evaluations
are still valid after fifteen years, but most of the rest of the book has changed.

The material on jug wines, wine labels, and addresses and the bibliography have all been superseded.

187.   Brennan, John M., ed. **Buying Guide to California Wines**. 3d ed. San Francisco, Calif.: Wine Consultants of California, 1983. 256p. index. $25.

A basic series of wine evaluations for the novice, expressing several good choices for wines to consume now and to lay down, and for "best buys." This is advice that is always needed, since there are so many different styles of wines in California.

188.   Caldeway, Jefferey. **Napa Valley Wine Tour**. San Francisco, Calif.: Wine Appreciation Guild, 1983. 94p. illus. $4.95 paper.

This tour guide to the Napa Valley provides a description of wineries, gourmet shops, gift shops, food, and lodgings. It is not for the budget traveller, since most items here are on the expensive side. But presumably, by doing the tour yourself you get a chance to save money over what the innumerable touring companies charge for their services. And you get your own choice of companions (or none at all).

189.   Csavas, Zoltan. **The Louis M. Martini Winery: St. Helena, Napa Valley, California, 1933-1983**. St. Helena, Calif.: Martini Winery, 1983. 96p. illus. $7.95 paper.

This is a corporate history, much in the style of the European books authored by Ray, et al., who celebrate the French châteaux. There are many photographs of the vineyards, chapters on food and wine matchups, and a 12-page pamphlet of recipes that comes with the book itself. Celebrating fifty years of business, this excellently produced book won a Gold Medal for Typographical Excellence from the International Typographical Association.

190.   Gillette, Paul. **Buyers Guide to California Wines**. Los Angeles, Calif.: Camaro Publications, 1983. 212p. illus. index. $7.95 paper.

In many respects, this book is quite similar to Brennan's (see entry 187). It is a basic text on California wine evaluations for the novice, giving several choices for wines to buy and drink now, to store and age, and even to forget about. "Best buys" are also indicated.

191.   Hinkle, Richard P. **Central Coast Wine Tour**. St. Helena, Calif.: Vintage Image, 1980. 112p. illus. maps. index. $5.95 paper.

191a.   Hinkle, Richard P. **Napa Valley Wine Tour**. St. Helena, Calif.: Vintage Image, 1980. 88p. illus. maps. index. $4.95 paper.

Both of these books are straightforward guides to touring the wine counties of California. The other book in the series has been written by Latimer (see entry 193). The guide has some suggested tour routes, along with maps, wineries and their telephone numbers and addresses, visiting hours, restaurants in the areas, and hotels and motels for lodgings.

192.　　Kaufman, William I. **Pocket Encyclopedia of California Wine**. 2d ed. San Francisco, Calif.: Wine Appreciation Guild, 1983. 236p. illus. maps. index. $4.95 paper.

Here are compact, informative details on about five hundred wineries in California. This is basic information such as name, address, and phone number. Data is given on which wines were medal winners in the various competitions (1,387 wines were tasted, but no ratings are given here). Maps and directions for travelling are also here. There is also a guide to touring wineries in the state.

193.　　Latimer, Patricia. **Sonoma-Mendocino Wine Tour**. 2d ed. St. Helena, Calif.: Vintage Image, 1983. 88p. illus. maps. index. $4.95 paper.

Like Hinkle's books (see entries 191 and 191a), this is a straightforward guide to touring a wine-producing area within narrowly defined limits. It has some suggested tour routes, along with maps, wineries and their addresses and telephone numbers, visiting hours, restaurants in the area, and hotels and motels for lodgings.

194.　　Melville, John. **Guide to California Wines**. 5th ed. rev. by Jefferson Morgan. New York: E. P. Dutton, 1976. 237p. illus. index. $4.95 paper.

This classic was first published in 1955, when there was little else available on California wines for the consumer. Parts of it are still valid because the book contains no tasting notes and no recommendations. The first section describes wine varietals and generics (table wines, sparkling wines, aperitifs, dessert and fruit wines). The section that follows gives a brief description of wineries by region (from north to south) and histories. Given the profusion of other California books, there may not be a sixth edition of the late Melville's book. But the material is still valid for the discussion of the larger wineries.

195.　　Millner, Cork. **Vintage Valley: The Wineries of Santa Barbara County**. Santa Barbara, Calif.: McNally and Loftin, 1983. 150p. illus. maps. index. $8 paper.

Similar to Hinkle's, Latimer's, and Caldeway's books on California wines, this guide is restricted to one small area. It is a better model than the other books because it has more historical material about the county and the wineries (most of which started since 1970). Seventeen wineries are listed, along with the appropriate tour information of maps, names, and addresses and phone numbers, and where to eat, where to stay, and so forth.

196.*　　Olken, Charles, et al. **The Connoisseurs' Handbook of California Wine**. 3d ed. New York: Knopf, 1984. 230p. illus. maps. index. $6.95 paper.

First issued in 1980, this updated text is based on the authors' bimonthly newsletter *Connoisseurs' Guide to California Wine*, a publication that reviews about fifteen hundred vintage dated wines a year. The book itself is arranged alphabetically, and lists all the wineries of North America. Despite its title, there is also a large section on non-California wines that also includes Canada. Each entry in either section discusses, describes, and evaluates the types of wines available, indicating "best" years and "best buys." This handy pocket book has increased in size from 182 to 230 pages in four years. The vintage tables and notes have been brought forward to 1983. While the data on California wine has increased by 30 pages, that on the other wines in North America have shrunk by 7 pages. Another dramatic figure: the number of bonded wineries in the United States increased from 729 to 1,037 in four years from 1979 to 1983 (153 of these new wineries were in California). This book is one of the best of the pocket guides, and certainly one of the better of the California wine guides.

197.* **Sunset's Guide to California's Wine Country**. By the Sunset Editorial Staff, under the direction of Bob Thompson. Menlo Park, Calif.: Lane Books, 1983. 160p. illus. maps. index. $7.95.

First issued in 1968 and regularly revised (this time with a new title), this large-format book travels through California by region, from north to south, with much updated information. The twenty-seven maps have accompanying tourist data for the wineries located within the area shown. Information is given about picnic areas, bicycle tours, and so forth for the *en famille* tours. There are many color photographs. The book has almost doubled since it first came out; indeed, there are a hundred more wineries listed here than in the 1979 edition.

198. Taylor, Sally and Lena Emmery. **Grape Expeditions**. 3d ed. San Francisco, Calif.: Taylor and Friends, 1983. 62p. illus. $5.95 paper.

Here are some fifteen bicycle tours to some of California's most reclusive wineries. The tours have all been carefully plotted, locating wineries on a route, places to eat, and relatively inexpensive lodgings. Sixty-one wineries in all are covered, mostly in the Napa and Sonoma areas.

199.* Teiser, Ruth and Catherine Harroun. **Winemaking in California**. New York: McGraw-Hill, 1982. 256p. illus. index. $24.95.

This is a well-produced general history of grapes and wines in California. It grew out of an oral history project of some years back, and it has been augmented by many rare but vital photographs and decorative drawings of bygone eras. It clearly shows the scope of the industry, from the mission wineries of the late eighteenth century, through the Italian influences of family-run businesses, to the large conglomerate takeovers of the late 1960s and early 1970s, to the rise of the "boutique" wineries in the 1970s, with their French influences. Tragedies are discussed as well, such events as combatting diseases and phylloxera, the dreadful Prohibition period and World War II, and the lack of proper marketing strategies of the "product." The only drawback for the book is the lack of sources for facts and figures (no footnotes, no bibliography). All data is presumably derived from the oral histories. Still, a very interesting and informative book on the inside stories behind California wines.

200. Thompson, Robert. **The Pocket Encyclopedia of California Wines**. New York: Simon and Schuster, 1980. 128p. illus. maps. index. $4.95 paper.

This is a typical pocket guide, done in the style of Johnson (for the world), Read (for Spain), and Anderson (for Italy). General material and grape varieties and maps are presented at the front, while the index contains all the names of grapes, products, and wineries in one alphabetical sequence. The main text is a region-by-region listing of the various wineries, highlighting their production and their good years, rating the wines for consumption and value.

201.*   Wine Appreciation Guild. **California's Wine Wonderland: A Tour Guide to California Wineries Open to the Public.** San Francisco: 1972- . Annual. 32p. illus. maps. Free.

With 393 entries in the 1983/84 edition, this is an exceptionally useful pamphlet (and the price is right). By restricting this annually revised list to only those wineries that are open to the public, the W.A.G. has forestalled many harassments and embarassments. There is certainly enough here to choose from, no matter where you are in California. The introduction discusses the characteristics of vintners and wineries, tastings, cellarage, and restaurants, and gives a mileage chart for motorists. Arrangement is by the major producing areas, with the name, address, phone number, hours of opening, and public facilities available (picnic grounds, retail sales, washrooms, tasting rooms).

Non-California Regions

202.   Cattell, Hudson and Lee Miller. **Wine East of the Rockies.** Lancaster, Pa.: L & H Photojournalism, 1983. 160p. illus. index. $17.50.

This book is mainly photographs—about 450 photos of people, wineries, and labels. It is a pictorial account of some 325 wineries, some of the wine makers, some festivals and fairs, a few competitions and tastings, and items pertaining to societies and research institutes. There are text chapters on the history of wine making, particularly on the East Coast and Canada. This book has been published by the editors of *Eastern Wines* magazine.

203.   Church, Ruth Ellen. **Wines of the Midwest.** Athens, Ohio: Ohio Univ. Press, 1982. 248p. $21.95; $9.95 paper.

Here is good historical and current data for the three major types of vines growing in North America: vinifera, labrusca, and hybrids. Church covers twelve states (Illinois, Kentucky, Michigan, Wisconsin, Pennsylvania, Arkansas, and others), listing vineyards for each one, along with addresses, visiting hours, and types of wine produced. Cheeses are also included and make up about 15 percent of the book. This is all directory-type data.

204.   Crosby, Everett. **The Vintage Years: The Story of High Tor Vineyards.** New York: Harper & Row, 1973. 176p. illus. index. $12.50.

For twenty-two years, Crosby and his wife ran a winery about thirty-five miles up the Hudson River. This is the story of their adventures in keeping the operation going. Interesting information includes the vagaries of wine, weather, hired help, and the federal and state liquor commissions. The meat of the book documents the selection of hybrid varieties, their proper cultivation and harvesting, and the processes involved from grape to bottled wine.

205.   Gohdes, Clarence. **Scuppernong: North Carolina's Grapes and Its Wines.** Durham, N.C.: Duke Univ. Press, 1982. 144p. illus. maps. index. $14.95.

This is a short evaluation and examination into the muscatine style òf grapes, the kind that grow singly like cherries rather than in clusters or bunches. This wine is over four hundred years old, since these were the grapes originally found by the first settlers of the East Coast. They are quite strong in flavor, and often they were (and still are) cut down with concord grapes in the production of wines. Virginia Dare was a successful wine name of the pre-Prohibition period, using both the muscatine and the labrusca grape varieties. This book does a good job of describing the history of this grape and its uses in the wines. Evaluations of the wine are given.

206.   Holden, Ronald and Glenda Holden. **Touring the Wine Country of Washington.** Seattle: Holden Pacific Inc., 1983. 240p. illus. maps. index. $7.95 paper.

The Holdens are wine and food writers with a P.R. and publishing firm. In 1982 they wrote a guide to Oregon wines; here they tackle the larger area of Washington wines. This is a description of that state's wines and wineries, along with a history of wine making in the regions. Included, for the sake of completeness, are some breweries and four wineries in Idaho. They recommend, as a travel guide, about fifty places to stop for the night, 125 restaurants, 65 wine and food shops, and 75 picnic areas.

207.*   Kaufman, William I. **Pocket Encyclopedia of American Wine East of the Rockies.** Watkins Glen, N.Y.: Association of American Vintners, 1984. 128p. illus. maps. index. $4.95 paper.

This book is pretty much the same as his *Pocket Encyclopedia of California Wine* (see entry 192), except that the latter only dealt with California. Here is compact information about three hundred wineries ranging from New Mexico to New England. These are basic details such as names, addresses, and phone numbers. Data is given on which wines were medal winners in the various competitions, but no wine ratings are given in the book. Maps and directions for touring are also presented. Highly useful for non-California wines.

208.*   Meredith, Ted. **Northwest Wine.** 2d ed. Kirkland, Wash.: Nexus Press, 1983. 256p. illus. index. maps. $8.95 paper.

Adding new wineries, this book is in its second edition. Basically, his guide is to the Pacific Northwest of the United States, since Canada is not here, except obliquely as an influence on Washington state wine (especially the lemberger grape variety) and as an importer of grapes and grape juice. This is a highly useful little directory for those who need hard data about this area. Described herein are the twenty-eight wineries of Oregon, the twenty-seven wineries of Washington, and three wineries from Idaho. For each is given the name the founding date, address and phone number, the hours open to the public, travel directions and maps, some narrative prose about the owner's philosophy of growing grapes and creating wines, and some general tasting notes. Illustrations comprise mostly recent labels and line maps for state locations. All of the wineries grow *vitis vinifera* grapes; these are the wine grapes of cabernet sauvignon, chardonnay, pinot noir, and riesling.

209.   Purser, Elizabeth J. and Lawrence J. Allen. **The Winemakers of the Pacific Northwest.** Vashon Island, Wash.: Harbor House, 1977. 224p. illus. maps. index. $30.

Time has overtaken this book: the changes in the Pacific Northwest have been so vast that while most of the wineries described here are still in operation, more than twice as many have come "on stream" since the 1977 publication date. The large-format book concentrates on color and black-and-white photography, and maps. Covered, of course, are those wineries of Oregon and Washington that were in business by 1976.

210.   Valchuis, Robert F. and Diane L. Henault. **The Wines of New England.** Boston, Mass.: Wine Institute of New England, 1980. 44p. illus. $2.95 paper.

This interesting little book deals with commercial wine production as found in six states in 1980. It is a good resource tool, presenting the histories of the wineries, tasting notes, a grape index of all the varieties cultivated, and general information on the growing cycles.

Canada

211.*   Aspler, Tony. **Vintage Canada.** Scarborough, Canada: Prentice-Hall Canada, 1983. 213p. illus. index. $9.95 paper.

About half of the wine consumed in Canada is "Canadian"; this is a low figure when compared to the rest of the world's consumption of local wines. This is also why there are few materials about Canadian wines. Aspler, wine writer for the Toronto *Star*, has done Canadians a favor by writing on an obscure topic. His book is in three sections. One is a general history of wine making in Canada, while another gives corporate minihistories for all the Canadian wineries that started before 1982 (these latter are arranged by province), with an indication of their storage capacities, locations, types of brands produced, and specializations. Ontario and British Columbia are the most important, since these are the large grape-growing areas. But Quebec, with no such area, is also included because of the enormous quantities of foreign juice and concentrates from abroad that are used. The third section—all of seventy-five pages—covers hundreds of wines tasted by Aspler between October 1982 and May 1983, reflecting the 1980, 1981, and 1982 vintage years. This section is arranged by province, subarranged by winery, and then alphabetically arranged by the name of the wine. For each (and he includes the 7 percent wines, sherries, ports, vermouths, cracklings, sparklings, proprietary names, and varietals) he evaluates on four basic points: color, bouquet, flavor, and overall impression. He indicates the types of grapes, percentages of the blended grapes, percentages of alcohol, and some one-or-two-star recommendations. There are some unusual surprises here from what is basically a bland wine industry.

212.   Nichol, Alexander E. **Wine and Vines of British Columbia.** Vancouver, B.C.: Bottesini Press, 1983. 168p. bibliog. index. $12.95 paper.

The British Columbia vinelands that are suitable for the production of wines cover about 3,200 acres, which is larger than what Oregon has. Most of it is in the Okanagan Valley, and most of it is of the French hybrid type. Permissive legislation in British Columbia allows for the import of grapes to be crushed locally; thus, every fall, grapes are trucked in from Washington and blended with the French hybrids. Occasionally, just the juice of the imported grapes is bottled. But this results in a highly priced bottle of wine, since the difference on the exchange rate of the countries' dollars is around 30 percent. Nichol, with assistance from his wife Kathleen, covers all this and more: he presents minihistories of the different wine makers, comments on all types of wines, and deals effectively with both the large and the small wineries.

213.   Rannie, William F. **Wines of Ontario: An Industry Comes of Age.** Lincoln, Ontario: W. F. Rannie, 1978. 171p. illus. $6.95 paper.

Rannie takes a historical approach, describing the early experiments with grape growing, especially by the Horticultural Institute of Ontario (the prime research station dealing with vines), the establishment of wineries after 1860, Prohibition, the postwar boom, and home wine making. He presents corporate histories of Ontario wineries, from 1811 through 1977, and lots of historical photographs. Generally laudatory in tone (Lincoln is in the heart of the Niagara Frontier Peninsula where the grapes are grown and the wineries reside), the book does a good job on background knowledge of Ontario's wineries, but it has no tasting notes.

214.   Rowe, Percy. **Red, White and Rosé: Enjoying Wines in Canada.** Toronto: Musson Books, 1978. 228p. index. $7.95 paper.

215.   Rowe, Percy. **The Wines of Canada.** New York: McGraw-Hill, 1970. 200p. illus., color. index. $12.95.

In a history that closely parallels that of the United States, immigration brought a healthy onslaught of both wine makers and wine consumers to Canada. Both books give a short history of wine making and the wine areas and wine stores, with details on modern vineyards at Niagara, Ontario, and Okanagan in British Columbia. The 1970 book examines the technical side of quality controls, as well as planting, tending, and harvesting. There is material on fruit wines (loganberries, strawberries, blueberries, and honey), sweet wines, and dessert wines, and how to sell vinous products abroad. The 1978 book adds to this by surveying and describing Canada's wine-drinking habits, with material on wine clubs, wine bars, and how to store wine in the home, as well as a guide to purchasing some Canadian wines and home wine making.

216.   Schreiner, John. **The World of Canadian Wine.** Vancouver: Douglas & McIntyre, 1984. 286p. illus. maps. index. $19.95.

Schreiner is western editor for Canada's *Financial Post.* This is a first-rate history of the wine business in Canada: the people behind the wineries and the government control; the moves to upgrade both the vines and the wines in view of the new demand for quality wines; an explanation of the liquor laws; and the business of producing a wine. There is, of course, a guide to the wines themselves, with his recommendations and buying tips.

217.   Sharp, Andrew. **Vineland 1000.** Toronto: Andrew Sharp Publications, 1977. 200p. illus. $10 paper.

Sharp is a syndicated wine columnist in Canada, with a wine education course and touring company as sidelines. Vineland, of course, was Canada's first name, acquired in 1000 A.D. (or so) by the Viking explorers who noted the vast quantities of labrusca grapes growing so close to the shores of the land. This book, then is about the grape in Canada. Part One covers Canadian wines and their consumption, the *vitis labrusca* varieties, the newer French hybrids, and a history of wine making and Prohibition. Part Two is largely derived from his columns, and covers wine lore through about a hundred questions and their answers. Part Three covers the government monopolies, the controlled distribution of alcohol, and the state pricing policies.

SOUTH OF THE EQUATOR

Australia and New Zealand

218.* **Australian Wine Industry Directory, Incorporating New Zealand, 1984.** Thebarton, South Australia: Australian Industrial Publishers, 1983. various pagination. $25.

This is a new book, but already it is a standard reference text for the Australian wine industry. It has details on all Australian and New Zealand wineries: resumés of the operations of wineries that detail suppliers, list personnel, and supply information on laws, taxes, and tariffs; there are also reference tables for wine makers.

219. Beckett, Richard and Donald Hogg. **The Bulletin Book of Australian Wineries.** Ultimo, Australia: Gregorys' Publications, 1979. 276p. illus. index. $17.99 Austr.

These are profiles of the various wine makers and their wineries, as derived from the periodical *Bulletin of Australian Wines.* It is mostly intended for the consumer, showing the different styles of wine and different methods of production, but without releasing any trade secrets.

220. Bradley, Robin. **The Australian Wine Pocket Book.** 2d ed. London: Macmillan, 1979. 115p. $5.95 Austr. paper.

A highly useful little book, describing most of the Australian wine characteristics and presenting ratings of the wines and their producers in the same manner as the Mitchell Beazley–Simon and Schuster series that began with Hugh Johnson's *Pocket Encyclopedia.*

221.* Evans, Len, comp. **Complete Book of Australian Wine.** 3d ed. Sidney, Australia: Paul Hamlyn, 1978; distr. by Mereweather Press (New York). 512p. illus. maps. charts. index. $15 Austr. paper.

This book is largely an encyclopedia to the Australian wine industry (the first edition in 1973 also had Frank Thorpy writing on New Zealand wines). Evans has about 215 pages on wines, arranged in dictionary fashion, which comment on the styles of wines, the grapes, geographic names, the names of the valleys and the wineries, and so forth, heavily illustrated with reproductions of wine labels and biographic details on the vintners. Other chapters—the other 300 pages—have been written by others, depending on the topic. Jaki Ilbery has written a large section on the history of wines and grapes in Australia, as well as profiles of wine makers and firms in the large areas within each state: New South Wales, Victoria, South Australia, Western Australia, Queensland, and Tasmania, while Anders Ousback writes on the technology of the vinification processes and Australia's contribution to the worldwide changes. Other writers comment on the climate, the business, home wine making, and how vineyards and wineries function. The changes, though, have been enormous in the past six years, with mergers and acquisitions, different grape-growing styles, and surging increases in foreign wine imports, with the result that some of the facts and figures here are definitely dated. Still, there are many color and black-and-white illustrations scattered among the double-columns of type, and much attention has been devoted to the development of wine making.

222.   Halliday, James. **Coonawarra.** Australia Square, New South Wales: Yenisey
        Ltd., 1983. unpaged. illus. maps. index. $35 Austr.
This is the story of a microclimate. The Coonawarra region is a strip of red soil, about 15 kilometers by 1.5 kilometers. The area is known as the "terra rosa soil of Coonawarra," east of Adelaide. As a vineyard, it makes Australia's best wines by far, and has since the 1960s. This history of a small area explains the geology of the region and the climate, as well as the histories of the various vignerons, wines, and vines. There are tasting notes back to the 1960s, as well as details on the corporate incursions made by the larger companies such as Wynn's, Penfolds, Lindemans, and Mildara. Good illustrations and maps complete the package.

223.   Halliday, James. **The Wines and Wineries of New South Wales.** St. Lucia,
        Australia: Univ. of Queensland Press, 1981. 165p. illus. index. $10.95
        Austr.

224.   Halliday, James. **The Wines and Wineries of South Australia.** St. Lucia,
        Australia: Univ. of Queensland Press, 1981. 144p. illus. index. $10.95
        Austr.

225.   Halliday, James. **The Wines and Wineries of Victoria.** St. Lucia, Australia:
        Univ. of Queensland Press, 1982. 152p. illus. index. $12.50 Austr.

226.   Halliday, James. **The Wines and Wineries of Western Australia.** St. Lucia,
        Australia: Univ. of Queensland Press, 1982. 119p. illus. index. $12.50
        Austr.
Halliday is one of Australia's leading wine writers (and wine makers: he owns Brokenwood Winery in New South Wales); he is also a full-time lawyer. Each of these books has a brief introduction to the wines of each state, followed by a listing of all the wineries located in that region. The listings are divided according to subregion, for example, in South Australia there are the Barossa Valley, the Coonawarra area, etc. Then the wineries are presented in alphabetical order within each subregion. The subregions are all described as to climate, soil, and grape varieties employed. Each winery listing begins with highlights about each one, plus some knowledgeable opinions about the wines, the date established, who the wine makers are, the size of the annual production, the principal wines and wine styles, and "best buys" with some tasting notes. This is a good, complete inventory of Australian wines, as of 1980 or so.

227.   Halliday, James and Ray Jarratt. **The Wines and History of the Hunter
        Valley.** Sydney, Australia: McGraw-Hill, 1979. 144p. illus. index. $15.95
        Austr.

With color illustrations and maps, this is a different but complementary book to the four described just above. It is a commercial book, produced about one of Australia's leading wine areas. It is more monographic in its treatment, although there is some of the inevitable duplication of data between this book and the one on New South Wales described above (of course, the Hunter Valley is where Halliday has his own winery, the Brokenwood). Still, though the University of Queensland book is smaller in size for the Hunter Valley area, its figures are a little more up-to-date.

228.   James, W. **Wine in Australia: The Complete Guide.** 5th ed. Melbourne, Australia: Sun Books, 1978; distr. by Tri-Ocean. 206p. illus., color. index. $3.95 paper.

This book has good applicability to North America, for it includes many wines that are available domestically in the United States and Canada. The basic descriptive data here includes how wine is made, the chief production areas, the chief wine makers, and tasting notes.

229.   **New Zealand Wine Annual, 1980-** . Auckland, New Zealand: New Zealand Wine Institute, 1981- . price not available.

This annual deals with the wines and their districts, and the production from the wineries: statistics, new regulations, the harvest, and so forth. About half of the white wine production is from the Müller-Thurgau grape, while half of the red wine production is from the cabernet sauvignon grape.

230.   Potter, Michael. **Wines and Wineries of South Australia.** Adelaide, Australia: Rigby Ltd., 1978. 226p. illus. maps. index. $19.95 Austr.

Potter here concentrates on the styles of wines found in the various areas. For example, around Adelaide there are the larger wineries of Penfolds and Seppelt; in the Barossa Valley, the small firms of Wolf Blass and Wynn's; in Watervale there is Lindeman's; in Coonawarra there is Mildara; and the McLaren Vale has Hardy's.

231.   Rankins, Bryce Crossley. **Wines and Wineries of the Barossa Valley.** Milton, Queensland: Jacaranda, 1971; distr. by Tri-Ocean. 114p. illus., part color. maps. tables. index. $9.95.

This slim book concentrates on the wine styles and family-owned groupings of the Barossa (in South Australia): Basedow, Wolf Blass, Hamilton's, Kaiser Stuhl, Orlando, Penfolds, Seppelt, Yalumba, and Wynn's, among others. The Barossa Valley is 35 miles from Adelaide; it is the oldest and most important region, most famous for its dessert wines and hard red wines that need considerable aging.

232.*   Saunders, Peter. **A Guide to New Zealand Wines.** Auckland, New Zealand: Wineglass Publishing, 1984. 128p. illus. index. $7.95 N.Z.

A basic book, up-to-date, and covering all of the 14,000 acres under production on the islands. Wineries include the largest, Montana (about 40 percent owned by Seagram's), as well as Corbans (the largest exporter), Cooks New Zealand Wine Company, and Nobilo Vintners.

233.   Simon, André L. **The Wines, Vineyards and Vignerons of Australia.** London: Paul Hamlyn, 1967. 194p. illus. maps, color. tables. bibliog. index. out of print.

This is a comprehensive work, sadly out of date, written by the notable wine scholar and commentator André Simon near the end of his life. Approaching 90, he decided to take up the offer of a trip to Australia to explore and comment on Australian wines. He went by boat, and wrote most of the material himself. Part One is a geographic description, with the maps of the vineyards. Part Two is about the wines, with a general survey of the types of wines and productions as compared to Europe. Part Three, almost half the book, discusses forty-three vignerons by region, from their early history through the cooperative marketing schemes. The appendices cover about one-third of the book, and contain: historical extracts, 1803-1866; Australian grape varieties and quantities produced; characteristics of what to look for in Australian wines; some recipes for cooking with wine; and a description of the Australian Wine Research Institute. The valuable bibliography is mainly historical; most references are to nineteenth-century publications.

234.   Thorpy, Frank. **New Zealand Wine Guide.** Auckland, New Zealand: Collins, 1976. 199p. illus., part color. maps. index. $12.95 N.Z.

This book details the history of the wine in New Zealand and its trade. The industry itself never really became established until after 1960; now there are 14,000 acres of land being cultivated to produce wines of a high, light style resembling the aromatic wines of the Loire, the Médoc, and Champagne. Thorpy's book is particularly good on the early struggles of the pioneers, most notably the Italians and the Dalmatians and Lebanese.

235.   **Wine Talk: Australian Winemakers and Their Art.** Canberra, Australia: Action Press, 1979. 176p. illus. price not available.

This is a collection of papers from a symposium held at the Australian National University Staff Centre in September of 1979, with such local authorities and wine makers as Brian Barry. It is a good book for details of production.

236.   Young, Alan. **Australian Wines and Wineries.** Cammeray, Australia: Horowitz Grahame Books, 1983. 200p. maps. charts. index. price not available.

This new, general book comes complete with vintage charts that should indicate when certain heavy red wines made from the Shiraz-Cabernet combination will be ready. It has a brief history of the major areas: Barossa Valley (South Australia), Hunter Valley (New South Wales), and sections of Victoria and Western Australia. Young shows, by describing the grape types and the vinification processes, how Australian wines differ from those of the rest of the world.

South Africa

237.   Biermann, Barrie. **Red Wine in South Africa.** Cape Town: Buren, 1971. 156p. illus., part color. price not available.

This is a short account of the history of red wine vinification, with particular detail on grape types, aging, and casks. It complements De Klerk's book (see entry 242).

238.   Brink, André P. **Dessert Wine in South Africa**. Cape Town: Buren, 1974. 136p. illus. price not available.

Brink's book opens up with a description of the sweet wine tradition: the history of sweet wines around the world, and then, more specifically, the history of sweet wines in South Africa. Strewn throughout the book are many facts, anecdotes, and legends, together with a collection of black-and-white historical photographs and color pictures of contemporary people and processes. There are also some recipes on foods that go with sweet wines, but unfortunately there is no index.

239.   Calpin, G. H. **Sherry in South Africa**. Cape Town: Tafelberg, 1979. 114p. illus. price not available.

Quite similar to Brink's book (see entry 238) in that it covers some of the dessert-wine status of sherry, this book by Calpin also emphasizes the aperitif characteristics of that alcoholic beverage. It presents the history, legend, and lore of Spanish sherry and then moves more specifically to the transposition of sherry-type wines to South Africa, especially from the K.W.V. at Paarl. The illustrations, as in Brink's book, contain black-and-white photographs of historical reproductions and color pictures of contemporary people and processes. And again, there is no index.

240.   De Bosdari, C. **Wines of the Cape**. 3d ed. Cape Town: Buren, 1966; distr. by International Publications Service. 100p. illus. index. $18.50.

A general book on a specific area (the Cape, or Paarl, wines), with a short history of the K.W.V. wine-growers cooperative (see also entry 246). There is much detail here on the individual characteristics of individual grapes and wine types, as well as statistics of the wine trade. There are chapters on the climate of the Cape, the making of both red and white wines, the fortified wines, and the nomenclature involved in the regulation of the wine industry.

241.   De Johngh, Fanie. **Encyclopedia of South African Wine**. 2d ed. Durban, Pretoria: Butterworths, 1981. 171p. illus. bibliog. index. $20.

This book was first published in 1976. It is a basic, A-through-Z arranged tool with identification of wine types, production processes, serving and evaluation of wines, geographic areas, grapes, estates, and so forth. There are many cross-references, with illustrations of labels in black-and-white and color photographs of the grape clusters. The entries all explain the styles of wine. At the back of the book there is a series of addresses useful for contacting sources in the South African wine industry.

242.   De Klerk, Willen Abraham. **The White Wines of South Africa**. Cape Town: A. A. Balkema, 1967; distr. by International Publications Service, 1971. 110p. illus. index. $18.

This is a short account of the history of white wine identification, with particular detail on grape types, sweet and dry qualities, and casks. Along with travel notes and tasting notes, it nicely complements Biermann's book (see entry 237).

243.*   **Decanter Magazine Guide to South Africa.** London: Decanter Magazine, 1984. 80p. illus. maps. magazine size, soft covers $5.

As one of a series of separately published and separately priced available regional guides, this specific issue excels in promoting the latest information about South African alcoholic beverages. There are profiles of the six main producers and the leading estates, covering ten areas such as the Bergkelder, Stellenbosch, the K.W.V. at Paarl, and Gilbeys. More than three hundred wines are assessed through tasting notes and descriptions of style and grape varieties. Spirits, liqueurs, and fortified wines are also covered. General material includes a history of South African wine making, climate, the grape varieties, the wine regions, a definition of the wines of origin system, and the structure of the industry. Also covered are wine auctions, tourism, restaurants and lodgings, and wine travel routes. A very good package for the newcomer to South African wines.

244.*   Kench, John, Phyllis Hands, and David Hughes. **The Complete Book of South African Wine.** Cape Town: C. Struik, 1983. 352p. illus. maps. bibliography. index. $35.

This is a definitive guide; this big book covers the history, the vineyard practices, the wine-making technology, the vine cultivars, the Estates, the cooperative wineries, the private cellars, the wholesalers, and the wines themselves. Over a thousand South African wines are assessed and rated. There are 16 maps for all of the wine districts, 700 photographs, and a glossary of 250 items. The arrangement of the book is principally by area: Stellenbosch, Paarl, Worcester, Robertson, Swellendam, etc. A very attractive book, making effective use of color.

245.*   Knox, Graham. **Estate Wines of South Africa.** 2d ed. Cape Town: David Philip, 1982. 240p. illus. maps. index. £ 23.

First published in 1976, this present book has been expanded and revised. It is a detailed description of each of the sixty-four Estates (forty-seven are registered with the Wine and Spirit Board of South Africa; the rest are intending to register). For each estate details are given about topography, climate, history, soil, tasting notes, etc., along with photographs and other illustrations of the vineyards, the owners, the homesteads, and wine labels. There are maps of the Cape, a brief outline of the South African wine industry since 1652, a description of eighteen white and twelve red varieties of grapes with photographs, and material dealing with the 1973 legislation that imposed strict conditions on the labelling terms of "Estate Bottled" (all of this is explained here, and there are illustrations of the guarantee stamps). This book is very much like Johnson's *The World Wine Atlas*, but for South Africa only. A good reference source for details about the better South African wines.

246.   Ko-operatives Wijnbouwers Vereniging van Zuid-Afrika. **The K.W.V. Wine Library.** Beperkt, Paarl, South Africa: K.W.V., 1982. 12 booklets, 24-28 pages each, slipcased. illus. maps. price not available.

These booklets are a hodgepodge of history, pictures, and anecdotes and a description of the markets for the wines of South Africa, especially those of the Cape and Paarl. Among the twelve are an explanation of the "Co-operative Winegrowers Association," the history of South African wines, a general wine guide, cultivars (grape varieties), red and white wines, fortified wines and spirits, Estate wines and their districts, a recipe booklet, and one on "Wine and Good Health." Excellently reproduced color photos and maps.

247.   Orffer, C. J., ed. **Wine Grape Cultivars in South Africa**. Cape Town: Human and Rousseau, 1979. 111p. illus., color. maps. index. price not available.

This is a technical book, covering forty-three of the grape varieties used in the production of South African wines. Each is given a description along with a color photograph plate, a history, some comment on the wine quality, and statistics. The basic division of the varieties is into red and white. Most of the materials and the support for the book came from the Stellenbosch Farmers' Wineries.

248.   Pama, C. **The Wine Estates of South Africa**. Cape Town: Purnell and Sons, 1979. 102p. illus. maps. index.

With color illustrations, this book is quite similar to Knox's (see entry 245), except that it is half as long. It has more opinionated commentary than technical explanations, and as such it serves as a useful complement to Knox's book.

249.*   Platter, John. **John Platter's South African Wine Guide, 1980-** . Maitland, Cape: Derek Butcher and Co., 1979- . 220p. (approx.). index. $10.

This annual has been modeled on *Hugh Johnson's Pocket Encyclopedia of Wine*, except that it concentrates on the South African industry: in its small print, and with ratings of all the applicable wines, its contents cover the estates, the cooperatives, and the merchants (with a directory of addresses to all three), the imported wines (about 40 pages), and other useful items on the Cape wines such as styles, grape varieties, tastings, scoring, wine areas of origin, wine tours, and the various wine makers themselves. An impressive record.

250.   Schultz, Merwe, ed. **Wine Country**. Cape Town: Buren, 1971. 240p. illus., part color. $12.

More of a tour book with lavish photographs, this tool details routes and journeys along the wine-growing areas and streams in the Cape area. Sixteen authors present their views on such areas as Paarl, Stellenbosch, and Swartland.

251.   **Spirit of the Vine: Republic of South Africa**. ed. by D. J. Opperman. Cape Town: Human and Rousseau, 1968. 360p. illus., part color. index. $35.

This book was published on the occasion of the Fiftieth Anniversary of the K.W.V. Each of the 14 chapters was written by a specialist in and on South Africa. With a large type face, large pages, and color illustrations, this book would be a coffee-table book were it not for its excellent text. Material covered includes a description of the parent wine and grape stock from the Near East and the historical development of wine from Europe through to South Africa. The problems of growth are covered, as well as marketing strength resulting from the founding of the K.W.V.—storage of fifty million gallons, wholesaler and exporter clout, vine development, and so forth. Several chapters relate visits and descriptions of members and the Estate wines. Only since 1965 has an effort been made to sell South

African wines in the United States. The technical section in this book details grafting stock and wine diseases, with the appropriate photographs. Closing chapters discuss wine in art, literature, and music, with fine detail paid to the Afrikaans literature and language.

⟦3⟧ *Books on Beers*

The books listed in this chapter actually consider "low alcoholic beverages." Most of the works deal with beer, but at the end of the chapter there is a section on ciders and mineral waters. Often it is quite difficult to separate book materials into different subcategories by topics because there simply is not enough such material to warrant a whole book. Hence, a "beer" book here may have all the pertinent details necessary for history, appreciation, techniques, collecting, and cooking, and its subcategories may or may not be reflected in the other chapters of this book. Many book items here deal with collectibles and price guides; they have all been collated into this chapter for the sake of convenience. Additional materials on beers will be found in chapter 7 on cooking with beer; chapter 10 on home brewing; and chapter 6 on legends and lore. Associations are in chapter 11, magazines in chapter 9, and the trade and technical side is covered in chapter 8. Also, many general reference books found in chapter 1 will also contain material on beers.

BEERS

252.   Abel, Bob. **The Beer Book.** New York: G. P. Putnam's Sons, 1981. 95p. illus. $12.95.
This particular book is in the shape of a beer bottle, with a plastic-and-vinyl cover. General material covered includes data on how beer is made, the history of beer, where beer is sold, types of beer as found in different countries, and many color illustrations.

253.   Alcorn, Alan J. and Paul F. Burden. **The Beer Tray Guide: The First Comprehensive Guide for the Beer Tray Collector.** Dover, Mass.: College Hill Publications, 1979. unpaged. illus. $5.95 paper.
This price guide gives a whole series of recommended prices for various kinds of trays (including some reproductions). Illustrations concern the original trays.

254.　　Anderson, Sonja and Will Anderson. **Anderson's Turn of the Century Brewery Directory: A Complete Listing of All U.S. Breweries in Operation in 1890, 1898, 1904 and 1910, as Listed in the Original Brewers' Handbooks for Those Years.** Comp. and published by Sonja and Will Anderson. Carmel, N.Y., 1968. unpaged. illus. price not available.

A straightforward historical document, as indicated by the subtitle.

255.*　　Anderson, Will. **The Beer Book: An Illustrated Guide to American Breweriana.** Princeton, N.J.: Pyne Press, 1973. 199p. illus. bibliog. $30.

The first 100 pages here are concerned with collecting: bottles, trays, advertisements, calendars, tap knobs, glasses and mugs, cans, signs, posters, openers, caps, labels, holiday items, cards, and coasters, with appropriate black-and-white and color illustrations of the historical materials. This is an excellent guide to the whole area of collecting materials about beers, with representative samples of just about every type of product. Then, 60 pages are devoted to "representative American breweries," both large and small. Here there are minihistories of the corporations, with pictures. Unfortunately, too, many of the companies are out of business. Then the last part of the book—about 25 pages—deals with the great brewing cities of America, such as Boston, Buffalo, Chicago, Cincinnati, Milwaukee, Philadelphia, and St. Louis. In its conception, this is a great book despite the price.

256.　　Baillie, Frank. **Beer Drinker's Companion.** North Pomfret, Vt.: David & Charles, 1973. 296p. illus. $9 paper.

This book deals primarily with breweries and industry in Great Britain. It discusses about 1,000 brands (all British), as well as some of the hotels and taverns in Great Britain. There is an excellent section on the efforts of the Campaign for Real Ale.

257.　　Baron, Stanley Wade. **Brewed in America: A History of Beer and Ale in the United States.** Fort Washington, Pa.: Ayer Co., 1972. 424p. illus. bibliog. $25.50.

This is a reprint of the 1962 classic originally published by Little, Brown. Since beer was the universal language of the seventeenth century, it was natural that the art of brewing would be carried on in the Colonial period. The brewing industry, as the author notes, has played a large part in the social and cultural growth of the United States. It slowly moved from the art of the 1630s to the science of 1819, when the first steam engine was installed in a brewery. Short biographies of the leaders in the field are given, and, of course, the impact of the introduction of German lager in the 1840s is assessed. This scholarly work details the advances made in science (pasteurization, refrigeration, transportation) and the Prohibition-Repeal period. An extensive 22-page bibliography, which also includes unpublished material, concludes this readable book.

258.　　Boston, Richard. **Beer and Skittles.** Glasgow: Collins, 1976. 221p. index. $9 paper.

This slim book presents much advice on the consumption of beer, anecdotes about beer and the saloon life, and some material about pub food. A fun book to read, even if the hard information is sparse.

259.   Bull, Donald. **Beer Advertising Openers: A Pictorial Guide.** Trumbull,
        Conn.: Bullworks, 1981. 120p. illus. $7 paper.
This book annotates, identifies, and describes over 2,000 types of "church keys";
3,000 openers are thus classified by type in arrangement. Bull has also published
A Price Guide to Beer Advertising Openers and Corkscrews (40 p. illus. $5 paper.),
which pictures over four hundred different types and gives a value guide, patent
data, and historical background to each.

260.   Bull, Donald, Manfred Friedrich, and Robert Gottschalk. **American
        Breweries.** Trumbull, Conn.: Bullworks, 1984. 400p. bibliog. index.
        $17.95 paper.
This directory is a boon for researchers in the field of American breweries. It is a
listing, by state and city, to some 6,000 breweries that have produced beer in
America, ranging from the first, in 1632 in New York (then New Amsterdam),
through to 1983. All name changes, ownership changes, and mergers are kept
together, as well as address changes. Dating is restricted to calendar years only;
there are no months or days indicated. Because of the dates, a researcher can
determine when a brewery existed; a collector can date an artifact; and a buff
can visit a site (if it is still standing). There is a name index to all the breweries,
and this provides access if you only know the name of the brewery, but not its
city of operation. Additional information here includes a 5-page chronology of
American brewing history (and this is useful for trivia fans) and a good bibliography of the source documents.

261.   Cady, Lew. **Beer Can Collecting.** 2d ed. New York: Charter Books, 1981.
        224p. illus. $2.95 paper.
Once billed as "America's fastest growing hobby," this particular book deals
with the fun and serious aspects of collecting beer cans. It is a basic handbook,
opening with a history of the can, and then going on to describe such data as what
to collect, how to spot fakes, how to date a can, how to barter and trade, how to
approach breweries for can samples, what to do at a convention (which the beer-can
collectors' group calls a *can*vention), how to restore cans, how to display cans,
and other general advice. There are many illustrations of the diverse kinds of cans,
as well as price ratings for over two hundred of the rarest cans in the United States.
For a book of this kind, though, there should be an index.

262.   Cameron, Jeffrey C. **The Class Book of U.S. Beer Cans.** Colman, Pa.:
        Class Publications, 1982. 128p. illus. $11.95 paper.
This is a price guide to beer cans, as of 1982 or so. Over four hundred of the rarest
cans known are depicted in color. And about 2,000 other cans are shown in black
and white. Grades, prices, and variations have been listed.

263.   Corran, H. S. **A History of Brewing.** North Pomfret, Vt.: David & Charles,
        1975. 303p. illus. bibliog. index. $20.
This basic history describes the technical developments of the brewing industry,
especially over the past two hundred years in Europe. There is little here on social
or economic history; most of the work deals with the impact of the Industrial
Revolution on the manufacture of beer. Most changes occurred in Britain until the

mid-nineteenth century, when advances in Germany, France, and later the United States began to be significant. Topics here include medieval brewing, the introduction of hops, the early-seventeenth-century patents, the techniques for porter production, steam, taxation, bottled beer, and appropriate legislation. The historical illustrations are highly useful, since they show a basic thematic history of science and technology for one product. These include the grinding of malt, the mechanical mashing rakes of 1798, the cellar beer pump, the siebe ice machine (for chilling), horizontal refrigerators, skimming yeast, and isobarometric bottle fillers.

264.   Donaldson, Gerald and Gerald Lampert, eds. **The Great Canadian Beer Book**. Toronto: McClelland and Stewart, 1975. 128p. illus. $12.50.
This book is much like the Anderson book (see entry 255), except that it concerns Canada. It is a history of Canadian beer, with some material about beer in other lands. It does a good job on Canadian hotels, pubs, and the blue laws. But essentially it is an eclectic collection, with information on labels, cans, and the distinctions between lager and ale, minihistories of the corporations (large and small, such as Molson, Labatt, and Moosehead), and even little snippets of poetry as part of anecdotal materials.

265.   Downard, William L. **Cincinnati Brewing Industry**. Cincinnati, Ohio: Ohio Univ. Press, 1973. 173p. illus. bibliog. index. $25.
This is a straightforward account of the history and development of the brewing industry in Cincinnati, showing the rise and fall of many local breweries, and attempting an explanation of why Cincinnati was considered a regional brewing capital. There are also many historical photographs.

266.   Downard, William L. **Dictionary of the History of the American Brewing and Distilling Industries**. Westport, Conn.: Greenwood Press, 1980. 268p. bibliog. $45.
This book begins with an introductory survey of both the brewing and the distilling industries in the United States. Basically, though, it is a dictionary-arranged reference tool that briefly identifies items such as technical terms used in the processes of obtaining alcohol, federal liquor legislation and regulation, Prohibition and general historical matters, specific institutions and persons, and brief histories of 180 breweries and 100 distilleries. The twelve appendices cover historical tables of facts and figures.

267.   **Elsevier's Dictionary of Barley, Malting, and Brewing, in Six Languages: German, English/American, French, Danish, Italian, Spanish**. Comp. by B. D. Hartong. Amsterdam: Elsevier Publishing Co., 1961. 669p. $76.75.
As one of Elsevier's authoritative multilingual dictionaries, this is a very helpful translation dictionary. It has not been revised for over twenty years (it may not actually need revision), but its price has tripled during that time. It is arranged in German alphabetical order.

268.   **Good Beer Guide**. St. Albans, Herts., England: CAMRA, 1980; distr. by Arrow Books (London). illus. £ 2.60 paper.

This book has been issued by the Campaign for Real Ale, a British consumer fight-back group that has done wonders in promoting good quality British ale with real flavor and guts instead of the watered-down, mass-marketed large-brewer products. Essentially, the book is a list of several thousand pubs in every part of the country that serve "real" draft beer in all of its regional varieties (there are over 1,500 different beers in Britain). Accompanying road maps are useful, as well as copious use of symbols to summarize the facilities (washrooms, hours, types of food, etc.). Under the names of each pub there are short descriptions in about six words or so, such as "historical," "back street," "friendly," "busy," "typical," or "basic." A good book for the traveller in England who wishes to sample pub grub and beer.

269.   **Good Pub Guide**. London: Consumers Association, 1983. £ 5.95 paper.
Unlike the *Good Beer Guide*, this book concentrates mainly on the facilities and food of about 1,000 general pubs: location, decor, food, drink, and other items. Brews are normally specified, and the beer and the pub are rated on a one- to three-star scale. It differs from the *Great Beer Guide* in that it assesses the quality of the entire operation, not just the beer. Hence, fewer pubs in Britain have been recommended here, but also recommended are some of the better pubs that sell mass-produced beer. For an adequate coverage of pubs in Britain, both books are needed. For instance, under Cambridge, eleven pubs within the area are recommended. There are almost three times as many Cambridge recommendations in the CAMRA book, but these are just for the service of "real" beer. And there is little overlap between the Cambridge lists.

270.*   Hillman, Howard. **The Gourmet Guide to Beer**. New York: Pocket Books, 1983. 96p. illus. bibliog. $3.95 paper.
Hillman is a wine and food critic. Here he gives advice on buying, storing, and serving beer. He tells you how to do beer evaluations based on appearance, bouquet, flavor, and aftertaste. There is also a glossary of terms. In addition to material on the ins and outs of the brewing business, Hillman also rates many beers here, on a one- to five-star scheme; these are for most of the domestic and imported beers available on a national basis in the United States. A miscellaneous section covers beer and health; beer and food in cooking, collecting beer cans and labels, and toasts.

271.*   Jackson, Michael. **The Pocket Guide to Beer: A Discriminating Guide to the World's Finest Brews**. New York: Perigee/Putnam, 1982. 138p. illus. index. $5.95 paper.
Jackson is one of the world's leading authorities on beers. His previous book on beer won a German literary prize in 1978. Here he concisely defines the whole beer-making process, describing types of beers and what to look for when tasting (all of this in two dozen pages). The balance of the book is a geographically arranged listing of the more interesting beers of the world, a few of which are not even available in the United States, but are worth tracking down in their country of origin. Europe gets most of the space, especially Britain and West Germany. Within each country he lists (alphabetically) the various breweries and describes their top products, giving each a ranking from zero to five. Over six hundred lagers, ales, and stouts are rated, and there is a brand-name index for quick location.

272.*   Jackson, Michael, ed. **The World Guide to Beer**. Philadelphia: Running
         Press, 1982. 255p. illus. $9.95 paper.
This book is complementary to Jackson's *Pocket Guide to Beer*. Although it, too,
is arranged with data on the history of beer making, styles and types of beers,
regional variations, and so forth, the book is arranged by country in ranked order
(Czechoslovakia is first, Africa is last). While there are tasting notes, none of the
beers are rated; just the country's beer-making qualities in general are rated. There
are lots of illustrations: historical drawings, color photos, local history, color
reproductions of bottle labels, and site maps for brewery locations.

273.   Marchant, W. T., comp. **In Praise of Ale: or, Songs, Ballads, Epigrams,
        and Anecdotes Relating to Beer, Malt, and Hops, with Some Curious
        Particulars Concerning Ale-Wives and Brewers, Drinking Clubs and
        Customs**. Detroit: Gale, 1968. 632p. $42.
This facsimile of the 1888 edition contains "rich, rare and racy songs," plus everything mentioned in the subtitle. The author dragged up as many references from
newspapers, friends, magazines, and books as he could find. This is an eclectic
hodgepodge for the true lover of beer who wondered what beer drinking was all
about a century ago.

274.   Monckton, H. A. **A History of English Ale and Beer**. London: Bodley
        Head, 1966. 238p. illus. maps. tables. bibliog. index. £ 15.
This is a fairly complete and chronological account of the beer trade in England,
and it also explains the process of malting and brewing in historical terms. It
describes the rise in popularity, economic importance, and consumption of ale and
beer, since the fifteenth-century development from the Lowlands. Monckton
explains such things as bride-ales, inn tokens, Assize of Bread and Ale in 1267, and
the changing shapes of vessels. Supplementary material includes beer consumption
figures for the past three hundred years. Appendices list the Acts of Parliament
that deal with beer. This is a readable book, lightened by the occasional anecdote.

275.   Morris, Stephen. **The Great Beer Trek**. Brattleboro, Vt.: Stephen Greene
        Press, 1984. 211p. illus. $10.95 paper.
This is a record of certain travels Morris made with his wife Laura, "to visit all
existing independent breweries and to hit as many highlights as possible in
between." In doing so he managed to cross forty-five states in the United States.
Topics covered include a brief synopsis on the art of home brewing, a history and
folklore of beer (including anecdotes and about a hundred line drawings), an inter-
view with beer owner Rudy Schaefer, and other miscellaneous items. The bulk of
the text concerns visits to both dormant and active breweries, both large and small,
with some tasting notes of mainly regional products such as Grain Belt Beer, or
Rainier Beer.

276.   **The Official 1984 Price Guide to Beer Cans and Bottles**. 2d ed. Orlando,
        Fla.: House of Collectibles, 1983. 204p. $2.95 paper.
This is one of a series of price guides issued by this publisher, which is concerned
with all sorts of collectibles, and not just beer items. The format is straightforward,
with a name and indication of the beers and the types of containers available,
whether a bottle or a can, and a range of prices for resale or retention value.

277.   Ojala, Reino. **20 Years of American Beers**. n.p.: Winslow Printing, 1983.
        100p. $9.95 paper.
This history of beer making briefly identifies about 3,000 brands produced during
the 1930s and 1940s.

278.   Orton, Vrest. **The Homemade Beer Book**. Rutland, Vt.: C. E. Tuttle,
        1973. 159p. illus. $3.75 paper.
As Orton states, this is a book "in which are included general principles and recipes
for making beer in the home, history of beer drinking customs of old New England,
brewing of the olden times, curious lore of old time brewing, etc. etc." It is a graceful social history, a fun book passed off as a reprint of the 1932 Proceedings of the
Company of Amateur Brewers. There is some excellent material here on New
England; this is mainly a history book, but there are a few beer recipes not only for
malted barley, but also for spruce beer and ginger beer.

279.   Osborne, Keith and Brian Pipe. **International Book of Beer Labels, Mats
        and Coasters**. London: Hamlyn, 1979. 93p. illus. £ 4.
An oversized book, full of the usual color photographs expected of book packagers.
The theme this time is, of course, beer and the accessory products from a variety
of countries. A good book for the collectors who need more pictures of beer labels,
mats, and coasters.

280.   Robertson, James D. **The Connoisseur's Guide to Beer: 1984**. 2d ed.
        Ottawa, Ill.: Green Hill Publishers, 1984. 300p. illus. $11.95 paper.
This book deals with obscure brewers and local brands, as well as nationally distributed American brands and internationally available imported brands. All beers
are described, rated, or ranked, and there are tasting notes. History and collecting
of brewing are also covered.

281.*   Watney, John. **Beer Is Best: A History of Beer**. London: Peter Owen,
        1974. 157p. $11.95.
This straightforward history, from the Egyptian *hek* made from fermented barley
in 3000 B.C., up through modern times with the big stainless steel tanks, has been
written by one of the successors to the Watney Beer Company in England. Topics
include, under history, the introduction of hops to England and the development
of alehouses; under social activities, the life of the public house, with entertainment, sports and games, inn signs, poetry and beer in cooking; and under finance,
the marketing of beer, the ownership of breweries, American beers, advertising in
Britain, and licensing hours in Britain.

282.*   Weiner, Michael A. **The Taster's Guide to Beer: Brews and Breweries
        of the World**. New York: Macmillan, 1977. 256p. illus. bibliog. $14.95;
        $7.95 paper.
Part One here details tastings of beer, storing, histories, medical aspects, and the
technical processes. Part Two concerns that alphabetical arrangement by country
in which Weiner discusses selected, leading breweries in terms that describe the
processes, the taste evaluations, bouquet, color, flavor, aftertaste, and finish. Each
beer is rated at 1 to 7 "beer mugs"; 225 beers are included in this test. Throughout

the text statistics are scattered, as well as black-and-white illustrations of labels, tankards, and bottles (and historical pictures). All the color photographs are of pre-Prohibition advertisements.

283.   Young, Jimmy. **A Short History of Ale**. North Pomfert, Vt.: David & Charles, 1979. 164p. illus. $7.50.
This is a book that treats ale lightly; it is a popular history covering only the British beers, but it is useful as a supplementary work to augment existing materials that are concerned solely with American beers or German lagers.

CIDERS AND WATERS

284.   Gault, Lila and Betsy Sestrap. **The Cider Book**. Seattle: Madronna Press, 1980. 166p. illus. index. $5.95 paper.
A standard but short book on ciders in America: how to make, how to store, how to cook with it, and so forth. Some recipes are concerned with the production of ciders, while most others are for using cider in food preparations. All courses are stressed, from soup to nuts.

285.   Orton, Vrest. **The American Cider Book: The Story of America's Natural Beverage**. New York: Farrar Straus Giroux, 1973. 136p. illus. $3.25 paper.
A short history of cider is presented (including both legends and American usage), along with general methods of amateur and commercial cider making, using both old-time and modern principles. The production of cider apples is noted; there are copious illustrations of cider presses and the names and addresses of manufacturers of such presses; there is a short discourse on fermenting sweet cider into hard cider; and, of course, there are simple directions on how to make cider at home. The book is completed by an extensive beverage and cooking section: thirty-four historic recipes for punches, nogs, and nightcaps (from 1745 through 1960), along with twelve modern ones, and fifty-nine recipes for food, including dried apple pie with cider, wild game basted with cider, apple bread, and an unbelievable sixteen recipes on the uses of boiled-cider pie! Although the entire book is mouth-watering, it warns the user that the results are not guaranteed.

286.   Proulx, Annie and Lew Nichols. **Sweet and Hard Cider: Making It, Using It, and Enjoying It**. rev. ed. Charlotte, Vt.: Garden Way Publishing, 1984. 188p. illus. bibliog. index. $14.95 paper.
The authors discuss the six basic ways to make cider, as well as how to produce it, the legality of "hard" cider, historical details from the past on the use of cider, and even some advice on how to start a home orchard. Auxiliary material concerns a glossary, a mailing list of equipment suppliers, and even apple-stock suppliers (for the home orchard). Information is also given for Quebec, Canada, and there is a 7-page bibliography of some 250 items dealing with cider and its production. The book contains fifty food and beverage recipes.

287.   Schwartz, Stephen. **The Book of Waters**. New York: A & W Visual Library, 1979. 95p. illus. $5.95 paper.

Twenty-one bottled mineral waters are covered in this book; six are American (such as the Saratoga Springs). For each is given the mineral content, a genealogy for changes of ownership, and health claims. There are also pictures of the label and of the bottle, plus other pictures associated with the water. Both black-and-white and color illustrations are here, and of course the emphasis is on waters that people either drink straight or mix with drinks. Imported waters include Perrier, Ramlosa, Vichy, Vittel, Apollinaris, and Fiuggi.

288.   Von Wiesenberger, Arthur. **Oasis: Guide to Bottled Water.** Santa Barbara, Calif.: Capra Press, 1978. 192p. illus. index. $6.95 paper.

Covering much the same ground as Schwartz's book, this little gem does give more space to the history of mineral waters in general, the health claims, and the trendy rise in consumption in North America as an alternative to either tap water or to cocktails. Although not as heavily illustrated as the above book, there is more thoughtful textual commentary. The two books are complementary and duplicative at the same time. Still, these two are the only on the market, and *some* people might like to read about mixers.

④ *Books on Spirits*

The books noted in this chapter actually consider "high alcoholic beverages." Most of the works deal with spirits and liqueurs, but there are three sections: one presents notes on general books, the second covers books dealing with specific types of spirits or concoctions (whisky/whiskey, brandy, rum, the martini), and the third itemizes books that are largely collections of cocktail recipes. Often it is difficult to separate book materials into different subcategories by topics, because there simply is not enough material to warrant a whole book. Hence, a "scotch" book here may have all the pertinent details necessary on history, appreciation, collecting, cooking, and so forth, and its subcategories may not be reflected in the other chapters of this source book. Many book items here deal with histories and recipes; they have all been collated into this chapter for convenience. Additional materials on spirits will be found in chapter 7 dealing with cooking and spirits and chapter 6 on legends and lore, while associations are in chapter 11. Magazines are in chapter 9, and the trade and technical side is covered in chapter 8.

GENERAL

289.   Barleycorn, Michael. **Moon-Shiner's Manual.** New York: Scribner's, 1975. 150p. illus. $3.95 paper.
The introduction to this book states that "the sole intention of this book is to preserve a dying art ... a rapidly fading folklore." And that the author does. Part One is a brief history of distilling and moonshining, with a discourse on the principles of distillation. Part Two tells how to build a still, with a description of its various components and some basic recipes for the mash. Part Three covers the legal aspects, with sixteen recipes for cocktails made with moonshine. The line drawings very adequately illustrate the techniques, but while there is a glossary, there is no index.

290.   Carr, Jess. **The Second Oldest Profession: An Informal History of Moonshining in America.** Englewood Cliffs, N.J.: Prentice-Hall, 1972. 250p. illus. bibliog. index. $9.95.

A totally fascinating book about the illicit distillation of whiskey. The author, a native of mountainous western Virginia, has produced a complete study that traces the history of moonshining from colonial times to the 1960s. His richly detailed chapters on producing "mountain dew" and on the types of stills in use are completely absorbing. One cannot go wrong by following Chapter 7, "Moonshining Methods and Equipment," or Chapter 12, "Types of Stills and Their Application." However, if one reads the other chapters one will find out what happens to someone who "runs off a little brew now and then."

291.*   Cooper, Rosalind. **Spirits and Liqueurs.** Tucson, Ariz.: HP Books, 1982. 112p. illus. index. $5.95 paper.
Cooper's book is a standard, no-frills introduction to the variety of spirits (whiskeys, vodkas, gins, rums, brandies, tequilas) and liqueurs: it has much to recommend it, such as the low price, good photographs, and a brisk writing style. In addition to a history of each category of product, its origin, and how it is made, there are details about many nationally distributed brands. These are mainly short notes to distinguish one label of, say, Scotch, from another. Although written for the American market, most of the brands (at least the imported European ones) are to be found throughout the world. There are also some serving suggestions in the form of cocktail recipes for standard preparations, but experienced mixologists already know these.

292.   Dabney, J. E. **Mountain Spirits, I and II.** Lakemont, Ga.: Copple House, 1978, 1981. 2 vols. (228p., 242p.) illus. $6.95 paper (each).
These two volumes are admirable histories that chronicle the rise of corn whiskey from King James' Ulster plantation to America's Appalachians and the moonshine life.

293.   Erdos, Richard. **One Thousand Remarkable Facts about Booze.** New York: Rutledge Press, 1981. 192p. illus. $5.95.
In crisp form this slim book attempts to crowd together a useful number of historical, technical, and social facts about drink (largely about spirits). Highly useful for answering questions, and perhaps for playing "trivia" games.

294.   Farrell, John P. **Making Cordials and Liqueurs at Home.** New York: Harper & Row, 1974. 156p. illus. $9.95.
This useful little book presents a variety of recipes for the home reconstruction of liqueurs, using diverse sugars and syrups, flavorings, and commercially available spirits. It does not give "moonshine" data; this is not a book for those who want to learn from scratch.

295.*   Greenberg, Emanuel and Madeline Greenberg. **Pocket Guide to Spirits and Liqueurs.** New York: Perigee/Putnam, 1983. 144p. illus. $5.95 paper.
Although there are other, similar "pocket" guides to spirits and liqueurs available these days, this is one of the better reference works in this area because it gives more details in the tasting notes, both in what to expect and in what there actually is in the brand-by-brand comparisons. Over five hundred brands are rated and discussed, all arranged by type, e.g., whisky/whiskey, brandy, clear spirits, rum,

tequila, and liqueurs. Even vermouths are included, for they are part of every well-stocked bar. The alphabetic range is from "Armagnac" through to "vodka," and there is a lot of information on how the particular spirit has been made and on government regulations. The 4.5-inch width, though, is a tad too wide for pockets (except for the Scottish Tweed jackets) and may present some problems for the library shelf and/or rack.

296.*   Hallgarten, Peter A. **Spirits and Liqueurs.** London: Faber and Faber, 1983. 188p. illus. index. $16.95.
The Faber books on wine, of which Hallgarten's book is one, is a first-rate series. This contribution, first published in 1979, is by the son of the founder of Hallgarten wine shippers. Part One describes distillation processes and kinds of spirits (whiskies, gin, brandies, tequila, rum, etc.), along with a history and a description of production techniques. The second part delves into the art of the liqueur: how blending is determined, the use of aromatics and sugars, and the raw materials (leaves, barks, roots, flowers, seeds, fruit) as well as different classifications as to types. This is a very interesting book to read; the new edition contains updated figures, new cocktail configurations, and material about the dairy liqueurs.

297.   Hannum, Horst and Robert S. Blumberg. **Brandies and Liqueurs of the World.** Garden City, N.Y.: Doubleday, 1976. 278p. $15.
This is a comprehensive history of distillation and its modern technology. The evolution of modern brands is shown, as well as material on how each should be served. There are chapters on how to blend drinks at home, as well as how to use drinks in cooking. The bulk of the text is in two parts. Part One covers "brandies," such as Cognac, Armagnac, Calvados, California brandies, and fruit eaux-de-vie. Part Two looks at "liqueurs" (herbal, seed, plant, fruit, brandy-based, etc.). Each is arranged alphabetically within, by name or by proprietary name.

298.   Henriques, Frank. **The Signet Encyclopedia of Whiskey, Brandy, and All Other Spirits.** New York: New American Library, 1979. 243p. $2.95 paper.
All the generic varieties such as brandy, gin, and rum are covered here, as well as the nationally distributed brands, corporate histories, and histories of cocktail mixes and their standard recipes. The book is arranged alphabetically, with pronunciation guides, too. There are internal cross-references, but no index. There is one highly useful feature here: there is quite a lot of material about ordinary brands.

299.   Kellner, Esther. **Moonshine: Its History and Folklore.** Indianapolis: Bobbs-Merrill, 1971. 235p. bibliog. $6.50.
A reasonably good, well-written history on the activities of moon-shining in America, with of course the emphasis being on history and not "how to."

300.   Lord, Tony. **The World Guide to Spirits, Liqueurs, Aperitifs, and Cocktails.** New York: Sovereign, 1979. 256p. maps. illus. $25.
Lord, the editor of *Decanter* (the leading English-language wine magazine), here covers any materials that have spirits added. "Distillation" is the key word, and

hence fortified wines such as ports and sherries and madeiras are also displayed. Lord tells where and why, all nicely arranged and photographed in coffee-table-book style.

301.   Meilach, Dona and Mel Meilach. **Homemade Liqueurs.** Chicago: Contemporary Books, 1979. 72p. illus. $9.95; $6.95 paper.
The stress here is again on blending: flavors and syrups with alcohol bases, to create reasonable knockoffs of the popular brands. Sometimes it works, especially the orange- and menthol-based drinks and liqueurs; but the drier the liqueur, the less successful will be the final product.

302.   Ray, Cyril. **The Complete Book of Spirits and Liqueurs.** New York: Macmillan, 1978. 139p. illus. $10.95.
This highly prolific author has produced yet another readable, well-illustrated book giving the facts and specifics of the distilled spirits industry and their products.

303.   Sale, Jacques. **Dictionnaire Larousse des Alcools.** Paris: Editions Larousse, 1982. 256p. illus. price not available.
This heavily illustrated book is reminiscent of Larousse's earlier dictionary of wines. The emphasis is, of course, quite naturally on French products such as Cognac, Armagnac, Calvados, and Benedictine, with hardly anything on various knockoffs or competitors from other countries. Production figures are useful.

304.   Tritton, S. M. **Spirits, Aperitifs, and Liqueurs: Their Production.** London: Faber and Faber, 1975. 82p. illus. £ 2.35.
This little book is more along the technical line, with material on how to make the products rather than on the art of blending. The section on aperitifs is highly useful; somehow it is often neglected in books dealing with homemade alcohol-enhanced products. Tritton was well-known as a British amateur wine maker, with several books to his credit (see Chapter 10 of this book).

SPECIFIC (Whisky/Whiskey, Brandy, Rum, the Martini, etc.)

305.   Andrews, Allen. **The Whisky Barons.** London: Jupiter Books, 1977. 148p. illus. $10.
This illustrated history concentrates on the great names in Scotch manufacturing. The biographies are illustrated with many photographs, and there are reproductions of diverse documents.

306.   Barnard, Alfred. **The Whisky Distilleries of the United Kingdom.** New York: A. M. Kelley, 1969. 457p. illus. maps. $25.
Originally published in 1887, this reprint presents corporate histories of the distillation industry in Ireland, Scotland, England, and Wales. The maps give precise and concise data.

307.   Barty-King, Hugh and A. Massel. **Rum: Yesterday and Today.** London: Heinemann, 1983. 264p. illus. $23.

This is one of the first detailed books on rum: history, lore, how it is made and how it is used, and the trade routes from New England to Barbados to India. Illustrated plates.

308.   Brander, Michael. **The Original Scotch**. London: Hutchinson, 1974. 150p. illus. £ 3.50.
A concise, straightforward account of the history of Scotch making and manufacture, from its beginnings up through the present day.

309.*   Carson, Gerald. **The Social History of Bourbon: An Unhurried Account of Our Star-Spangled American Drink**. New York: Dodd, Mead, 1963. 280p. illus. index. $6.95 paper.
Utilizing vintage photographs for this history of the all-American drink, Carson details the Whiskey Rebellion, the Whiskey Ring, and the Whiskey forts of the fur trade, using both anecdotes and straight facts. American drinking manners are covered up to 1920, but only 11 pages are devoted to the period since. Chapter notes are given in lieu of a bibliography, and these notes are mainly to older accounts.

310.*   Cooper, Derek. **The Century Companion to Whiskies of Scotland**. London: Century Publishing, 1983. 168p. illus. maps. bibliog. index. $7.50 paper.
This brief history of Scotch (first published in 1978) also describes, in some detail, how malt and grain whiskies are made and blended. About one-third of the book is devoted to a gazetteer of the Scottish malt and grain distillers, with names and addresses. There are cocktail recipes as well as material about whisky around the world.

311.   Crowgey, Henry G. **Kentucky Bourbon: The Early Years of Whiskey Making**. Louisville, Ky.: Univ. Press of Kentucky, 1971. 171p. illus. bibliog. index. $9.75.
A scholarly history of the early production of bourbon, complete with derivation of name and government controls of the initial product.

312.   Daitches, David. **Scotch Whisky: Its Past and Present**. New York: Macmillan, 1970. 168p. illus., part color. maps, part color. index. $9.95.
This is the grand tour of malt distilleries. Daitches studied the complex manufacturing processes in 1967, and here gives his account, along with a social and economic history (taxes to be collected, malt and barley processes). The inventions of stills (pot versus patent) and the discovery of blending are both covered. The two significant highlights in history—the amalgamation of the Big Five into the Distillers' Corporation, and the 1907 decision allowing blends—had the direct result of making Scotch the second largest United Kingdom export. Statistics, a glossary, old cartoons, and photographs by the author's son complete this compact book.

313.* Doxat, John. **Stirred—Not Shaken.** London: Hutchinson Benham Ltd., 1976. 192p. illus. $5.95 paper.

Doxat tries to cover every single aspect of the martini cocktail, as found in both fact and fiction. Here then is a collection of eclectic writings on historical materials, the martini's associations with John D. Rockefeller and others, various cocktail recipes and proportions, some material on related gin drinks such as the Gibson and the Murphy, and some gin humor (as opposed to "wry" humor). Jokes and stories abound (here called "fun and games" in a Monty Python nudge-nudge, wink-wink fashion). The international scene is covered as well, for Doxat poses the question: what is the dry martini like around the world? For an answer, he gives black-and-white photographs of bartenders pouring drinks in foreign bars. 'Nuff said.

314. Gorman, Marion and Felipe Padilla de Alba. **The Tequila Book.** Chicago: Contemporary Books, 1976. 184p. illus. index. $6.95 paper.

A basic description of Tequila, with its various permutations and qualities on the North American marketplace. Cocktail recipes are included, as well as tasting notes.

315. Herzbrun, Robert. **The Perfect Martini Book.** New York: Harcourt, 1979. 117p. illus. $5.95.

This has a large-print format, with photographs and cartoon illustrations. It gives a short history of the martini, both in fact and in fiction. There are 268 recipes and variations for the martini and gin-based drinks.

316. Kroll, Harry Harrison. **Bluegrass, Belles, and Bourbon: A Pictorial History of Whiskey in Kentucky.** South Brunswick, N.J.: A. S. Barnes, 1967. 224p. illus. index. $12.

As a social history of drinking styles, this book also describes the production of bourbon in context with the life-style of the time. Many of the illustrations are rare, having been collected by the author from many personal files.

317. Lafon, René and Pierre Couilland. **Le Cognac, sa distillation.** 4th ed. Paris: J. B. Baillière, 1964. 270p. illus., color. maps. bibliog. 40 French francs.

This is the definitive book about Cognac, detailing its history, the discovery of double distillagion, and the effect of storage in a cask. There is some description of present-day Cognac houses, along with an introduction by Maurice Hennessy.

318. Layton, T. A. **Cognac and Other Brandies.** London: Harper Trade Journals, 1968. 153p. illus. £5.

This basic and factual description of the history and manufacture of brandy (world-wide) also includes some "must" items for the tourist in France.

319. Lockhart, Sir Robert Bruce. **Scotch: The Whiskey of Scotland in Fact and Story.** 6th ed. London: Chatto, Bodley Head, and Jonathan Cape, 1982; distr. by Merrimack Book Service. 184p. index. $12.95.

The late Sir Robert, who was previously the owner of Balmenach Distillery, first published this book in 1951; it was last revised in 1974. It is a slight book that defines the process of making Scotch, and also presents a very readable account of its colorful history as told in terms of the "whisky barons." There is also important material here on the huge Distillers Company Ltd. (which bought Sir Robert's distillery), and on the impact that American Prohibition had on the Scottish distillers in general. Sir Robert even traces the decline of overall quality and the necessity for blending whiskies. But he does commend the era of specialization to single malts. Much of the updating of this book was worked on by Sir Robert's son, but the flavor of the original still shines through in biographies of Dewar, Buchanan, Walker, and Haig (all real people).

320.*   Long, James. **The Century Companion to Cognac and Other Brandies.** London: Century Publishing, 1983. 98p. illus. maps. bibliog. index. $7.50 paper.
Century Publishers in Great Britain have been busy issuing and reissuing short, crisp materials covering the world's wines and spirits. The series of books are edited by Pamela Vandyke Price; some of the material appeared earlier in the Pitman Publishers series of wine books. Long was the British wine buyer for the International Distillers and Vintners Group, and his book does indeed cover the world, albeit in a brief format. Brandies include Cognac from France (as well as pomace, marc, and Armagnac), pisco from Peru, and vinjak from Yugoslavia. Other countries here include South Africa, portions of Europe, and North America. He presents material on how to taste, how to store, stemware, recipes, drawings of stills, maps of the various regions, and the names and addresses (and some description) for the principal producers of Cognac and Armagnac. The book concludes with a glossary and with a listing of still more names and addresses of groups that will supply additional data.

321.   McCreary, Alf. **Spirit of the Age: The Story of Old Bushmills.** Belfast, Northern Ireland: Blackstaff Press, 1983. 356p. illus. index. £ 12.95.
Bushmills, founded in 1608, celebrated its 375th birthday in 1983; it is the world's oldest licensed distillery (the Scottish ones did not get licenses until a hundred years later). This basic history covers how the whiskey is made, the story of the area around the distillery, and profiles of the people involved in the distillery. There are over two hundred illustrations in this historical panorama.

322.*   McDowall, R. J. S. **The Whiskies of Scotland.** 3d ed. London: John Murray, 1975. 168p. illus. maps. bibliog. index. $5.75 paper.
This extensively revised book (with new maps and illustrations) details malt whiskey (from barley) in part One. McDowall visited all the distilleries concerned, commenting on each and relating their histories. The book concentrates on these single-malt whiskies. Part Two is about grain whisky (from maize). Part Three concentrates on the blended whiskies. The author visited 28 of over 2,000 different blending distilleries, and he gives a description of each as in part One. Part Four, the technical section, discusses the making of whisky, the choices of grain, the final product available for the consumer, and government controls. There are some

comments about the Scotch Whisky Association, a concluding chapter on the economics of whisky production (by I. A. Glenn) and material on the large distillery groups.

323. McGuire, E. B. **Irish Whiskey: A History of Distilling, the Spirit Trade and Excise Controls in Ireland.** New York: Barnes and Noble, 1973. 462p. illus. bibliog. index. $20.50.

Originally published in Dublin by Gill and Macmillan, this text was written by the former Collector of Customs and Excise in Northern Ireland. It is a comprehensive account, as he states that "corruption, illicit distilling, lawlessness, political jobbery, antagonism to English rule were all accentuated in government attempts to control the manufacture and consumption of Irish whiskey." The growth and effect of these laws are traced, as well as the thorny problem of revenue versus sobriety. There is an analysis of the expansion of the Scottish industry at the expense of Irish whiskey. The author also goes into the evolution of distilling plants and their techniques as they move from primitive apparatuses to the modern continuous still.

324. Magee, Malachy. **One Thousand Years of Irish Whiskey.** Dublin, Eire: O'Brien Press, 1980. distr. by Merrimack, 1982. 144p. illus. index. $15.95.

This is a very popular account of the rise of the whiskey spirit in Ireland, with illustrations of the distillation method, people, places and things. Concentration, of course, is on Eire rather than Northern Ireland. This is a more popular account than the McGuire book (see entry 323), but of course more brief, extolling the virtues of Irish whiskey.

325. Morrice, Philip. **The Schweppes Guide to Scotch.** London: Alphabet and Image, 1983. 416p. illus. £ 8.95; £ 4.95 paper.

Morrice's book concentrates on blended brands and the proliferation of scotches; very few single malts are actually covered here. After a brief history of the industry, market, and trade, he gives a dictionary-arranged listing of the main whisky companies, incorporating a minihistory of each with a sublisting of their main brands and where they are sold in the world today.

326. Moss, Michael and John R. Hume. **The Making of Scotch Whisky: A History of the Scotch Whisky Distilling Industry.** London: James and James, 1981. 304p. index. $40.

A much more technical history than any of the others described above, this text contains many facts and figures, along with tables of statistics detailing the growth and export market of Scotch whiskey. A very comprehensive and thorough book, well written and well researched.

327. Murphy, Brian. **The World Book of Whisky.** Glasgow: Collins, 1978. 192p. illus. bibliog. £ 10.95.

A coffee-table book, full of colorful stories and illustrations, pictures of the whisky barons, maps of the distilleries' locations, and even music—for songs to sing while drinking!

328.   Pack, J. **Nelson's Blood.** Havant, Hampshire, England: Mason, 1982; distr. by State Mutual Books. 160p. illus. $50.
This is one of the few books written about rum. It is a brief, but thorough account of the rum trade as well as the materials that go into making high-quality rum products and cocktails.

329.   Ramos, Adam and Joseph Ramos. **California Brandy: The Wine Drinker's Spirit.** Berkeley, Calif.: Padre Productions, 1982. unpaged. illus. $12.95.
A very posh book, suitable for gift giving, about the California brandy industry and subcultures. A few recipes for cooking with and drinking such brandies are included. A useful book, since it deals with a low-profile and unexciting product.

330.   Rannie, William F. **Canadian Whisky: The Product and the Industry.** Lincoln, Ontario: Rannie Publications, 1976. 169p. illus. index. $6.50 paper.
This is the history of whisky in Canada, including some corporate histories of twenty-two distilleries (Seagrams, Walkers, Corby, Gilbey, Schenley, and McGuinness). Modern technology is discussed, as well as the enormous government taxes and regulations (and the history behind these). Rannie also has a chapter on Prohibition as well, and separate little sections dealing with odds and ends and statistics.

331.   Ray, Cyril. **Cognac.** New York: Stein & Day, 1974. 171p. index. $7.95.
A brief but informative book by an erudite and prolific wine writer. Techniques are explained, the various houses of production in the Cognac area are described, and certain categories of Cognac are tasted and rated.

332.   Ross, James. **Whisky: The Story of Scotch Whisky from Its Beginning.** London: Routledge and Kegan Paul, 1970. 158p. illus. index. $9.95.
A history of Scotch, very basic, much like Daitches' book. It covers the invention of stills, the discovery of blending, the extent of government involvement, and the impact of exports.

333.   Samalens, Jean and Georges Samalens. **Armagnac.** London: Christie's Wine Publications, 1983. 64p. illus. $11.
Armagnac is not too well known in America; it is quite similar to Cognac in that it is made the same way (double distillation), but the finished product has a stronger taste. This little book deals with the making of Armagnac with historical background, customs, traditions, and technology explained (including the soils, the oak used, the pot stills). This English edition has been edited and expanded by Jill P. Goolden based on the original 1974 French (the authors are from an old established Armagnac family).

334.   **Scotch Whisky.** London: Macmillan, 1974. 120p. illus. $10.
Seven different authors produced this book. Theodora FitzGibbon contributes 15 pages of recipes for food and drink; Bill Simpson writes on the history of Scotch; Anthony Troon comments on the land and the materials; S. Russell Grant

goes into the details of the distillation process; Donald MacKinley talks about blending; and Hugh MacDiarmid and Jack House have separate chapters on the big corporate houses. One hundred twenty-nine distillers are listed and shown on a map. There are lots of pictures (historical reproductions), drawings, and much use of color.

335.   Spencer, Herbert and Fred Mayer. **Cognac Country**. New York: Universe Books, 1983. 159p. illus. $29.50.
This is basically a photographic essay (there are 170 color plates) with text. The latter covers the history, the vineyards, the distillation, and the making of Cognac, while the former shows the Charentes countryside and the town, the stills and the cellars of the houses. Some material on Armagnac is also included.

336.   Wilson, Ross. **Scotch: The Formative Years**. London: Constable, 1970. 502p. illus. index. $25.
This economic history is largely an extended version of the author's *Scotch Made Easy* (1960). It is a massive work chronicling the early developments, the discovery and use of the pot-still method, and the various attempts at government intervention by the English.

COCKTAIL RECIPE BOOKS

337.   Arthurs, Stanley C. **Famous New Orleans Drinks and How to Mix 'Em**. Gretna, La.: Pelican, 1977. 98p. illus. $2.95 paper.
A collection of recipes, about seventy-five, devoted to the New Orleans style of fizzes and Creole concoctions, plus the trendy jazz drinks such as the Hurricane and various coffees associated with New Orleans.

338.*   Berberoglu, Hrayr. **The Professional Bartender**. Scarborough, Canada: Milmac Communications, 1983. 133p. illus. $7.95 spiralbound.
This is a good basic book on the art of mixology, suitable for any community college or skills exchange course. Topics handled include bartending training, personal work habits, service and dealing with people, types of bars (layout and equipment), ingredients (foodstuffs, garnishes, wines, ice, liquor), the art of mixing through stirring, shaking, blending, and building, and finally, price controls. The recipe section is about one-half of the book; there are about two hundred recipes here, although at any one time only about two dozen or so cocktails will be popular, such as the martini, the whiskey sour, the Bloody Mary, the screwdriver, and the daiquiri. Both avoirdupois and metric measurements are employed, as well as boldface type for the ingredients and an outline sketch of the glasses needed. Unfortunately, the recipes need an index, but there is still much material here that is good data for home parties as well.

339.   Brandy Advisory Board. **California Brandy Drinks, Cocktails, Punches, Coffee and Hot Drinks**. ed. by Malcolm P. Hebert. San Francisco, Calif.: Wine Appreciation Guild, 1981. 160p. illus. index. $4.95.

Hebert has done yeoman service for California brandy (see also his books in chapter 7, dealing with food). This particular one deals with brandy as a beverage in a variety of hot and cold drinks and, of course, the brandy need not necessarily be "California" brandy. In essence, the book was put together as one of a series that mainly dealt with food, in an attempt to push the California wine industry. The more uses, of course, the more brandy that will be sold.

340.*   Braun, Lionel and Marion Gorman. **The Drink Directory**. Indianapolis: Bobbs-Merrill, 1982. 415p. illus. index. $5.95 paper.
This book is a good value. Mixologists can always use many of these cocktail recipe books, because quite often what is not in one such book will be in another. Parenthetically, it should be noted that there are over ten thousand mixed drinks recognized by the New York Bartenders' Guild. Braun and Gorman have listed about 1,025 recipes, each illustrated with the type of glass shape to be served to the customer. One such recipe, entitled the French Lieutenant's Woman, contains maraschino liqueur, Calvados, and hazelnut liqueur. But then, everybody has their own poison, and that's the fun of drinking out at a bar, especially at a well-stocked bar. The book is arranged by product, with an alphabetical index to the name of each type of drink. There are also sections here devoted to glassware, bar snacks, measurements, and calories.

341.*   Buller, Jon. **Buller's Professional Course on Bartending for Home Study**. Boston, Mass.: Harvard Common Press, 1983. 152p. illus. index. $11.95.
This is a guide to bartending, either for the home or for gainful employment. It is full of techniques for the novitiate and for the professional alike: stirring, shaking, blending, or building drinks. Unfortunately, Buller only concentrates on the thirty basic drinks that make up the majority of American bar orders, but then recipes and cocktail preparations can be found elsewhere in other books. Other good data, extremely useful for the professional side, is on "office administration": cash register, tips, problem customers, measuring waste, cleaning up, ice and fruit, and laying in the supplies. As well, there is some slight material on wines and beers. This mixology book reads far more enjoyably than other such textbooks; it can be useful for the professional as a "brush up" or as a text for home use.

342.   **Cocktails**. ed. by Helen Chester. New York: St. Martin's Press, 1982. 80p. illus. $5.95 paper.
This really appears to be an international book: it originated in Great Britain, with the illustrations copyrighted by a German publisher; it was printed and bound in Spain, and made available in the United States. Nevertheless, it serves some useful purpose in that the 250 or so cocktail concoctions are the more common ones, and they are available in both Imperial and Metric measurements. Each recipe is squared off on a page, and sometimes there is an illustration showing the glass and the look of the finished product. In fact, because there are four recipes on a page and because they are neatly displayed, the home consumer may want to cut out favorites and retain them in a file. This book is certainly useful, since all the bar recipes are for the tried-and-true cocktails.

343.   Cowan, Thomas. **The Gourmet Guide to Mixed Drinks**. Scarborough,
        Canada: Prentice-Hall Canada, 1984. 128p. illus. index. $7.95 paper.
Believing that mixed drinks and cocktails are on the way back as part of the
nostalgia scene and a reverence for anything from the past, Cowan presents a guide
to the liquors used in drinks, including wines, liqueurs, brandy, and tequila. He has
recipes for over three hundred drinks from "Amaretto Sour" to "Zombie," and
he also includes specialty drinks from renowned hotels. Professional suggestions are
offered for stocking a bar, preparations, and service devices for garnishes, and there
are words of wisdom about choosing the appropriate cocktail for different seasons
and occasions. The format is in the shape of a pocket guide.

344.   Craddock, Harry. **The Savoy Cocktail Book**. New York: Arno, 1976.
        204p. illus. index. $10.95.
This book was originally published in 1930 with material by Craddock, who was
then the head of the American Bar at the Savoy Hotel in London. He was
succeeded by John Johnson, who also made contributions here. This book is a
reprint (not a facsimile) done up in trendy art deco style, and containing the
original old-fashioned recipes for products that are (usually) no longer consumed.

345.   DeWulf, Lucienne M. L. and Marie-Francoise Fourestier. **Adventures
        with Liqueurs**. New York: Books in Focus, 1979. 196p. illus. index.
        $14.95.
Another spirits book, chock-full of recipes and cocktail ideas for the home
consumer.

346.   Dickens, Cedric. **Drinking with Dickens**. New York: Hippocrene Books,
        1983. 127p. illus. $9.95.
Cedric is a great-grandson of the writer Charles Dickens, and he has here produced
an unusual sourcebook. These are recipes and cocktails based on the drinks of
Dickensian England and America (Dickens travelled to North America). As such,
the book becomes a good guide to drinking habits of the Victorian era with their
fondness for mixed drinks such as "Smoking Bishop," "Dog's Nose" (with hot
Guinness stout and gin), and "Shrub." Other types of drinks are American-based:
the dry Martini, the mint julep, the Rock Mountain Sneezer (made with fresh
Rocky Mountain snow, brandy, rum, bitters, sugar, and lemon juice). Material has
been derived from the notebook of Georgina Hogarth, a one-time nanny to
Dickens' children, Dickens' own 1870 wine-cellar book, some of the Dickens
Fellowship Branches from around the world, and the Dickens House Museum.
There are also some literary references from his books, stories, and excerpted
speeches. The arrangement is by type of drink (e.g., beer, brandy, cider, gin,
Madeira, port, wine, etc.). There are some seventy cocktail recipes, including variations, and these should prove satisfactory for the dead of winter when the body
needs either heat or sugar.

347.*   Duffy, Patrick Gavin. **The Official Mixer's Manual**. 7th ed. Garden City,
        New York: Doubleday, 1983. 190p. illus. index. $10.95.

The first edition of this book was in 1934, called the *Standard Bartender's Guide*; it was revised and enlarged by James Beard in 1955 as the third edition. This current version has been considerably revamped and rescaled by critic Robert Jay Misch. Here are some 1,200 mixed-drink recipes, with chapters on wine and food combinations. The arrangement is by base: gin, wine, brandy, liqueurs, rum, vodka, whiskey, and so forth. And it is unusually well indexed. It is interesting to compare this edition with previous ones, to see the changes in drinking preferences (no more long drinks, more vodka-based drinks, and some dairy drinks are now emerging).

348.   Embury, David. **The Fine Art of Mixing Drinks**. rev. ed. Garden City, New York: Doubleday, 1958. 362p. illus. index. $4.95 paper.

Still in print after all these years (albeit in a paperback edition), this work by Embury has been hailed by Michael Jackson as "the most detailed work." Many of the recipes, of course, are quaintly old-fashioned, but of course they still work. This "latest" work has been based on the earlier 1948 and 1952 editions, with added new illustrations.

349.   Haimo, Oscar. **Cocktail and Wine Digest: The Barman's Bible**. New York: self-published, 1979. unpaged. illus. $6.

This book is regularly updated (the "39th Edition" was the one published in 1979); it is available in English or in Spanish. As a standard guide, it has all the standard recipes and notes for making drinks. It has all the "latest" drinks as well, because of its policy of regular updating and revision.

350.   Hewitt, Edward and W. F. Axton. **Convivial Dickens: The Drinks of Dickens and His Times**. Athens, Ohio: Ohio Univ. Press, 1983. 196p. illus. index. $14.95.

This book competes head-on with the one by Dickens' great-grandson. While there is some duplication in the inventory of Dickens' own cellar and the recipes based on gin, rum, cordials, liqueurs, ales, wines, and vintage Champagnes, there is some different material in the exploration of the importance of eating and drinking in Dickens' England. Many of Dickens' settings and plots and characterizations were played out in taverns and inns (indeed, some recipes here have been gathered from innkeepers and butlers of the day). This book traces the history of the social class structure through the alehouses and the pubs, with many of the drawings and illustrations of the period coming from Dickens' published works.

351.   Hogg, Anthony. **Cocktails and Mixed Drinks**. New York: Larousse, 1981. 128p. illus. $7.95 paper.

A concise, deftly written work by an experienced wine and spirits writer. The illustrations, of labels and glasses and products, nicely complement the recipes that are furnished for cocktail preparations.

352.*   **International Guide to Drinks**. comp. by the United Kingdom Bartenders' Guild. London: Hutchinson, 1979; distr. by Merrimack Book Service. 238p. illus. index. $4.95 paper.

This classic was first issued in 1953. It serves admirably as a manual for all types and levels of bartending. Material includes historical notes, stocking the bar, wine information, descriptions of liquors and beers (and even cigars!), and tables and glossaries. The heart of the book is the collection of drink recipes: cocktails, aperitifs, punches, sours, highballs, Collins, etc., and using gin, rum, vodka, whiskey, liqueurs, and brandy. Twenty-five bartender associations from as many countries have contributed their prize-winning cocktail preparations derived from diverse competitions held in order to find new and different drink mixtures. Excellent value for the price.

353.*   Jackson, Michael. **The Pocket Bartender's Guide**. rev. ed. New York: Simon and Schuster, 1984. 144p. illus. bibliog. index. $9.95.

The blurb here says "everything you need to know about drinks, mixers, wines, and beers." And that is true. Here is material about drinking habits around the world, how to serve liquors and mixed drinks, what to do about hangovers, and so forth. There is even a country-by-country survey of drinking products, as well as glasses and stemware and equipment (all illustrated in outline form), and sketch maps for rudimentary locations. The bulk of the book is in two parts. The first, alphabetically arranged section defines terms and drinks, with an indication of whether the product has a generic or a proprietary name, the percentage of alcohol, and whether it is basic to a bar or not. The second, alphabetically arranged section contains 350 recipes—the basic—with an indication of ingredients, type of glass needed, which ones are "standard" or not (some atypical variations are appended here), and which ones are "sweeter" cocktails than the norm. Excellent comments by Jackson throughout the book.

354.   Kaufman, William I. **California Wine Drinks, Cocktails, Coolers, Punches and Hot Drinks**. San Francisco, Calif.: Wine Appreciation Guild, 1983. 128p. illus. index. $4.95 paper.

This book is quite similar to the California brandy book noted above, except, of course, it is concerned with California's wines. But the setup and the scope and the illustrations are quite similar. Kaufman gives some two hundred recipes, plus instructions and bar hints. Typical drinks include "Monterey Cocktail" and "California Martini"—all using local wines, which of course the home consumer need not duplicate exactly.

355.   Mario, Thomas. **Playboy's New Host and Bar Book**. 2d ed. New York: Simon and Schuster, 1979. 520p. illus. $19.95.

The first edition of this book was in 1971; Mario is a consultant for the industry and he was Food and Drink Editor of *Playboy* for twenty-five years. The book includes background information on spirits, wine and beer, comprehensive liquor and garnish lists, suggestions for starting a wine cellar, a glossary of wine terminology, a description of bar equipment, liquor anecdotes and history, a short course on mixology, a chapter of hors d'oeuvre recipes and suggestions for fifteen parties (from a brunch to a wine tasting to an urban luau). The color photographs are stunning, even if they are lavish and somewhat garish. There is much useful advice for the host here. The book has been expanded to include new material on wines (especially white wines), and the number of drink recipes have been increased from 800 to 1,000. Also, the print size has been increased (a sign of readers' advancing age?).

356.   Morelli, Carmine. **A Guide to Bartending Principles.** 2d ed. Vancouver, Canada: C. Morelli and Associates, 1984. 164p. illus. index. $16.95 paper.

Morelli is an instructor in the Food and Beverage program at British Columbia Institute of Technology; he teaches bartending courses. This book is geared primarily to schools and mixologists, and it is especially useful for its in-house training programs. Essentially, it satisfies the need for product knowledge while on the job, the type of bar equipment and accessories needed, and one hundred common cocktail recipes, illustrations, and a glossary.

357.*   **The Official Harvard Student Agencies Bartending Book.** New York: St. Martin's, 1984. 192p. illus. index. $5.95 paper.

The Harvard Student Agencies have been responsible for the enormously popular series, Let's Go Budget Guides. After some years of offering a mixology course, they have put together a manual for commercial distribution. All the usual data is here: the equipment needed, the setups (all nicely diagrammed), the principles of mixology, the recipes for drinks that are blended, stirred, shaken, or built, hot or cold, flamed, or wine-based. What is new and different is the text on cocktail party setups (and the diagrams), the health data on alcohol abuse, and the procedures for tapping a keg, getting a job as a bartender, and how to handle customers. More material, though, could be useful on the issues of ethics and liability, especially since this was a recent topic. Apparently, though, there are enough bartenders in the United States; that occupational classification appears on the "not wanted" immigration prohibition list, along with unskilled labor. The Harvard Book has some 275 cocktail preparations.

358.   **Old Mr. Boston Deluxe Official Bartender's Guide.** 61st ed. New York: Warner Communications, 1981. 216p. illus. index. $4.95.

This is Old Mr. Boston's first commercial trade issuance. It has been published since 1935 and has sold over eight million copies. This "1981" book is actually a reprint of the 1979 edition. Here are about a thousand traditional and trendy cocktails, complete with mixing directions and listed alphabetically by common name (and cross-referenced in an index arranged by category). There is also a photographic guide to the glassware needed, techniques such as flaming liquor, and a buying guide. The ingredients specify any of the 148 products put out by Mr. Boston, but of course the equivalent can be substituted from whatever is to hand.

359.   Poister, John J. **The Wine Lover's Drink Book.** New York: Collier Macmillan, 1983. 160p. illus. index. $5.95 paper.

These are two hundred recipes for mixed drinks made with wine, but of course they also contain recipes for drinks made with wine and a hard liquor of some type (brandy, bourbon, whiskey, rum, gin, liqueurs, fortified wines). The arrangement is by type of drink, beginning with the most popular wine coolers and named drinks, and then moving on to "elegant cocktails" (usually with Champagne or Cognac), then punches, aperitifs, and finally hot drinks. This is a handy book to have if you want basic alternatives to hard drinks and long cocktails.

360.   Ramos, Adam and Joseph Ramos. **Mixed Wine Drinks**. 2d ed. Berkeley, Calif.: Padre Productions, 1981. unpaged. $9.95 paper.
This collection contains about seven hundred recipes for a variety of concoctions such as punches, hot drinks, coolers, and cocktails. The emphasis is of course on the uses of wine, and how it all fits into the California life-style.

361.   **Trader Vic's Bartender Guide**. ed. by Victor J. Bergeron. rev. and enl. Garden City, N.Y.: Doubleday, 1972. 442p. illus. index. $7.95.
Originally published in 1947, this book now has over a thousand recipes, with 143 originals as served in the Trader Vic restaurants. There are no variations given— just one standard drink per recipe. Passé drinks have been dropped, but they are now coming back into style, at least among the younger generation.

362.*   Walker, Michael. **The Cocktail Book: The Complete Guide to Home Cocktails**. Tucson, Ariz.: HP Books, 1980. 96p. illus. $5.95 paper.
This book has excellent color photographs, illustrating nearly all the two hundred drinks listed. Included is standard data on equipment, stemware, garnishes, terminology, and so forth. Entertainment suggestions include how to give a successful party, what advanced preparations are needed, and the types of drinks to be served. Fifty food recipes are included for canapés, pastries, dips, cones, rolls, and stuffings. The measurements for the cocktails are given in proportions, which is a good idea in that you can increase the total quantity as much as you want.

Tasting, Comparing, and Evaluating Wines (Consumer Guides), Including Humor and Health Issues

One of the most important aspects of alcoholic beverages is their consumption. There are many guides to tasting and to consumer education; what follows are only the better ones that are almost completely "evaluative." Notes on tasting are scattered widely in the literature of wines, beers, and spirits. For instance, additional material can be found in chapter 9, which deals with magazines and newsletters (although the indexes to these magazines are described below, in this chapter); in chapter 11, which presents material on auction and sales catalogs; in chapter 2, for general books on wines and for wines of a particular country; in chapter 8 for the technical books that explain how we taste and why we sense diverse stimuli (material can also be found in chapter 10, which deals with amateur wine making); and in chapter 6, with evaluations and opinions and book listings of personal observations and historical accounts.

Contained here, then, are books and other materials concerned with the appraisal of alcoholic beverages, principally wine. Described are books that tell you what to look for when you are tasting, books that contain a great number of recommended wines to drink, wine cellar and wine record books in which to jot down your impressions while maintaining your wine cellar inventory, books dealing with humor (where you should know the rules before you break the rules—the easiest way to get rid of a wine snob), and some material about the therapeutic health aspects of alcoholic consumption.

CONSUMER GUIDES AND TASTING

363.*   Amerine, Maynard A. and Edward B. Roessler. **Wines: Their Sensory Evaluation**. rev. and enl. San Francisco, Calif.: W. H. Freeman, 1983. 448p. illus. bibliog. index. $19.95.
A highly technical, but readable book. Sensory analysis is arrived at through knowledge of sensory physiology, psychology, and perception. Outside aid is provided for by careful statistical analysis of the data. The sole difficulty appears to be in measuring consumer acceptance for a product. The complexity of a wine bouquet and taste are examined through various topics such as wine quality (aesthetics,

pleasure, complexity), sensory responses, the composition of wines, and the types of wines available. Other chapters deal with how to do statistical analyses, and there are appendices of tables of mathematical distributions. There is a glossary that is ideal for tasting notes, since the book is restrictive in its use of terminology. The authors condemn the use of certain words because they mean different things to most people. Such intangible words include: "big," "harsh," "noble," "severe," "tangy," "warm," "and "zestful" (among others).

364.　　Bespaloff, Alexis. **Alexis Bespaloff's Guide to Inexpensive Wines.** New York: Simon and Schuster, 1975. 160p. $2.95 paper.

In addition to covering the basics of tasting, storing, and serving wines, Bespaloff comments on retail wine prices and how to read a label. He gives some evaluation for a range of two thousand specific wines and fifty jug wines. Not current, but useful for information about the state of the wines being consumed in the mid-1970s.

365.　　**Bottles and Cellars Index to California Wine, 1982-** . Norwalk, Calif.: California Wine Consultants, 1983- . various pagination. $32.

The 1982 edition of this new index covered six hundred different wines, along with tasting notes and a listing of wine awards.

366.*　　Broadbent, Michael. **The Great Vintage Winebook.** New York: Knopf, 1980. 432p. illus. index. $25.

Broadbent is head of the Wine Department at the auction firm of Christie's, and he is Chief Auctioneer of the annual Heublein Wine Auction in the United States. This book is essentially thirty years' worth of wine tastings and ratings from his notebooks. It is a description of fine wines, covering the vintages from 1653 to 1979. For example, he covers eighty different vintages of Château Lafite. This book is one of the few totally new wine books of the past several years because it embraces virtually totally new material, that is, an experienced taster's thoughts on a variety of wines such as reds, whites, Champagnes, ports, and other fortified wines. But it is limited in that it covers only some of the wines of France (70 percent of the book), some from Germany (39 pages), and rare wine types from California (9 pages) and Australia. Missing are all the fine Italian brunellos, and chianti classico riservas, as well as the Spanish Riojas, the pre-phylloxera Chilean wines, and so forth. Still, for the areas that he does cover (and for France, this is only the Bourdeaux and Burgundy table wines), he discusses every vintage since 1945, as well as quite a few from the past. His coverage also includes tasting the same vintage of the same wine, but several years apart. His tasting notes rate wines at one to five stars, and there is a 150-item glossary. The appendix identifies thirty-three wine groupings. The maps are good for identification and locations, and the index covers châteaux, wine makers, and specific vintages.

367.*　　Broadbent, Michael. **Michael Broadbent's Complete Guide to Wine Tasting and Wine Cellars.** New York: Simon and Schuster, 1984. 272p. illus. bibliog. index. $12.95.

First issued in 1968 by Christie's, the 1984 updating includes more material about North America, since this is its first commercial distribution by an American publisher. Since it first came out, Broadbent's writings on sensory evaluation have proved to be the best source for the technical enjoyment of all kinds of wines. When one expertly employs all of the senses, and encounters the expected grape characteristics of the varieties used in the production of the world's best wines, there is no reason why one cannot develop a discriminating palate through the use of this book. Additional information is given on how to organize a tasting, how to record tasting notes, how to use "words" properly in communicating the description of sensations, and the appropriate terminology as used locally in France, Germany, and Italy. The thirty-one color photographs show the variations in both white- and red-wine colorations. At the back there is an excellent bibliography on other wine tasting books and books containing technical data on the production of wine, as well as space for recording your own notes.

368.* **Consumer Index to Product Evaluations and Information Sources, 1973- .** Ann Arbor, Mich.: Pierian Press, 1974- . $69.

The value of this book is that it is an index to individual products, listed under product name, with full references to the periodical (title, issue date, and page number) in which the product appeared. For comments on the wine, you have to look up the article itself. Thus, in section 5, under "Food, Beverages and Tobacco," there is a subunit entitled "Alcoholic Beverages," further broken down into "Brewed Beverages," "Spirits/Distilled Beverages," and "Wines." About fifty pages of this index cover around 3,200 wines annually, indexing such magazines as *Consumer Reports, Consumers Digest, Which ?, Bon Appetit, The Friends of Wine, Gourmet, Vintage, Wine World,* and general magazines (food magazines, *Vogue, Esquire, House and Garden,* etc.). For all these, it will pick up references to any wines evaluated and tasted, and list them in alphabetical order by name of the wine. No newsletters are covered, except for *Robert Balzer's Private Guide,* and there are also sections indexing general wine articles and books covered (in addition to just the tastings and evaluations).

369.   Ensrud, Barbara. **The Pocket Guide to Wine.** rev. ed. New York: Perigee/ Putnam, 1982. 138p. illus. maps. index. $5.95 paper.

As a competitor to *Hugh Johnson's Pocket Encyclopedia of Wine,* Ensrud's book is more restricted to evaluations. About 1,500 wines are briskly described, with their producers and vintages rated through the 1981 harvest, and ranked as to dollar value. The arrangement is by country, with France first, followed by Italy, Germany, etc.

370.   Fadiman, Clifton and Sam Aaron. **Wine Buyers Guide.** ed. by Darlene Geis. New York: Abrams, 1977. 159p. illus. index. $8.95 paper.

This is a condensed, popularly priced version of *The Joys of Wine* published in 1975 at $45 by Abrams. It lacks the in-depth treatment of the original, but it is a solid guide to wines around the world (how to read the labels, wine recommendations, vintage charts, price guides, etc.). One chapter here is by James Beard, on wine and food affinities; and there are many maps, charts, and color illustrations.

371.   Fingerhut, Bruce and Steve Haskin. **Read That Label: How to Tell What's Inside a Wine Bottle from What's on the Outside.** South Bend, Ind.: Icarus, 1983. 128p. illus. index. $4.95 paper.

A neat, crisp little book that describes what the wine label is supposed to do in describing what is on the inside of the bottle. There are examples given of poor labels and of good labels. A useful book.

372.*   Johnson, Hugh. **Hugh Johnson's Pocket Encyclopedia of Wine.** 1985 ed. New York: Simon and Schuster, 1984. 191p. illus. maps. $8.95.

This was the first of the pocket guides to wines and other beverages and foods (there are several dozen of these books now available from different publishers). Johnson has extensively revised this book, since he was also working on a companion volume (his *Modern Encyclopedia*). In this edition ratings and rankings of top California cabernet sauvignon and chardonnay vintages are given for the first time. The book itself appears about every year, and each edition is needed for the updated thoughts and opinions of previous and new vintages. The beginning materials cover the nature of wine, with the usual data on tasting, buying, serving, storing, and terminologies. The country-by-country arrangement begins with France and ends with minor countries. The illustrations are mainly sketch maps of a locational nature, and the individual entries are short and to the point, with no mincing of words, including some "personal choices" for consumption in 1985.

373.   Kaufman, William I. **The Whole-World Wine Catalog.** New York: Penguin Books, 1978. 224p. illus. $5.95 paper.

This is an assortment of 2,500 wine labels, arranged by country beginning with the United States (California has 50 pages here), and then France, Italy, Germany, Spain, Portugal, England, Australia, New Zealand, Canada, and fifteen others. Within each county, arrangement is by producer, with a label illustration followed by brief data on the type of wine (such as "red," "white," "sparkling"), grape variety, district, tasting notes, vintage notes, and price ranges. Sherries, sparkling wines and jug wines are also included. There is no index, but the book is certainly useful for label identification in a wine store.

374.   Marcus, Irving H. **How to Test and Improve Your Wine Judging Ability.** rev. ed. Berkeley, Calif.: Wine Publications, 1984. 96p. illus. $6.00 paper.

Twenty-five short chapters describe the basics and give tips. Marcus outlines the professional's approach to wine judging and describes the tasting tools and patterns. He gives a detailed explanation of the 20-point score card, and suggests ways of testing an individual's wine-tasting ability. This former editor of *Wines and Vines* has devised a series of six sensory tests to measure taste thresholds for total wine evaluation. After describing the major components of wine, he analyzes the physiological capabilities and limitations of sight, smell, taste, and touch in judging wines.

375.   Nelson, James. **Everybody's Guide to Great Wines under $5.** New York: McGraw-Hill, 1983. 256p. illus. index. $6.95 paper.

This book is a guide to some of the more easily available, nationally distributed cheap ("jug") wines in the United States, both imported and domestic. But of course the California wines predominate in this rating and tasting list of some 505 wines.

376.   Peppercorn, David, Brian Cooper, and Elwyn Blacker. **Drinking Wine**. New York: Harbor House Books, 1979. 256p. illus. maps. $14.95.
Originally published in Britain, this ratings guide to wine covers some three thousand different labels. Thumbnail sketches of different areas are presented, as well as glossaries of terms, and notes on how to taste, buy, serve, and store. Label reproductions, charts, photographs, and sixty-five full-color maps are among the over two hundred illustrations.

377.*   Peynaud, Emile. **Le Gout de Vin**. 2d ed. Paris: Editions Bordas, 1983.
A French-language classic by one of the leading French oenologists: this is a highly technical book detailing the full range of sensory evaluations of wines. The stress, of course, is on French wines.

378.   **Pocket Wine Record**. Montreal, Canada: Kylix International, 1982. unpaged. illus. $5.95 paper.
This is a pocket cellar book to record data when you are away from home; it is a good idea for portability. There is space on each lined page for name, place, date, price of wine, and comments. Highly useful for tastings at another person's home or in a restaurant, not only for the space but also for the basic text that serves as an aide-memoire (vintage charts, maps, label notes, and descriptions of nose and color and taste, but no tasting glossary, nor any explanation of tasting terms).

379.*   Price, Pamela Vandyke. **Enjoying Wine: A Taster's Companion**. London: W. Heinemann, 1983; distr. by David & Charles. 202p. illus. bibliog. index. $18.95; $12.95 paper.
Price is an exceptionally talented food and wine writer; this is her twelfth book. She presents copious notes on the sensory analysis and tasting of wines, with much detail on how to gain experience, how to do "homework," how to arrange blind tastings, and how to make notes. There are also chapters on specialized wines and spirits to taste, e.g., port, sherry, vermouth, and Madeira, and on the use of equipment and glasses, the affinity of wines to food, and last, but not least, how to "learn" about wine through books, courses, lectures, and teachers. This last part is of particular value to keen students in order to derive maximum benefit from any courses: be prepared before you attend. Some of it is fun, but you do take these courses and read books to learn!

380.*   Puisais, J. and R. L. Chabarron. **Initiation into the Art of Wine Tasting**. Madison, Wis.: Interpublish Inc., 1974. 96p. illus. bibliog. index. $8.95 paper.
Originally published in France in 1969 by the Institut Technique du Vin, this short book (one of the best on the subject) covers the following topics: sensory system (tasting, smelling, and the breakdown of the various esters), applying senses to food and drink, getting ready for a tasting (emphasizing room conditions), how to taste

wines, choosing the wines to taste, and the influences of wines on food. There is also a how-to-section on exercises for "scoring."

381.   Quittanson, Charles. **Connaissance et Gloire du Vin**. 2d ed. Paris: Editions Bres, 1979. 176p. illus. 30 French francs.
Although in French, there is a highly modified version of the text in English included. Topics include: a discussion of French wines, what to look for in these wines, grape varieties and characteristics, ratings and rankings in scoring, and material on storage, serving, and buying.

382.   Robards, Terry. **California Wine Label Album**. New York: Workman, 1981. 176p. illus. $10.95 looseleaf.
Basically a text descriptive of the California wines, plus a sketch outline of the various labels, and space for the consumer to add his own labels and tasting notes.

383.   Robinson, Jancis. **Masterglass**. London: Pan Books, 1982. 176p. £ 2.95 paper.
This is a practical course in wine tasting by a leading British wine taster and wine writer. The emphasis is on European wines, notably French, Italian, and German. Material covers buying, storing, serving, tasting, and evaluating.

384.   Sarfati, Claude. **La dégustation des vins: méthode pédagogique et exercices pratiques**. Suze-la-Rousse, France: Université du vin, 1981. 155p. illus. index. price not available.
This excellent little book, although in French and useful only with a translating dictionary, delves into all the aspects of tasting: what to look for, organization of tastings, organoleptic qualities, vocabulary for description, and so forth. There are thirty exercises against which the reader can test himself, all concentrating on tasting, smelling, seeing, analyses, and character of the wine.

385.*   Sharp, Andrew. **Winetaster's Secrets: The Consumer's Guide to Wine-tasting**. New York: Sterling Press, 1982. 144p. illus. $6.95 paper.
Written in a colloquial manner (and obviously taken from his class notes, for he is a wine teacher and syndicated columnist), this book deals with the "how to" of wine appreciation. By using sight, smell, and taste, one learns what to look for in fine wines, and what to avoid in mediocre wines. Sharp presents a number of evaluation forms and systems that a serious taster can use, plus the technical advice on what each grape variety should smell and taste like once it has been made into wine. The work is uncomplicated and of good value. He also includes a detailed description of the major grape varieties and a glossary of terms to be used in the descriptions.

386.   Sichel, Peter and Judy Ley Allen. **Which Wine? The Wine Drinkers Buying Guide**. New York: A & W Visual Library, 1977. 288p. illus. $12.50.
A fairly good book written by an importer of European wines (principally German). The details cover much the same ground as the other books do, and the heavy concentration is on product availability in New York City and on imported wines.

387. Sutcliffe, Serena. **The Wine Handbook.** New York: Simon and Schuster, 1982. 224p. illus. maps. $14.95 looseleaf.
With sections on wines of the world, maps, art work for labels, and a three-ring binder, this useful tool has much space to add your own comments and tasting notes for other wines that you can try.

388. Treber, Grace. **World Wine Almanac and Wine Atlas.** New York: International Wine Society, 1976. 2 vols. 944p. illus. $30.
This was a useful reference book, but it needs some updating if it is to remain current. There are 4,172 wines of the world described and evaluated as to how, where, and when to drink. There are photographs of specific labels, as well as a directory of American wine shops and maps.

389. Waugh, Harry. **Bacchus on the Wing: A Wine Merchant's Travelogue.** London: Wine and Spirit Publications, 1966. 203p. illus. £ 5.

390. Waugh, Harry. **The Changing Face of Wine: An Assessment of Some Current Vintages.** London: Wine and Spirit Publications, 1968. 109p. illus. £ 5.

391. Waugh, Harry. **Diary of a Wine Taster: Recent Tastings of French and California Wines.** New York: Quadrangle, 1972. 228p. illus. $9.95.

392.* Waugh, Harry. **Harry Waugh's Wine Diary,** vol. 1- . London: Christie's Wine Publications, 1970- . $11.50 each.
In some form or another, Harry Waugh has published his "wine diary" containing vinous information going back to 1960. All of these books are very similar, having been written for the current times with up-to-date tastings in mind. They are systematic assessments of French wines (usually), district by district and year by year, with comparative data. Other countries are also here: Australia, America, Germany, Italy, and Portugal. Current vintages are stressed; this is an inimitable record of visits to wine areas, memorable meals, comparative tastings, and personalities in the wine world. All are well illustrated, with photographs, maps, and charts. Waugh was a wine merchant, a consultant to the industry, and a director of Château Latour. When Christie's took over the publication of his notes, he kept them in the rough form in which they now appear, as a diary. Volume 8 was issued in 1978 at 164 pages, while volume 9 came along in 1981 at 208 pages and covered the April 1978 to February 1981 period.

393. Waverman, Lucy. **The Pennypincher's Wine Guide.** Toronto, Canada: Avon Books of Canada, 1983. 213p. index. bibliog. $5.95 paper.
Originally published in 1975 and updated since then, this current consumer guide to wines under eight dollars in Canada has a wrap-up section entitled "Best Buys." There are very few American wines here, but most of the imports should also be available domestically. The prime value here might be for the tastings of Canadian wines. There is an 80-page summary of the wines available across Canada, tasted by an ever-changing wine panel. Rated are bouquet and taste, plus what they are

suitable with in the way of food. Some wines, of course, are specifically made for cheap markets, and obviously they are going to taste "cheap," but that does not excuse the cheap shots taken here when Waverman writes that one particular wine is fine with "mother-in-law at lunch," or about one with a bouquet of "rotting leaves" being recommended as going with "thousand year old eggs." The book concludes with 70 pages of food recipes.

394.   **Which ? Wine Guide, 1984.** ed. by Jane MacQuitty. London: Consumers' Association, 1983. unpaged. maps. £ 6.95.

All wine-producing countries of the world are covered here, as well as sherry, port, Cognac, and aperitifs. Various listings here include recommendations for 250 wine merchants, 200 wine bars and 60 restaurants with good wine lists, and over 1,000 best buys. The wine merchants were judged on the length and range of wines; the wine bars on their wine lists and accompanying food. Other material here covers wines at auction, considerations of vintages, the English wine industry (its history and a directory of addresses), and basics of service and food. There is a town directory as well as three sets of maps: of England, of English vineyards, and of European wine-producing areas.

395.   **Wine Album.** New York: Metropolitan Museum of Art and Coward, McCann & Geohegan, 1982. 160p. illus. $15.95 boxed.

This has been adapted from *Monseigneur Le Vin* (Paris, 1927) as written by Louis Forest and illustrated by Charles Martin. The first 80 pages are a text on preparing (wine cellars, decanting, temperature), serving (stemware, food, and menus), and drinking (appreciation and vocabulary). There are excellent 1920s-style illustrations on every page. The last 80 pages are a record for your own wines and meals, about 40 double pages. The left side (verso) has space for the name of the wine and the region, and space for the label. The right side (recto) has space for food, rating, shared with (somebody), address, date, menu, etc., and there are decorative illustrations again. The handy book is nice because it has the space to deal with forty dinners and makes a good gift, and one can use the interleaving pages for one's own wine labels.

396.   **Wine Cellar Album: A Personal Record of Purchases and Usage of Wine for Your Greater Enjoyment of Nature's Unique Beverage.** San Francisco, Calif.: Fortune House, 1970. unpaged. illus. $10 looseleaf.

Arranged in a looseleaf format (with room for extra pages to be added later), four sections cover appetizer wines; shite, rosé and red wines; dessert wines; and sparkling wines. For each section there are purchase records on one side of the page (reference number, quantity, wine types, brand, purchase source, date, price, comments) and use records on the other side (reference number, wine type, number used, stock balance, rating, occasion, guests, food, comments). A miscellaneous section has guidelines for choosing glasses, and suggestions for rating, starting a cellar, and building a rack storage. There is a glossary, a bibliography, and space reserved for photographs and memorable labels. A very comprehensive tool, extremely useful for the larger cellar.

397.   **Wine Record Book.** 3d ed. London: Wines and Spirits Publications, 1972.
         144p. £ 5.

In addition to a layout similar to that of *Wine Cellar Album* (see entry 396),
this book contains hints on recording and rating wines, a glossary of tasting terms,
a stock analysis, vintage and vinification charts, pages of descriptive matter for
bottles, glasses, and openers, and an index page.

398.   **Wine Spectator's Guide to Selected Wines, 1982-** . New York: Wine
         Spectator, 1983- . $7.95 paper.

This is a compilation of every "Highly Recommended" and "Recommended"
wine reviewed in the periodical *The Wine Spectator.* In 1982, there were 596
wines from around the world, in 48 pages.

399.*   **The Wine Tasting Index, 1978-** . San Francisco, Calif.: Bacchus Data
         Services, 1979- . $13.95 paper.

This is a computerized listing of all wines and wine tastings reported and rated
and/or ranked in some seventeen (as of 1983) wine guides and newsletters of the
previous year. Each issue has about 150 pages, and the latest for 1982 had 11,000
citations, all sorted by region, variety, vintage, and producer. The overall rating
of the wine is noted, as well as the page and the month of the magazine. Thus, no
recourse to the original article is really necessary if all you are interested in is some
kind of numeric value.

HUMOR

400.   Bernstein, Leonard S. **The Official Guide to Wine Snobbery.** New York:
         Morrow, 1982. 160p. illus. $10.95.

Bernstein (no relation to the conductor of the same name) has packaged many of
his humorous articles for *House Beautiful* and the New York *Times* into this handy
book. His essays are serious at the same time as they are funny: how to put down
wine stewards and friends, how to play around with the unusual bottle (such as
Beaujolais Blanc), how to find the correct ponderous adjectives and wine words,
how to conduct blind tastings to your advantage, plus discussions on vintages,
etiquette, wine breathing, and so forth. This is all an exercise in one-upmanship
and forms a good read. There is lots that can be learned from this book, by novice
and expert alike.

401.   Clarke, Nick. **Bluff Your Way in Wines.** New York: Crown, 1971. 63p.
         illus. maps. tables. $1.95.

Originally published in England, this amusing little book is dedicated to the lady
who described an inoffensive Mosel as being "tender, without being mawkish."
The inclusion of inside jokes makes this book a jewel for the professional, the
advanced amateur or the wine snob, with added tips on how to combat such
snobbery. Plentiful information is presented, in almost point-by-point form. The
book deals with: selection of wine, tasting, merging of food with wines, choosing
a wine in a restaurant, and dominating a wine steward. Despite such obvious state-
ments as "wine glasses should be water tight," it does include facts not commonly
known, such as a description of a white Beaujolais. Coverage is worldwide, with
some detail on sherry and port. The book closes with a "Totally Useless Glossary."

402.   Outerbridge, David. **The Hangover Handbook**. London: Pan Books, 1982. 96p. illus. $2.95 paper.
This is supposed to be the definitive guide to the causes and cures of mankind's "oldest" affliction. It does list causes and excellent solutions. Written in a humorous style, with some history of excessive drinking (such as the Navy Grog), the book does show what causes a "high" and what causes a "hangover." In German the word is "katzenjammer" (a wailing of cats); in Italian, hangover is "stonato" (out of tune). In whatever language it is sheer hell, and Outerbridge gives good advice on what to do before you start drinking, and of course ninety-three remedies on what to do the morning after. All of these are graded from poor to fair to good to excellent. Most of these solutions are common sense, others involve some alcohol—a hair of the dog, such as Bloody Mary or Between the Sheets. My own favorite is from Puerto Rico: "Take half a lemon and rub it in the armpits."

403.   Searle, Ronald. **The Illustrated Winespeak**. London: Souvenir Press, 1983. 100p. illus. £ 6.95.
Searle explores the wicked world of wine tasting. He matches descriptive phrases meant to accompany wines (e.g., "somewhat lacking in finesse") to people drinking these very same wines (e.g., a wino). The line drawings are amusing, and most are in color. Searle, of course, was the artist behind the girls of St. Trinians.

HEALTH

404.   Baus, Herbert. **Gateway to Wine and Health**. Montreal: Kylix International, 1983. 179p. illus. bibliog. $12.95 paper.
Originally published in 1973 by Mason and Lipscomb as *How to Wine Your Way to Good Health*. Baus in middle age had to change his diet for reasons of health. He switched to a regular consumption of wine, albeit in a moderate sense, and when this created a weight loss that he has since managed to maintain, he decided to write a book about the therapeutic value of wine. This, then, is a book written for a broad audience, with notes on how wine helps the digestive system, the circulation and the respiration, and contributes to a balanced diet and controlled appetite. There is also material about doctors, hospitals, hangovers, drugs, and so forth. He uses medical quotations and the appropriate sources to back himself. The bibliography is useful, but most imprints are dated before 1973.

405.   **Proceedings of Wine Health and Society: A Symposium**. San Francisco: Wine Institute, 1983. 147p. $6.95.
This is a transcript of a symposium held in November, 1981, jointly sponsored by the Wine Institute, the University of California at San Francisco, and the Society of Medical Friends. Thirteen papers were presented, on a number of topics: absorption of alcohol from beverages; alcohol and heart diseases; wine and diabetes; wine and nutrition; wine and drugs; wine and allergies; drinking and pregnancy; neurological disorders caused by alcohol; and a history of wine as medicine. Good, substantial presentations that should be of interest to all serious wine drinkers and to doctors.

6 Wines, Beers, and Spirits in History

This chapter is divided into 4 sections. Section 1 concerns materials dealing with the history of wine, and it includes original documents and primary sources of the day. The books here have been carefully selected out of the hundreds of social and economic histories available. Temperance, Prohibition, and Repeal—indeed, almost everything dealing with alcoholic abuse—have been eschewed. Further investigation into these fields will be found by consulting the books listed here, or by checking the bibliographic section in chapter 12. Typical material excluded would be along the lines of Henry W. Lee's *How Dry We Were* (Prentice-Hall, 1963), a history of Prohibition, or H. F. Lutz's *Viticulture and Brewing in the Ancient Orient* (Macmillan, 1922). Regional histories that are part of a larger general study will be found under the appropriate geographic section of chapter 2, as will be found corporate histories or histories of a particular breed of wine. Some historical materials about beer can be located in chapter 3, while items on spirits can also be discovered in chapter 4.

Section 2 in this chapter covers pubs and inns; at best, these are regional histories of the hospitality trade. Taverns became important because they were the way stations on a long and arduous journey, a place that provided food and accommodation, news and information.

Section 3 here describes collecting and collectibles—a very small but growing literature on the collecting possibilities affiliated with alcoholic consumption.

And finally, section 4 has material descriptive of personal observations from the past, full of anecdotes, reflections, tastings from an older time, and so forth. These books, while not technical, do presuppose a knowledge of alcoholic beverages. Indeed, the books often give the impression of being letters from one friend to another. Topics include art, literature, and music, and deal with *bon vivant* life-styles, the great vintages of pre-phylloxera wines of the past, the great vintages of the 1920s, legends and lore, and so on.

HISTORY

406.   Adlum, John. **A Memoir on the Cultivation of the Vine in America, and the Best Mode of Making Wine.** Washington, D.C.: 1823; reprinted Hopewell, N.J.: Booknoll Reprints, 1971. 144p. $12.50.

This is a diverse collection of papers that includes the first book printed in the United States on wine (with the addition of a biography and bibliography by Dorothy Manks); a facsimile of Thomas Jefferson's letter of April 1823 to Adlum regarding his book and some of his wine; and Adlum's "Petition to Congress" of April 30, 1828, regarding the book and his pioneering efforts in making wine from native grapes.

407.   Butler, Frank H. **Wine and Wineland of the World, with Some Account of Places Visited.** New York: Finch Press, 1971. 271p. illus. $25.

This is a reprint of the 1926 edition originally published in London by T. Fisher Unwin. It opens with a discussion of religious and health reasons for consuming wines. Most of the fifty-five photographs are the author's, and together with the text they cover Portugal, Spain, France, Italy, Algeria, Morocco, Russia, South Africa, Australia, Argentina, Chile, Canada, and other places. Covered are brandy, Cognac, whisky, Irish whiskey, rums, ales, perries, gin, drinking songs, and even fashions in drinking wines.

408.   Carosso, Vincent. **The California Wine Industry: A Study of the Formative Years, 1830-1895.** Berkeley, Calif.: Univ. of California Press, 1976. 241p. bibliog. index. $27.50.

This is a reprint of the 1951 edition, which was a scholarly account of the early beginnings of the California wine-making industry.

409.   Crawford, Anne. **A History of the Vintners' Company.** London: Constable, 1978. 319p. illus. index. £ 10.

This is a history of the London wine trade. The Company regulated the quality of the wine and enforced fair prices and true measures. Its trade functions died down over the centuries, and it became more social and educative in nature.

410.   DeRothschild, Phillipine. **Mouton-Rothschild: Paintings for the Label, 1945-1981.** Boston, Mass.: New York Graphic Society, 1983. 144p. illus. $35; $14.50 paper.

This is mainly a collection of colored plates, one per year, illustrating the art work used for the unique labels on the Château Rothschild Bordeaux wine. Thus, there are labels that have been designed by Andy Warhol (this seems out of balance), Marc Chagall, and two from the Canadian artist Riopelle (in the same year). Other illustrations include materials of rarity in the Mouton wine museum.

411.   DeTreville, Lawrence R., ed. **Jefferson and Wine: Thomas Jefferson the Wine Connoisseur and Wine Grower.** The Plains, Va.: Vinifera Wine Growers Association, 1976. 192p. illus. bibliog. index. $4.95 paper.

This was a special issue of *The Vinifera Wine Growers Journal* (vol. 3, combined issues of nos. 1 and 2), and it describes sixty-one years of Jefferson's love of viticulture and buying, storing, and making wine. There is lots of material here on the efforts Jefferson made to induce the growth of European wines in the United States. Twenty illustrations are useful.

412.   Francis, A. D. **The Wine Trade.** London: Adam and Charles Black, 1972. distr. by Humanities. 353p. bibliog. index. $11.25.
This is a British economic history text that covers the major developments of the spread of English commercial influence in the fifteenth and sixteenth centuries, with the import of wine and the export of wool. It deals with the increase of trade with Portugal and Spain, to about 1850. There are many contemporaneous accounts reproduced here, as well as statistics and an extensive bibliography of both primary and secondary sources. Major topics include method of shipment, customs and excise, and the production and blending of wines.

413.   Grace, Virginia R. **Amphoras and the Ancient Wine Trade.** Princeton, New Jersey: American School of Classical Studies at Athens, 1979. 69p. illus. $1.50 paper.
As one of the series dealing with the excavations of the Athenian agora, this small booklet consists mainly of pictures of wine containers, with little text.

414.   Haraszthy, Agostin. **Father of California Wine.** Santa Barbara, Calif.: Capra Press, 1979. various pagination. illus. bibliog. $20.
This is a reprint of the 1862 edition, originally published by Harper Brothers as *Grape Culture, Wines and Wine Making, with Notes upon Agriculture and Horticulture.* Haraszthy was a Hungarian vintner whose family produced Tokay wine. In 1857 he discovered the Sonoma Valley's wine-making potential, and from 1859 through 1868 he was a commercial California wine maker—the first. He has been called "the father of modern California viticulture," for he was commissioned by the California legislature to gather information on European wine-making methods. This book was the result of a tour through France, Italy, Germany, Spain, and Switzerland. He brought back over 100,000 cuttings representing 300 varieties, which formed the base of California's modern industry. His own winery subsequently became Buena Vista Winery, and it produced many of the wines from these initial cuttings. This book is his story of scientific findings and applications of European stock to California conditions.

415.   Haynes, Irene W. **Ghost Wineries of Napa Valley.** San Francisco, Calif.: Taylor and Friends, 1980. 64p. illus. maps. $4 paper.
A nifty little book that presents details on former wineries located in the Napa Valley area. There are full maps with suggestions of tours.

416.* Hyams, Edward S. **Dionysus: A Social History of the Wine Vine.** New York: Macmillan, 1965. 381p. illus. maps. $25.
An exemplary history of viticulture, with 130 reproductions of paintings and other artworks, maps, eight color plates, and a good index. As a basic historical work concerning the consumption of wine, the book details *vitis vinifera:* how it was cultivated in the past, what sort of wines were drunk, how they were made and taxed, how all of this affected people's lives. An interesting approach since it is an account of a single plant species through eighty centuries.

417. James, Margery Kirkbride. **Studies in the Medieval Wine Trade.** Oxford, England: Clarendon Press, 1971. 232p. illus. maps. bibliog. index. £ 14.
These are four papers and material from James' unpublished doctoral dissertation. She pays particular attention to the Anglo-Gascon fourteenth- to sixteenth-century wine trade, from the production of wine in Gascony to its retail sale in England. Covered, then, are materials on the transit of wine and the English ports of entries, the distributive trade of wine in England, and some profiles of London wine merchants. Twenty-five appendices record various tables of statistics, such as the numbers of wine ships entering English ports in different years, overseas freight charges, wholesale and retail distribution prices in England, and values of sales.

418. Lamb, Richard and Ernest G. Mittelberger. **In Celebration of Wine and Life.** 2d ed. San Francisco: Wine Appreciation Guild, 1980. 255p. illus. bibliog. $19.95; $9.95 paper.
Originally published by Drake in 1974, this book was put together with the assistance of Mittelberger, who was then Director of the Wine Museum of San Francisco. That Museum provided the illustrations here (there are also 35 color plates), which appear on virtually every page. Topics include the origins, customs, and traditions of wine making and wine drinking, as well as wine and health and wine and love. Practical data is also given, such as how to select wines, what to serve and drink at appropriate times, and why wines can be so different. In 1984, most of the Museum's contents were transferred to Waterloo, Canada.

419. Lesko, Leonard. **King Tut's Wine Cellar.** Providence, R.I.: B. C. Scribe, 1977. 124p. illus. maps. $3.95 paper.
Lesko is a professional Egyptologist; this is an account of the wine industry as it existed in King Tut's time. There is material on wine-jar labelling, vintage dating, vineyards, and even a wine list from King Tut.

420. Loubere, Leo. **The Red and the White: History of Wine in France and Italy in the 19th Century.** Baltimore, Md.: State Univ. of New York Press, 1978. 401p. illus. index. $32.50.
A fairly comprehensive and interesting history of the interplay between these two countries as they aggressively promoted their wine trade.

421. Mishkin, David. **The American Colonial Wine Industry: An Economic Interpretation.** Fort Washington, Pa.: Ayer Co., 1975. 2 vols. (232p.; 630p.) bibliog. index. $61.

This book was originally issued by the University of Illinois Press in 1966. It is an economic history of the American wine industry under the French, English, Spanish, and Dutch policies of the sixteenth to eighteenth centuries. The bibliography forms a substantial part of this doctoral dissertation: 1,200 entries on early American attempts to produce wine.

422.* Ordish, George. **The Great Wine Blight**. New York: Scribner's, 1972. 237p. illus. bibliog. index. $12.95.
This is a fascinating account of the phylloxera blight on European vineyards in the late nineteenth century, and of the subsequent attempts to eradicate the pest. Chapters discuss the first bumbling, panic-stricken efforts to find a remedy—just about everything was tried except grafting (which was delayed fifteen years because of local opposition). In France alone, 11 billion cuttings were needed to "reconstitute" the vineyards.

423.   Peninou, Ernest P., and Sidney Greenleaf. **A Directory of California Wine Growers and Wine Makers in 1860**. Berkeley, Calif.: Tamalais Press, 1967. 84p. illus. bibliog. index. $15.
Much biographical and historical detail is given "to commemorate the names of those Californians who more than a century ago were engaged in the growing of grapes and the making of wine." This directory lists 262 names, mostly gathered from the Census of 1860. Information also concerns acreage, gallons of wine on hand, pounds of grapes sold, and money received for grapes. Only six sites that were occupied in 1860 are still producing wine. Arrangement is by county, and then alphabetical by grower (some names of whom were obtained from additional sources such as county histories and agricultural societies).There are four black-and-white illustrations of wine labels from this period.

424.   Seltman, Charles. **Wine in the Ancient World**. London: Routledge and Kegan Paul, 1957. 196p. illus. bibliog. index. out of print.
The author describes wine-drinking habits of the ancients, with an emphasis on Greece and Rome. He guesses at what ancient wine must have tasted like, and provides a description of various illustrated amphorae. Other material includes mention of the gods and saints of wine in the Homeric epics, a description of a fifth century B.C. Athenian banquet as contrasted to a vulgar Roman feast, and some details on the Italian, French, and German beginnings of wine after the collapse of the Roman Empire.

425.* Seward, Desmond. **Monks and Wine**. New York: Crown, 1979. 208p. illus. maps. index. $14.95.
The cultivation of the vine has occurred wherever the Church sent its missions, such as to California, and for a variety of reasons, such as use for the sacraments, agricultural work, medical aid, and business interests. Covered in this book is material on the impact of monks on wine, especially in the Dark Ages, wines and spirits (*eiswein,* liqueurs, beers) and so forth. There are maps of wine-producing monasteries in Europe and California.

426.   Simon, André L. **The History of the Wine Trade in England.** London: Holland Press, 1964. 3 vols. bibliog. index. $60.

427.   Simon, André L. **Bottlescrew Days: Wine Drinking in England During the 18th Century.** New York: Finch Press, 1971. 273p. illus. index. $24.

The *History* book is a reprint of the 1906 edition, with a new index. It is a good scholarly work, leaning towards the economic history side. It was originally meant as a text for the trade, and there are chapters on port, sherry, Madeira, brandies, and other products that used the grape. The *Bottlescrew Days* book is a reprint of the 1926 edition. Here, from the days of Queen Anne, he investigates and tells the story of smuggling, excise taxes, customs duties, the shipping of French wines during those troubled times, plus details on port, the wines of Spain, Madeira, Italy, and Germany. A description of wine glasses, wine labels, and bottlescrews follows, along with a concluding chapter on drinking songs and toasts.

428.   Warner, Charles N. **The Winegrowers of France and the Government since 1876.** Westport, Conn.: Greenwood Press, 1975. 303p. bibliog. index. $19.

Originally published by Columbia University Press in 1960, this specialized study in business history details the trials and tribulations of the French in combatting phylloxera with government assistance, the demarcation of the grape growth areas, the involvement in tariffs and trade by the government, and the inside stories concerning the newly emerging "Appellation Contrôlée" laws.

429.*   **Wine and the Artist.** New York: Dover, 1979. 135p. illus. $5.95 paper.

This is a record of 104 of the prints and drawings contained in the Christian Brothers Wine Museum, with a commentary by Joseph Armstrong Baird Jr. It starts with the vine and the harvest, and then moves on to the making and the selling of wine. There are chapters on wine in mythology and religion, as well as a celebration of wine in life and humor. The reproductions are all in black and white.

430.*   Younger, William A. **Gods, Men and Wine.** Cleveland: World Publishing Co., 1966. 516p. illus. bibliog. index. out of print.

This is probably the definitive one-volume history of wine. When Younger died in 1961, the book had been completed but not corrected. John N. Hutchinson contributed an 11-page chapter on wines in America. Most of the history is Greek and Roman; since then viticulture staggered about until the eighteenth century. Younger called on a wide range of source material, and some of this has been incorporated into the eight appendices: wines of Egypt and the ancient Middle East; ancient Greek wines; ancient Roman wines; medieval wines; medieval English vineyards; Renaissance wines; and tables of measures and money for both the medieval and the ancient worlds. In addition, Younger speculates on the beginnings of wine making.

INNS AND PUBS

431.*   Ade, George. **The Old Time Saloon; Not Wet, Not Dry, Just History.** New
        York: Ray Long and Richard Smith, Inc., 1931; reprinted Detroit: Gale,
        1975. 176p. illus. index. $34.
A basic, readable account of the history of the American saloon in the American
West.

432.   Burke, John. **The English Inn.** London: Holmes and Meier, 1981. 240p.
        illus. index. $29.50.
A basic, readable account of the development of the English public house.

433.   Chidsey, Donald Barr. **On and Off the Wagon: A Sober Analysis of the
        Temperance Movement from the Pilgrims through Prohibition.** New York:
        Cowles, 1969. 149p. bibliog. index. $14.95.
This is the story of the corner saloon (bar, tavern, taproom, nightclub) and of
people's attitudes towards private and public drinking. Material covered also
includes the Women's Christian Temperance Union (W.C.T.U.), the Whiskey
Rebellion, and the Anti-Saloon League.

434.   Clark, Pete Allen. **The English Alehouse: A Social History, 1200-1830.**
        London: Longmans, 1983. 384p. index. $25; $13.95 paper.
Another interesting account of the social phenomenon of drinking in England.

435.   Crawford, Mary Caroline. **Little Pilgrimages among Old New England
        Inns; being an account of little journies to various quaint inns and
        hostelries of Colonial New England.** Detroit: Gale, 1970. 381p. illus.
        $34.
This is a reprint of the 1907 edition, one that deals with material about the
hospitality of the wayside inns of New England.

436.   Dallas, Sandra. **No More Than Five in a Bed: Colorado Hotels in the Old
        Days.** Norman, Okla.: Univ. of Oklahoma Press, 1967. 208p. illus. maps.
        index. $13.95.
An account of the hospitality trade in the Western United States, principally
Colorado.

437.   Duns, Perry R. **The Saloon: Public Drinking in Chicago and Boston, 1880-
        1920.** Urbana, Ill.: Univ. of Illinois Press, 1983. 376p. illus. bibliog. index.
        $24.95.
A highly useful account of the history of social drinking in two cities, reflecting
the comparative nature of the contrast between Chicago and Boston.

438.   Earle, Alice Moore. **Stage Coach and Tavern Days.** New York: B. Blom,
        1969; distr. by Ayer Co. 449p. illus. $25.

This reprint of the 1900 edition is important since it was written near the end of the stagecoach days, in a period when travellers still had memories fresh in their minds. Sources and illustrations were also still available.

439.   Endell, Fritz A. G. **Old Tavern Signs; An Excursion into the History of Hospitality.** Detroit: Gale, 1968. 303p. illus. bibliog. index. $34.
This reprint of the 1916 edition is an illustrated history, with many reproductions of actual signs.

440.   Firebaugh, W. C. **The Inns of Greece and Rome.** New York: B. Blom, 1972; distr. by Ayer Co. 271p. illus. $18.
Covering social life and customs of ancient times, this book was originally published in 1928. Firebaugh also wrote *Inns of the Middle Ages* (1924), but it has not yet been reprinted.

441.*   Guillet, Edwin C. **Pioneer Inns and Taverns.** Toronto: Univ. of Toronto Press, 1964. 2 vols. illus. maps. $50 boxed.
First published in five volumes from 1954 through 1962, these books cover the main pioneer routes in Ontario, *Quebec, and New York State.* Detailed references are made to Toronto, Yonge Street to Penetanguishene, and to the New York-Buffalo route via the Hudson River and the Erie Canal. There is a concluding estimate of the position of the innkeeper in community life, plus a large section (the entire original fifth volume) on the origins of tavern names and signs in Great Britain and America.

442.*   Jackson, Michael. **The English Pub.** London: Quarto, 1976. 170p. illus. $20.
Jackson describes the unique social phenomenon of 60,000 public houses in England: their history, food, ales, graphic art, architecture, and activities (sports, contests, singing, dancing). There are lots of historical pictures and illustrations here. Other books that do a similar job include Eric Delderfield's *Inns and Their Signs* (David & Charles, 1976), Brian Spiller's *Victorian Public Houses* (David & Charles, 1972), and Mark Girouard's *Victorian Pubs* (Studio Vista, 1975).

443.   Lathrop, Elise L. **Early American Inns and Taverns.** New York: B. Blom, 1968; distr. by Ayer Co. 365p. illus. bibliog. index. $17.50.
The arrangement here is by colony and state; it was originally published in 1935.

444.   Rice, Kym. **Early American Taverns: For the Entertainment of Friends and Strangers.** Chicago, Ill.: Regnery-Gateway, 1983. 174p. illus. index. $12.95 paper.
Another basic, enjoyable book about the American tavern.

445.   Richards, Timothy M. and James S. Curl. **City of London Pubs: A Practical and Historical Guide.** New York: Drake, 1973. 216p. illus. maps. bibliog. index. $12.95.

This is the brief history of some 1,153 taverns as found in the City of London (seventeenth century). There are descriptions of 162, as of 1971, with a mini-history for each, a photo of the facade, and a walking-tour map arranged in pub-crawl order, beginning with Fleet Street (west) to Bishopsgate (10 areas, 10 tours). Ambience, decor, and service are described for each. But of course some of them are no longer with us, or have been renovated.

446.   Richardson, Sir Albert E. and H. Donaldson Eberlein. **The English Inn, Past and Present.** New York: B. Blom, 1968; distr. by Ayer Co. 307p. illus. maps. index. $22.

447.   Richardson, Sir Albert E. **The Old Inns of England.** New York: B. Blom, 1972; distr. by Ayer Co. 275p. illus. maps. index. $16.
These two books deal with inns in a social context; both have maps of exceptional detail and architectural plans. The 1968 book is a reprint of the 1925 edition, while the 1972 book is a reprint of the 1934 edition.

448.   West, Elliott. **The Saloon on the Rocky Mountain Mining Frontier.** Lincoln, Neb.: Univ. of Nebraska Press, 1979. 197p. illus. bibliog. index. $14.50.
A highly useful book descriptive of drinking in one part of the Western frontier, complementing Dallas' book on Colorado hotels.

449.   White, Arthur. **Palaces of the People: A Social History of Commercial Hospitality.** New York: Taplinger, 1970. 180p. illus. $5.50.
This is a good introductory text, covering the hospitality trade of hotels in general.

COLLECTING AND COLLECTIBLES

450.   Ash, Douglas. **How to Identify English Drinking Glasses and Decanters, 1680-1830.** London: G. Bell, 1962. 200p. illus. index. £ 12.

451.   Ash, Douglas. **How to Identify English Silver Drinking Vessels, 600-1830.** London: G. Bell, 1964. 159p. illus. £ 13.
These two works, part of Bell's "How to Identify" series, deal with descriptions of various vessels that were used for drinking. Both are well illustrated and cata-loged, with tradesmen's marks clearly identified, location of deposit, manner of drinking, and other aspects that help to identify the vessels. The section on decanters is particularly interesting since they are rarely used today, except for spirits. The second book is broader in scope, involving what today are called soup containers. No duplication in coverage.

452.   Davis, Derek C. **English Bottles and Decanters, 1650-1900.** New York: World, 1972. 80p. illus. bibliog. $5.95.
Here is good visual identification, but not everything here qualifies as "drinking" bottles. Some are scent bottles. Davis gives a short history at the beginning of glassmaking. Then come sixty plates with detailed captions and color photographs. The last section is "Collections on View," a listing of European and North Ameri-can sources for viewing glassware.

453.   Dumbrell, Roger. **Understanding Antique Wine Bottles.** Woodbridge,
        England: Antique Collectors' Club; Ithaca, N.Y.: Antique Collectors'
        Club, 1983. 338p. illus. bibliog. index. $29.50.
This work has a more narrow scope than is indicated in its title: it concentrates
on English bottles produced from around 1630 through to 1900, with about 12
pages for European bottles that are commonly found in England and that may
be mistaken for English bottles. The evolution of the elusive English wine bottle
is explored, with individual chapters covering a period of about two decades and
more. There are numerous line drawings and black-and-white photographs of
bottles, as well as an extensive listing of seals. Topics also include dating procedures, shapes of bottles (shaft, globe, onion, mallet, octagonal, cylindrical,
decanter), fakes and forgeries, rarities, how to form a collection, data on prices
and auction-house records, and a chronology of historical developments.

454.   Hartshorne, Albert. **Antique Drinking Glasses: A Pictorial History of
        Glass Drinking Vessels.** New York: Brussel and Brussel, 1968. 490p.
        illus. $50.
First published in 1897 as *Old English Glasses,* this classic and monumental work
contains 67 plates and 366 illustrations to identify vessels. Hartshorne gives a
history and use of drinking vessels and glasses from Roman times to 1800 in Great
Britain.

455.   Heckmann, Manfred. **Corkscrews: An Introduction to Their Appreciation.**
        San Francisco: Wine Appreciation Guild, 1981. 124p. illus. $12.95.
Originally published in German, this new English edition covers all the basics of
corkscrews: history, science, design, and illustrative materials.

456.   Penzer, Norman M. **The Book of the Wine Label.** 2d ed. London: Howe
        and Van Thal, 1974. 144p. illus. bibliog. $45.
With 28 plates, this book deals with the history, collecting, and classification of
wine labels on decanters. Material also includes items about porcelain and enamels.
Designs, lists of names, and identification techniques are covered.

457.   Preston, William A. **Cork and Wine.** St. Helena, Calif.: Illumination Press,
        1983. 64p. illus. $12.
This book was written by the Chief Executive Officer of APM Inc., the principal
supplier of corks and stoppers to the American wine industry. With 29 full-color
illustrations, Preston gives data about corks, both historical (e.g., twenty bottles
of wine corked in 1789 were discovered in a French cave in 1956; the corks were
still perfect) and technical (e.g., a single wine cork has about 800 million fourteen-
sided cells, each capable of acting like a suction cup).

458.   Victoria and Albert Museum. **Bottle Tickets.** London: H.M.S.O., 1958.
        32p. illus. £ 1.
"Bottle ticket" was the first name for wine labels, as they were simply items
attached to bottles to identify them. Twenty-six pages of this catalog are photographs from the permanent collection.

459.   Watney, Bernard M. and Homer D. Babbidge. **Corkscrews for Collectors.**
         London: Philip Wilson, 1981. 176p. illus. index. $35.
This is a comprehensive history of the corkscrew, covering developments in design
and in the mechanical principles. The inventions are here traced from England,
the United States, and Europe.

460.   Whitworth, E. W. **Wine Labels.** London: Cassell, 1966. 63p. illus., part
         color. £ 3.
This work presents the historical development of labels for bottles. The reader is
told where he may view the rarer pieces, and an identification list is given. Most
of these "decanter labels" are silver. Whitworth shows how to date labels, describes
types (e.g., shield, vine and tendril, goblet, etc.) and lists up to twenty makers.
Material also includes mother-of-pearl, Sheffield plate, and enamel. Bin labels,
which are used to identify wines stored in wine cellars, are also discussed (they are
not as elaborate as wine labels).

PERSONAL OBSERVATIONS FROM THE PAST

461.   Allen, H. Warner. **A Contemplation of Wine.** London: Michael Joseph,
         1951. 232p.

462.   Allen, H. Warner. **A History of Wine: Great Vintage Wine from the
         Homeric Age to the Present Day.** New York: Horizon Press, 1962. 304p.
         illus. bibliog. index. $8.95 paper.

463.   Allen, H. Warner. **The Romance of Wine.** New York: Dover, 1971. 264p.
         illus. $3.50 paper.

464.   Allen, H. Warner. **Through the Wine Glass.** London: Michael Joseph,
         1954; distr. by Transatlantic Arts. 244p.
These books by Allen contain a potpourri of his thoughts and ramblings concerning
wine appreciation and its history. Allen describes in his *A History of Wine* the
rediscovery of the Greek airtight amphorae used to preserve the wine against
spoilage (the long series of experiments culminated with vintage port in the later
half of the eighteenth century). Eventually the glass bottle replaced the earthenware jar. His scholarly but easy-to-read book covers mainly up through 1900, with
a few concluding pages to 1960. Throughout, there are 228 illustrations. The series
of short chapters in the other books contain diverse themes such as minihistories
of cocktails, Roman wines, corkscrews, and other accoutrements of alcoholic
beverages. He also presents sketches of noted chefs such as Billat-Savarin, and food
writers and other wine writers such as George Saintsbury and André Simon. There
are tales of wine drinking, wine appraisals, and wine tastings.

465.   Arlott, John, ed. **Wine.** New York: Oxford Univ. Press, 1984. 112p. illus.
         index. $9.95.
This brief, literary compilation ranges from short one-liners to several pages from
one source. Material has been taken from letters, poems, general thoughts, essays,

fiction, and so on. The excerpts are mainly from European sources, and most are in the form of poetry. Good enough, though, for a bedtime read. Typical quotations are from Colette, Virgil, Keats, Omar Khayyám, Ben Johnson, Rabelais, Tennyson, Chaucer, and Shakespeare, with contributions by the "experts," André Simon, Cyril Ray, Raymond Postgate, Patrick Forbes, and others.

466.* Bespaloff, Alexis, ed. **The Fireside Book of Wine.** New York: Simon and Schuster, 1977. 445p. illus. $12.95.

This is a collection of writings about wine, celebrating the glories and the pleasures of drinking and eating. Stories are by Joyce, Franklin, Hemingway, Byron, Buchwald. Strange company, but all united by the sauce.

467. Dali, Salvador. **Dali: The Wines of Gala.** New York: Abrams, 1978. 269p. illus. $50.

This is a paean of praise to wine, and is a companion volume to his *Diners de Gala,* which concerned food. The plates are in color, of course, and in that surrealistic style so closely associated with Dali. The text was translated from the French by Olivier Bernier.

468. Holland, Vyvyan Beresford. **Drink and Be Merry.** London: Victor Gollancz, 1967. 173p. maps. tables. £5.

The author, once a vice president of the Circle of Wine Writers, has collected a number of personal recollections that form a knowledgeable book. The bits and pieces of information are gathered in colloquial and anecdotal style. The commonsense wit, though, does tend to go off on a tangent from time to time, dealing with such topics as sardines, Chinese wine, vintage olive oil, vinegar, and mineral waters.

469.* Hunt, Peter, comp. **Eating and Drinking: An Anthology for Epicures.** London: Ebury Press, 1961. 320p. illus. out of print.

This is one of the nicest compiled sourcebooks for literary material about "eating and drinking." The literature of different periods and countries and languages is presented through poetry, prose, observations, and drawings—all on the theme of bon vivants! As a bedside book it is a classic. Topics include memorable meals, banquets, romantic meals, proper behavior, drinking, and all the opposites: desert island deprivation, appalling meals, overindulgence and gluttony, and strange food. Throughout there are cartoons and sketches by such as James Thurber and Ronald Searle, *Punch* artists of the past, and color reproductions of paintings associated with wine and food. A good collection notable for its wine appreciation material.

470. Marcus, Irving H. **Lines about Wines.** Berkeley, Calif.: Wine Publications, 1971. 214p. illus. $5.95 paper.

This is a collection of almost a hundred editorial pieces written for *Wines and Vines* when Marcus was its editor. Material ranges from cellar practices to public attitudes toward wines. These informative, chatty columns were written from 1956 to 1970, primarily for California wine makers.

471.   Mendelsohn, Oscar A. **Drinking with Pepys.** New York: St. Martin's, 1963. 125p. illus. $3.95 paper.

Here Mendelsohn has collated all of Pepys' allusions to alcohol, to possets and syllabubs, cellerage and cooperage. Through Pepys, then, he covers taverns, taphouses, the cellars of the Restoration in London, and some vineyards of Europe and of historical antiquity.

472.   Mew, James and John Ashton. **Drinks of the World.** Ann Arbor, Mich.: Gryphon Books, 1971. 366p. illus. $25.

This reprint of the 1892 London edition was intended for the general but informed reader. In coverage, the last hundred pages deal with nonalcoholic drinks such as tea, coffee, and chocolate. The history itself begins with antiquity: the Egyptian method of making wine, beer vessels, and goblets; the Greek spiced wines, resin, amphorae; Scandinavian meads and ales; wine growing abroad in Africa, Australia, and the United States. Large sections are devoted to ciders, brandies, gins, whiskies, rums, and liqueurs, along with many older recipes. The last chapters, on beer, are international, with coverage extending to China and Borneo. There are many mini-histories for each type of drink; there is a wealth of source materials here.

473.*   Morny, Claude, ed. **A Wine and Food Bedside Book.** Newton Abbot, England: David & Charles, 1973. 334p. illus. £ 10.

These are seventy short essays from the *Wine and Food* magazine that existed in the 1930s and 1940s. It is recommended as bedtime reading, as Harry Yoxall suggests in his foreword, with the book propped on a "happily but lightly filled stomach." Morny has selected E. M. Forster on sausages, Hilaire Belloc on wine, Osbert Sitwell on stage food, and Cyril Connolly on old restaurants; there are also several selections by André Simon, the founder of the magazine.

474.   Pellegrini, Angelo M. **Lean Years, Happy Years.** Seattle: Madrona Publications, 1983. 180p. illus. $12.95.

Pellegrini was a Professor of English at the University of Washington. This autobiographical series of commentaries is largely in three parts. First, he writes about establishing a kitchen garden of vegetables and fruit (and how he tends them). Secondly, he writes about how he cooks in his kitchen. And thirdly, he discusses how he makes and drinks his own wines. The author espouses the "conservor society" and with good reason, justifying his existence by delving into the simple life of wine, cheese, bread, fruits, and vegetables.

475.*   Saintsbury, George. **Notes on a Cellar Book.** New York: Mayflower Books, 1978. 231p. illus. $12.50.

Originally published in 1920 by an authority on the art of good living, this reprint (with an introduction by Harry Yoxall) is a classic series of reminiscences based on the premise that wine is what "God sends to make men glad." Literary allusions abound in this book, which covers wine, beer, spirits, and cider. Bottles and glasses are discussed, as well as methods of starting a cellar and creating classic menus. Saintsbury's erudite style led the way for today's modern wine appraisal.

476.　　Simon, André L. **The Art of Good Living.** 2d ed. London: Michael Joseph, 1951. 197p. illus. out of print.

477.　　Simon, André L. **In the Twilight.** London: Michael Joseph, 1969. 182p. £ 7.

André Simon died in 1970 after ninety-three years of living a full life. Over the course of that time he wrote a number of histories of the wine trade and of specific wines, a number of synoptic surveys dealing with wines of various countries, many books and articles on food, many reference books on wines and food (usually dictionaries), and even two bibliographies. Most of these will be found annotated elsewhere. These two books contain "observations" and general comments. His philosophy is expounded in *The Art of Good Living* (original c. 1929): "Thought and care in the matter of eating and drinking offer far greater rewards than mere satisfaction of appetite." He would wish to eliminate the snobs and the restaurants' attitudes to them. How to live well is always good advice. *In the Twilight* serves as his epitaph: it describes his life in wine, reflections, and second thoughts on what he had said over the past seventy years of his life.

478.　　Waugh, Alec. **In Praise of Wine and Certain Noble Spirits.** New York: Morrow, 1959. 304p. $3.95 paper.

A very readable autobiography by a well-travelled novelist; it is essentially a paean to wine. He begins with his own discovery of wine, then provides a history of wine making and a discussion of individual wines found on his travels, e.g., of a $1.30 New York State Port, he writes at p. 101: "The first sip was one of the biggest shocks my palate has sustained ... it bore no resemblance to anything." He concludes with a serious discussion of fallacies about wine. Tasting notes, food notes, and menus are scattered throughout.

7 *Food with Wines, Beers, and Spirits*

Wine and some spirits demand food, for they are the ultimate digestive beverages. At the same time, there are many cooking methods that utilize the distinct flavor enhancement of wines, beers, and spirits. Out of literally thousands of cookbooks, here is a highly selective list of those that concentrate on good food *with* alcoholic beverage flavor, and an alcoholic beverage flavor *in* good food. There are also comments on wine and food pairings and matchups in chapter 2, particularly on regional foods and wines. Chapters 3 and 4 have additional material on food with beer and spirits (the latter contains cocktail recipe books and, occasionally, books with recipes or suggestions for parties and canapés). Consumer evaluations in chapter 5 pair off wines with appropriate foods, particularly foods that will show off a wine to its best potential. And of course magazines in chapter 9 print recipes and alcoholic beverage recommendations. Thus, in many cases, materials in other sections also contain recipes, just as cookbooks often devote a chapter to wines or spirits.

479.   Allison, Sonia. **Spirited Cooking, with Liqueurs, Spirits and Wines.** North Pomfret, Vt.: David & Charles, 1982. 128p. illus. index. $18.95.
Although written for the British market, as are so many of those cookbooks that use alcoholic beverages, Allison's book is still highly relevant for North America. Obviously there is a de-emphasis on Bourbon and types of wines native to the United States, but this is more than compensated for by the other drinks and spirits. One just simply has to substitute. Many of these recipes were developed for *Decanter* magazine, especially for her column.

480.*   American Heritage. **The American Heritage Cookbook and Illustrated History of American Eating and Drinking.** New York: American Heritage, 1964. 640p. illus., part color. index. $25.
Part 1, the historical section, is in narrative form and includes anecdotes and superb, lavish illustrations. Each chapter has been written by a different person, and each presents character sketches of leading historical characters and places such as Mark Twain, Diamond Jim Brady, Delmonico's, and so forth. Progression is from the Indians, through the Colonial period to the Old South, cosmopolitan (i.e., European and Asian) tastes, and chapters on eating out and at home. Part 2

is the recipe section, which gives five hundred historical and unusual tested recipes, and thirty re-created menus from the past. Unlike European cookery, American cookery seems to concentrate on the culinary uses of beer and bourbon. For a history of European eating and drinking, see the companion volume below, by William Hale.

481.*   Ballard, Patricia. **Wine in Everyday Cooking: Cooking with Wine for Family and Friends.** ed. by Pamela Kittler. San Francisco, Calif.: Wine Appreciation Guild, 1982. 122p. illus. index. $5.95 paper.

The Wine Appreciation Guild was formerly the California Wine Advisory Board; under the earlier name it had sold over one million copies of all its cookbooks. Ballard's book is the Guild's eighth book, and here the stress is on *en famille* dining with a French and Italian orientation. The publisher, of course, would prefer that you use California wines, but any comparable kind can be used. Ballard has apparently collected and tested the recipes on her own, since they come from the many wineries in California, and they include such goodies as cold cantaloupe soup, baked sherry chicken, gumbo, and sweet-and-sour cabbage. The book contains about 135 easy recipes, and more such books can be found under the entry for the collective name of the Wine Appreciation Guild.

482.   Barbour, Beverly. **Cooking with Spirits.** San Francisco, Calif.: 101 Productions, 1976. 168p. illus. index. $7.95 paper.

These recipes were developed from her *Vintage* magazine column. Most of them appear to be mainly the use of spirits as flavor enhancers in cooking; this can be very inexpensive if you settle for the cheaper or comparable brands to the big names. Otherwise, an ounce here and an ounce there do add up when drawn out of a $30 bottle! The arrangement is by type of cordial, liqueur or liquor, and the cuisine is international in scope. One interesting example, chosen at random from the 165 recipes, is Chartreuse bread.

483.   Bennett, Bev and Kim Upton. **The Joy of Cocktails and Hors d'oeuvre.** Woodbury, N.Y.: Barron's, 1984. 218p. illus. index. $13.95.

This informative book opens with about 60 pages of "classic" cocktails, such as mulled cider, the Bloody Mary, the mimosa with Champagne and orange juice, and the martini. Some nonalcoholic drinks are also included. But the bulk of the book concerns appetizers, especially for cocktail parties. Chapters cover topics such as foods wrapped in dough, no-cook dishes, deep-fried canapés, quick and easy preparations, stove-top foods, and some desserts (for those sweet events). There are about 75 cocktail recipes and 125 food preparations. There are foods that one would like to serve as a spectacular offering, such as steamed broccoli with gorgonzola mayonnaise or chocolate truffles with hazelnut liqueur. Bennett and Upton conclude their book with a discussion of glass shapes and sizes.

484.*   **Beverages.** Alexandria, Va.: Time-Life Books, 1982. 176p. illus. bibliog. index. $14.95.

This is one of The Good Cook Series, a subscription book program from Time-Life also available separately through bookstores. Richard Olney is the series consultant. The basic idea is to take a type of food—salads, fish, cookies, beverages (in this case)—and present encyclopedic, summary-type background data about it, with a selection of good recipes from a wide-ranging collection of existing cook-books. And, of course, the editors provide appropriate illustrations of the techniques—in color. The *Beverages* book deals mainly with nonalcoholic drinks such as coffees and teas, but it also has a large section on spirits and making cordials at home. It can be extremely useful. A companion volume in this series covers wine (see entry 514).

485.   Beveridge, N. E. **Cups of Valor.** Harrisburg, Pa.: Stackpole Books, 1968. 106p. illus. index. $7.95.

This slender book concerns the procurement of drinking alcohol by America's armed forces since the Revolution. It is colloquial in style, describing the liquor lore of the Army and Navy. Anecdotes relate alcohol's use in easing the pain of battles and fatigue, and regimental celebrations. Interesting concoctions were made as the result of a lack of proper ingredients (such as the chicken marengo of Napoleon's chef). There are thirty-three contributed recipes from the eras of the Revolution, the Civil War, the Indian wars, the Spanish-American War, and the two World Wars.

486.   Chirich, Nancy, ed. **Life with Wine: A Self-Portrait of the Wine Business in the Napa and Sonoma Valleys.** Oakland, Calif.: Edit Productions/Straw-berry Hill Press, 1984. 192p. illus. index. $7.95 paper.

Chirich interviewed people associated with about a dozen wineries (out of the eighty-three wineries located in the Napa and Sonoma Valleys). These interviews—not given sources—are scattered about various topics such as vineyards, wine making, computers and wine, cycles of productions, government regulations, merchandising, and wine and food writing. About a hundred recipes are also pre-sented, using wines in the process of cooking: ginger squash soup, marinated sweet-breads salad, walnut tarts.

487.   Church, Ruth Ellen. **Entertaining with Wine.** Chicago, Ill.: Rand McNally, 1976. 174p. illus. index. $16.95.

After brief synopses on the various types of wines in the world, Church goes on to deal with both formal and informal entertaining. She matches foods with wines as she covers all courses (there are about 175 recipes here). Christmas dinner is a highlight of the book.

488.*   **Cooking with Wine.** Menlo Park, Calif.: Sunset Books, 1972. 80p. illus. index. $3.95 paper.

This book is very similar in format and presentation to the Wine Appreciation Guild's series of cookbooks. But of course it is part of the large number of cookery items from *Sunset* magazine, and resembles that larger oeuvre (illustrations, double-column type, line drawings, hints, and sidebars). The introductory material here includes advice on the use of wine in cooking (including a detailed wine cookery chart with suggested quantities of wine to use per serving, idea for the cook who wishes to improvise) and aids in recipe reading, with names of the wines. The two hundred recipes, which cover all courses, are geared to California wines. Preparations also include information on making wine vinegar, deglazing, and marinating, as well as special dishes using buffalo or octopus meats. The book concludes with a dozen or so recipes for wine drinks.

489.　　Cordon Bleu Cookery School. **Wine.** London: Macdonald, 1974. 144p. illus. index. £ 3.25.

This is the text from the series for the Cordon Bleu Cookery course in London. It is standard in format with the other books (double-column type, color illustrations, etc.). A historical approach is taken for each country, with material on how wines are made, the shapes of the bottles, how to match foods and wines, and so forth. About two dozen recipes in the cookery section stress the elegant: salmon trout vin rosé, pork chops ardennaise, fillets of sole Dorothea.

490.　　Cullen, Mary Anne and Frank Cullen. **The 80 Proof Cookbook: An Introduction to Cooking with High Spirits.** New York: St. Martin's, 1982. 125p. illus. index. $6.95 paper.

This basic book is arranged by spirit—scotch, gin, bourbon, vodka, brandy, Irish whiskey, rum and tequila—with about ten recipes apiece. Some of the preparations do sound interesting, such as the acorn squash in "heather dew" or scotch; others are standard fare with a little liquor to jazz them up, such as "foolish raspberries" (instead of "raspberry fool"). There are about eighty recipes here.

491.　　Ensrud, Barbara. **The Art of Wine with Food.** New York: Congdon & Weed, 1984; distr. by St. Martin's. 224p. illus. index. $16.95.

Ensrud has been a nationally syndicated wine columnist. Here she writes about something that has not been too well covered before: the good marriage of food with wine. Her notes are presented in a confiding manner; her chapters consist mainly of menus of food, along with her recommendations for accompanying wines. Of value are the notes that describe precisely why certain wines would be better choices than others. She presents the outlines of a "classic" dinner, with five suggested menus, and then goes on to present menus for each of the seasons, about twenty-five menus in all. Throughout she distributes tips and advice on buying, storing, serving, and tasting wines, as well as some notes on what to serve for the larger gatherings and for desserts. At the back there are charts: one is dedicated to wine styles (arranged by name of the wine) with the comparable food, another is dedicated to food styles (arranged by name of the dish) with the comparable wine.

492.*　　Fahy, Carole. **Cooking with Beer.** New York: Drake, 1973. 144p. illus., color. index. $6.95 paper.

Originally published in England, this book stresses the three main beers: lager, ale, and stout. Only lager is generally available in the United States, so a few of the recipes may be difficult to execute. The three hundred recipes cover all courses, including dessert (with a very good date-nut bread). The barbecue section is also recommended. There is historical information, and there are quite a few recipes requiring the mere (optional) addition of beer for a "special" flavor.

493.   Greenberg, Emanuel and Madeline Greenberg. **Whiskey in the Kitchen.**
         Indianapolis: Bobbs-Merrill, 1968. 315p. illus. index. $12.50.
Believing that liquor is an extension of the herb shelf and can thus be used to
enhance the flavor of almost everything, the authors present four hundred basic
recipes covering every course. Additional material includes chapters describing
each liquor type, what spirits enhance the natural flavors of what foods, tips to
brighten up a dinner party, the mating of food and spirits, and a history of liquor
use since the beginnings of the United States.

494.*   Hale, William Harlan. **The Horizon Cookbook and Illustrated History
         of Eating and Drinking through the Ages.** New York: American Heritage,
         1968. 768p. illus., part color. index. $26.50.
Part 1 is the historical section, in narrative form, complete with anecdotes and
superb, lavish, illustrations. Part 2, the recipe section, includes six hundred historical and unusual tested recipes, plus nineteen re-created menus from the past. In
all, there are 570 illustrations, 110 in color. Most of the recipes are European in
origin, and many use alcohol in their preparation. For a history of American eating
and drinking, see the companion volume listed above (entry 480).

495.   Hallgarten, Elaine. **Cooking with Wines and Spirits ... and Beer and Cider
         Too.** London: Hodder and Stoughton, 1981. unpaged. illus. £ 6.95.
A general, all-purpose cookbook for alcoholic beverages. It includes such topics
as how to store leftover spirits and wines (which will keep well if chilled), recipes
for sauces, cocktails and punches, and traditional recipes for carbonnade,
scaloppini al Marsala, and the unusual, such as the jellied Bloody Mary. Published
in association with the Good Food Club.

496.   Hatch, Edward White. **The American Wine Cookbook.** New York: Dover,
         1971. 314p. index. $2.50 paper.
This is a reprint of the 1941 classic. At the time of publication, it was pretty daring
because it stressed American wines only—and this was shortly after Repeal when
the industry was just getting back on its feet. The seven hundred detailed recipes
cover all courses.

497.   Hébert, Malcolm R. **California Brandy Cuisine: Celebrating Two Hundred
         Years of California Brandy.** San Francisco, Calif.: Wine Appreciation
         Guild, 1983. 128p. illus. index. $6.95 paper.
This little book covers the history of California brandy (anecdotes and illustrations
included) as well as presenting about 120 recipes for using brandy in cooking:
flambéed desserts, brandied soups and sauces, and others from the full range of
soup to nuts. Menu suggestions are given as well as using brandy as a flavor
enhancer. Some of the better sections deal with appetizers and drinks (cocktails,
flips, and punches).

498.   Hébert, Malcolm R. **The Champagne Cookbook: Add Some Sparkle to
         Your Cooking and Your Life.** San Francisco, Calif.: Wine Appreciation
         Guild, 1980. 124p. illus. index. $5.95 paper.

Hébert uses California, French, and European sparklers here. The recipes are derived from food consultants and from magazines; all courses are covered Strewn about the two hundred recipes, there are tips and advice on how to serve Champagne and cooking with Champagne. This is a very specialized area, as it is expensive to boil off all that bubbly!

499.   Lewin, Esther. **Stewed to the Gills: Fish and Wine Cookery**. Los Angeles: Nash Publishing, 1971. 165p. illus. $7.95.
These easy and international recipes (about 225 of them) deal with all types of courses and make use of liquor and beer as well as wine. Arrangement is by type of fish. There are nineteen recipes for abstainers (including one using "near beer"). Humor is a little on the flip side.

500.   MacDonald, Barbara. **Wine in Cooking and Dining**. New York: Culinary Arts Institute, 1976. 96p. illus. index. $3.95 paper.
Part of the Culinary Arts series of thematic cookbooks centered around types of courses and foods. The recipes are useful, albeit plain and simple.

501.   McDouall, Robin. **Cooking with Wine**. London: Penguin Books, 1970. 144p. illus. index. $2.95 paper.
Both British and American measurements are used in the 250 recipes. Beer, cider, and spirits are also included, as well as some preparations for drinks. Emphasis is on French cuisine, with a good section on poultry and savories. One of the best of the wine cookbooks.

502.   McDouall, Robin and Sheila Bush. **Recipes from a Chateau in Champagne**. London: Victor Gollancz, 1982; distr. by David & Charles. 160p. illus. index. $24.95.
This is an exercise in elegant food, directed to those home chefs that try to excel in anything they do. By taking a strictly limited application (the food service offered by Moët et Chandron Champagne company in France) and exploring it in depth, the authors have come up with a specialty book that should appeal to those who are always demanding something new or different. The preparations are taken from the Château de Saran, the Trianon Restaurant, and the Royal Champagne Hotel—all in or around Epernay in France. There may be a slight problem in obtaining some of the products in North America, such as the "marc de Champagne," but substitutes are, of course, permissible. Champagne is the main wine to be featured in the preparations, as well as to be consumed as a beverage. Of the more than half dozen veal dishes, for example, only one concerns "meat": the rest are all "organs." The book has over one hundred enticing recipes, as well as material about Moët and Chandron.

503.   **Mr. Boston Cordial Cooking Guide**. New York: Warner Books, 1982. 138p. illus., color. index. $13.50.

504.   **Mr. Boston Spirited Dessert Guide**. New York: Warner Books, 1982. 120p. illus., color. index. $13.50.

Both of these fine books use liqueurs as flavor enhancers, and indeed the recipes have been designed to augment the flavors in food. Substitutes can be used, of course, since all the named products here are from the Mr. Boston stable. The first book covers entire courses, from soup to nuts (but not too many desserts here, since that comes later). There are 178 easy recipes. The second book covers desserts only, with a section on creating your own desserts by mixing and matching liqueurs and flavors. This is for your choice of spirits. This book has about 120 easy recipes.

505.* **The New Larousse Gastronomique: The Encyclopedia of Food, Wine, and Cookery.** New York: Crown, 1977. 1064p. illus. index. $25.

The first English translation of Prosper Montagne's 1938 French original was in 1961. In that edition there was a wine chart and much material on liqueurs; both have been excised from the new 1977 edition. This is regrettable. Still, the overall work is a masterpiece, with 8,500 recipes (sole has 122 all by itself, most calling for white wine). It is arranged in dictionary format, with entries for wine found by types, country, and grape. Wine diseases are discussed and diagnosed, with data on how to correct the diseases. The American edition is written with Charlotte Turgeon.

506. Petel, Pierre. **The Little Wine Steward.** Toronto, Canada: Personal Library, 1981. 155p. illus. $4.95 paper.

This is an international guide to food and wine, with many suggestions for harmonizing specific dishes with various wines. It is arranged by name of food dish (as found in a restaurant), with wine suggestions as per labels. These suggestions are further subarranged in different price categories, so that users can tell at a glance what is worth drinking with any particular dish at differing price levels. Many wine labels are illustrated (black and white only).

507.* Ray, Cyril and Elizabeth Ray. **Wine with Food.** London: Sidgwick and Jackson, 1975. 159p. index. £4.

Ray is a superb wine writer; Elizabeth Ray was the food writer for the *Observer* at the time. This book is a good sharing of experiences. Ray comments on manners and style associated with wines, and is devoted to discussions directly about and pertinent to "wine and food," stressing the matching of the wine and food in different combinations. Liz (as she is known) gives about one hundred international recipes (not all using wine, but certainly all having wine as an accompaniment to be drunk). These recipes are suggested to go along with Ray's choices, as well as her own observations from the food side. Topics include the whole range: red wines, white wines, rosé wines, sparklers, "bad companions," "befores and afters and in-betweeners," spirits, punches, toddies, and so forth.

508.* Salmon, Alice Wooledge and Hugo Dunn-Meynell. **The Wine and Food Society Menu Book: Recipes for Celebration.** New York: Van Nostrand Reinhold, 1984. 234p. illus. index. $25.

The International Wine and Food Society was founded in 1934 by André Simon in London; this book is one of the projects held to celebrate its fiftieth anniversary in 1984. Requests were made of the over seven thousand members to submit treasured "gourmet" recipes, and the team of Salmon and Dunn-Meynell would create menus and wine recommendations. Salmon is an established British food writer; husband Dunn-Meynell is a former Chairman of the I. W. & F. S. and a British wine writer. They have fashioned some six luncheons, nine dinners, a breakfast, a picnic, and other occasions. The wines are especially appropriate, and go well with the food. The meals are of course glamorous, but not too difficult, and the level of creativity and expressiveness even extends down to such mundane items as condiments such as plum chutney (a difficult recipe to locate elsewhere). Good, solid wine-drinking notes here, complementing the over two hundred recipes.

509.   Simon, André L. and Robin Howe. **Dictionary of Gastronomy.** rev. and enl. New York: McGraw-Hill, 1970. 400p. illus., part color. bibliog. $19.95.
The first edition was published in 1949. This one has 2,000 definitions, 600 line drawings, and 64 full-color illustrations. Most definitions include some historical references. There are complete discussions of wines and cheeses, as well as fruits, vegetables, meats, fish, and fowl.

510.   Stover, Annette A. **Cooking with Beer.** New York: Culinary Arts Institute, 1980. 96p. illus. index. $3.95 paper.
Like the MacDonald book (entry 500), this book is one of a series—here entitled "Adventures in Cookery"—that deals with type of food and type of courses. This is an effective book of standard recipes.

511.*   Taeuber, Dick. **Grand Finales.** Woodbury, N.Y.: Barron's, 1982. 234p. illus. index. $16.95.
This book deals with desserts and sweets flavored with liqueurs, rums, and brandies. In the food preparations section are covered such delights as mousses, meringues, pies, cakes, Bavarians and Charlottes, ice cream crêpes, fruit, and fondues. The color photographs here are excellent, and there is good detail on the techniques of dessert creation. The sections on drinks continue the "showing off" principles, with materials on garnishes, decorating, and flambéeing. There is a comprehensive chapter on "pousse-café," with the various types that can be made, with full and complete instructions—so long as hour hand is not shaky—that also include a density table of specified, *branded* liqueurs. This is useful because of course the densities of similar products will vary from brand to brand.

512.*   Taylor, Greyton H. **Treasury of Wine and Wine Cookery.** New York: Harper & Row, 1963. 278p. illus. index. $9.95 paper.
The author is from the Taylor Wine Company and of Bully Hill fame. Here are 400 recipes plus 150 drink concoctions, along with tips on the service of wine, stemware, and food ideas. There is a superb special section on barbecue cooking, marinades, and canapés. All recipes were tested at the Taylor Wine Company kitchen. The book is also a work of art, with champagne tinted paper, sepia ink, and border decorations.

513.   White, Marjorie. **Cordial Cookery**. Maplewood, N.J.: Hammond Inc.,
        1982. 160p. illus. index. $8.95 paper.
A useful little book detailing how to make cordials at home, and furnishing a
sufficient number of recipes to cook with a variety of them. Most cordials are
flavor enhancers.

514.*   **Wine**. Alexandria, Va.: Time-Life Books, 1983. 176p. illus. bibliog. index.
        $14.95.
This is one of the Good Cook series, a subscription book program from Time-Life
also available separately through bookstores. Richard Olney is the series consultant;
the special consultants for *Wine* were Frank Prial and Gerald Asher. The basic idea
is to take a type of food—salads, lamb, pastries, wine (in this case)—and present
encyclopedic, summary-type background data about it, with a selection of good
recipes from a wide-ranging collection of existing international cookbooks
originally written in many different languages. And, of course, the editors provide
appropriate illustrations of the techniques in color. The *Wine* book deals with
selecting, serving, matching food with wines, cooking, guidance for label reading,
and a bibliography. All of this is clearly illustrated, along with an excellent wine
dictionary. Half the book has recipes for cooking with wine, chosen from dozens
of international cookbooks. A companion volume covers beverages, see entry 484.

515.*   Wine Appreciation Guild. **Adventures in Wine Cookery by California
        Winemakers**. San Francisco, Calif.: 1980. 128p. illus., color. index. $5.95
        paper.

516.*   Wine Appreciation Guild. **California Winelovers' Cookbook**. San Francisco,
        Calif.: 1983. 174p. illus., color. index. $5.95 paper.

517.*   Wine Appreciation Guild. **Dinner Menus with Wine**. San Francisco, Calif.:
        1983. 126p. illus., color. index. $6.95 paper.

518.*   Wine Appreciation Guild. **Easy Recipes of California Winemakers**. San
        Francisco, Calif.: 1970. 128p. illus., color. index. $5.95 spiralbound.

519.*   Wine Appreciation Guild. **Epicurean Recipes of California Winemakers**.
        San Francisco, Calif.: 1978. 128p. illus., color. index. $5.95 paper.

520.*   Wine Appreciation Guild. **Favorite Recipes of California Winemakers**.
        San Francisco, Calif.: 1978. 128p. illus., color. index. $5.95 paper.

521.*   Wine Appreciation Guild. **Gourmet Wine Cooking the Easy Way**. 3d ed.
        San Francisco, Calif.: 1980. 128p. illus., color. index. $5.95 paper.
These books have all been published by the Wine Appreciation Guild, once known
as the California Wine Advisory Board. Over two million of these books have
been sold over the years as the Board attempted to promote California wines.
Of course, one can easily substitute other known wines for the branded bottle.
Still, all of these books give good value for the dollar. *Adventures in Wine Cookery*

has five hundred recipes and was collected from winemakers, from the University of California at Davis, and from Fresno State College. The recipes range from punches to jellies, jams, and desserts. Over 300,000 copies of this book were sold. The *California Winelovers' Cookbook* is the Guild's ninth book. Five hundred recipes were submitted to the 1981 Wine Institute Food and Wine Competition; those reproduced here were the better ones—about one hundred of these, one per page. Brian St. Pierre gives a California wine cooking chart, a general commentary and some history. The full range of meals is here, such as pumpkin ball stew and a California wine soup. Rather than note specific brands, this book merely indicates the general type of wine to be used in the recipe, such as "California white wine" or "California red wine." There are no recommendations on what to serve with the meal. The *Dinner Menus with Wine* book emphasizes menu preparation and the complementary wine to be served. Here are one hundred menus and five hundred recipes, with some contributions from Emily Chase. The *Easy Recipes of California Winemakers* has its recipes signed by the contributor. There are around five hundred recipes here, and everything is easy and straightforward. *Epicurean Recipes of California Winemakers* has more complicated recipes; it also contains a master, comprehensive index to the whole series (as far up as 1978). *Favorite Recipes of California Winemakers* also contains many prize-winning contributions; it has sold over 400,000 copies. *Gourmet Wine Cooking the Easy Way* also has five hundred recipes; it contains tested recipes from producers of convenience foods (e.g., powdered, frozen, freeze-dried, canned, etc.) to which wine was added. Brand names are given at the back. A worthy attempt to put more flavor back into food, although the changes in the convenience food industry necessitates a new edition or updating every now and then—to add new foods and to drop references to packages that no longer exist.

522.   Wood, Morrison. **More Recipes with a Jug of Wine.** New York: Farrar, Straus & Giroux, 1956. 400p. index. $8.95 paper.

523.   Wood, Morrison. **Through Europe with a Jug of Wine.** New York: Farrar, Straus & Giroux, 1964. 302p. index. $7.95 paper.

524.   Wood, Morrison. **With a Jug of Wine.** New York: Farrar, Straus & Giroux, 1977. 379p. index. $8.95 paper.

These three books detail Wood's wanderings through Europe, the people he met, the sights he saw, the food he ate, and the wine he drank. He had a syndicated weekly column, "For Men Only," which dealt with cooking and wines, and most of these books are from that series, which ran from 1946 to 1962.

The Technology and Business of Wines, Beers, and Spirits

TECHNICAL LITERATURE

For a proper understanding of wines, beers, and spirits, it is necessary to know something of the various components that go into the production of alcoholic beverages. Below is a select list of technical texts that detail information about viticulture, harvesting, production of alcohol (fermentation and distillation), diseases, and spoilage, with general notes on composition and nutrients. Chapter 10 on home wine making and home brewing contains additional material more useful to the home amateur or small producer, while magazines are discussed in chapter 9 and professional associations in chapter 11. Hugh Johnson in his 1984 *Pocket Encyclopedia of Wine* said, "Attempts to express the characters of wines used to get little further than terms as vague as 'fruity' and 'full-bodied.' Your modern wine-lover is made of sterner stuff. He is satisfied with nothing less than the jargon of laboratory analysis—which means talking about sugars (and the various types), must-weight, residual sugar, alcohol content, fixed acidity, volatile acidity, pH, sulphur dioxide, and a whole battery of wine diseases and their solutions."

525.   Amerine, M. A., ed. **Wine Production Technology in the United States.** Washington, D.C.:   American Chemical Society, 1981. 229p. index. $31.95; $17.95 paper.
This is part of the A.C.S. Symposium series, number 145. It deals with the state of the art of wine production in the United States, as reported at the Las Vegas 1980 conference. As such, it serves as a masterful updating of the wine books that follow in this section.

526.   Amerine, Maynard A. and H. W. Berg. **The Technology of Wine Making.** 4th ed. Westport, Conn.: Avi Publishing Co., 1980. 802p. illus. bibliog. index. $42.50.
First published in 1969, this is now a standard treatise on commercial wine making. The authors cover methods (composition and quality) used in all of the important wine regions of the world, with a special section on sherry processes: Bodega (Spanish), baking (California), and the rapid Tressler (New York and Ontario). New information here includes sections on wine yeasts (using the 1970 Lodder classification), winery design, equipment and operation, and the processing of

vermouth and other flavored wines using herbs and spices, with a subsection on the California "pop" wines. Three chapters are concerned with spoilage, prevention, and waste disposal.

527.   Amerine, Maynard A. and M. A. Joslyn. **Table Wines: The Technology of Their Production.** 2d ed. Berkeley, Calif.: Univ. of California Press, 1970. 997p. illus. bibliog. index. $35.

This standard reference work is now two-and-a-half times the size of its original 1951 edition. The massive changes in the past two decades through scientific discoveries in microbiology and biochemistry alone have shifted wine making from an art to a science. World wine areas and wine types are described here in detail, along with technical standards, automation, and instrumentation. There is a step-by-step guide to all aspects of wine making—winery construction, marketing, sanitation, grape juice, fermentation processes, preservations, aging, filtration, and finishing. Other chapters cover the technical processes for red, rosé, white, sweet, and sparkling wines. Special sections deal with commercial wine disorders (for personal solutions, see the *New Larousse Gastronomique* for its section on wine illnesses), summaries of research in wine tasting and evaluation, a 15-page selective bibliography, and 117 pages of literature citations.

528.   Amerine, Maynard A. and C. S. Ough. **Methods for Analysis of Musts and Wines.** New York: Wiley-Interscience, 1980. 341p. illus. charts. bibliog. index. $48.50.

This book provides analytical data required by the wineries in operating and conforming to state and federal regulations. There are many sections dealing with the hows and whys of chemical analysis, with an indication of the various methods used.

529.*   Amerine, Maynard A. and Vernon L. Singleton. **Wine: An Introduction for Americans.** rev. ed. Berkeley, Calif.: Univ. of California Press, 1978. 532p. illus. bibliog. index. $7.95 paper.

This is a popularly written textbook, suitable for undergraduates in wine making courses, and of course interested amateurs. This factual account deals mostly with the United States, since 85 percent of all types of wine consumed here are domestic. This lay guide to vinification practices (growing, fermentation, clarifying, distilling) also briefly mentions other countries of the world. An extensive bibliography is also included.

530.   Galet, Pierre. **A Practical Ampelography: Grapevine Identification.** Ithaca, N.Y.: Cornell Univ. Press, 1979. 248p. illus. bibliog. index. $28.

First published in France in 1952, this is the first English translation, and it is based on the 4th edition (1976). Supplementary material has been added, along with the appropriate illustrations for Canada and the United States. These are mostly hybrids. The book, in the main, describes and identifies those French and American grapevines likely to be grown on this continent, and likely to be of value to direct users—the grape growers, educators, and wine producers. It describes the varieties, based on the growing tips (shoots) and leaves of the vine. Each of the 155 types of vines has a line drawing of its leaf structure and a description. The arrangement is by broad category: vinifera wine varieties, table grape varieties, American species, French and American hybrids. Most of the illustrations are contained in twenty color plates.

531. Hough, James Shanks, D. E. Briggs, and R. Stevens. **Malting and Brewing Science.** 2d ed. London: Chapman and Hall, 1982; 1983. distr. by Methuen. 2 vols. illus. bibliog. index. $90 set.

A comprehensive, up-to-date account of the biological, biochemical, and chemical aspects of malting and brewing. It presents the scientific principles behind the selection of raw materials and their processing, including a description of equipment used. The details of practice are related not only to the scientific background but also to historical reasons and present economies. An international section describes current practices and methods used in other countries.

532. Joslyn, Maynard and Maynard A. Amerine. **Dessert, Appetizer and Related Flavored Wines: The Technology of Their Production.** Berkeley, Calif.: Univ. of California Press, 1964. 483p. illus. index. $25.

This book was to be an aid for the California wine industry, improving the stability of aperitif, dessert, and flavored wines, in increasing their acceptance and use by the consumer. Basic principles of wine making are emphasized. Other subjects covered: choice of grapes, sensory judging, economies, winery design, origins of dessert and aperitif wines; flor sherries in California; vermouth; and wine disorders.

533. Ramey, Bern C. **The Great Wine Grapes and the Wines They Make.** Burlington, Vt.: Great Wine Grapes, Inc., 1977. 256p. illus., color. index. $49.95.

This large-format, coffee-table book does a good job in illustrating "the great wine grapes" such as cabernet sauvignon, pinot noir, chardonnay, and riesling. The photographs of the grape clusters and shoots are in color.

534. **Répertoire des stations de viticulture et d'oenologie.** Paris: L'Office International de la Vigne et du Vin, 1972. 120p. 350 French francs.

This is useful information on 280 active research stations and laboratories dealing with viticulture or wine making in 35 countries. Arrangement is by country, and then alphabetically by name, with complete address, names of director and assistants, general program to be carried out, the manner of consultation, and working languages. An alphabetical index is included, and a subject index to type (e.g., viticulture, wine making, microbiology, table grapes, raisins, etc.).

535. Turner, Ben and Roy Roycroft. **The Winemaker's Encyclopedia.** London: Faber and Faber, 1979. 208p. bibliog. index. $19.95; $9.95 paper.

Six hundred entries, arranged alphabetically, deal with technical data and definitions. There are no illustrations. It also considers homemade wines, but not in too much detail. There are some pretty funny ideas as to what constitutes an entry, since the "bibliography" is normally at the back of a book (or as footnotes or appended to each article); here, it is entered under "B"—for "Bibliography"!

536.   Weaver, Robert J. **Grape Growing**. New York: John Wiley & Sons, 1976. 371p. illus. index. $29.95.
This is a grower's handbook, oriented to the Western United States. Topics include grape varieties, pruning, irrigation, and harvesting.

537.   Webb, A. Dinsmore, ed. **Chemistry of Winemaking**. Washington, D.C.: American Chemical Society, 1974. 189p. $29.95; $11.95 paper.
This is number 137 of the Advances in Chemistry series, and it relates the transactions of a conference on the chemistry of wine making.

538.*   Winkler, Albert J. **General Viticulture**. rev. ed. Berkeley, Calif.: Univ. of California Press, 1975. 633p. illus. index. $27.50.
As a comprehensive compilation of contemporary practices in wine making, this is an excellent manual for vineyard owners and grape growers. Pruning is discussed, as well as climate and reasons for growth (or lack of it). The description of various wine grapes and table grapes is very important for the amateur vine grower.

TRADE PUBLICATIONS

While this section deals more with business, exports and imports, sales, distribution, futures, and so forth, it is often of interest to the wine buff who is a completist, who is interested in what company is importing what products and in what quantity, and where all the sales are going. Some of this information is highly useful for "futures" and for investment, while the balance is highly regarded as data for conversation, to replace the older terms of wine appreciation. For in today's hard-edged world, you need to know the story behind or the drama of the packaging, the selling, the consumption rates, and so forth.

There are many state and regional publications and periodicals that interpret policies, legislation, programs, personnel changes, and other activities relating to liquor control. Such titles as *Alaska Beverage Analyst* (1934-), *Atlantic Control States Beverage Journal* (1967-), and *Kentucky Beverage Journal* (1949-) also cover price lists, new products, industry news, and wholesale and retail information on a state or regional basis. These are not annotated in this book. Also not itemized here are business periodicals such as *Beer Distributor* (1935-), *Beverage Dealer and Tavern News* (1970-), *Leisure Beverage Insider Newsletter* (1967-), or *Liquor Store Magazine* (1934-), because these are, for our purposes, too business-oriented. What follows are largely annuals and irregularly published items that contain directory-type data and statistics, market trends, and forecasts. Chapter 9 has some useful business and trade magazines, while chapter 11 has a listing of business associations and lobby groups. Both categories can furnish additional data to the serious student of the alcohol business.

539.   **Alcohol and Tobacco Summary Statistics, 1953- .** Washington, D.C.: Government Printing Office. $10.75.
Statistics in this annual cover U.S. production, withdrawals, and stocks of distilled spirits, wine, beer, and tobacco, with comparative data by states and by months. There are historical tables, as well, and over ninety statistical tables in total.

540.   **Alcoholic Beverage Industry Annual Facts Book, 1946-** . Washington,
D.C.: Distilled Spirits Council of the United States. Free.
The text concerns the role of the alcoholic beverage industry in the national
economy and in the social and cultural life of America. This is a promotional
effort, an annual for both the trade and the consumer.

541.   **American Brewer Annual World Directory of Breweries, 1954-** . American
Brewer Publishing Corp., P.O.B. 267, Kearney, NJ 07032. $15.
In addition to coverage of corporate names, there is also other relevant information
on key personnel and production.

542.   **Annual Survey of Illegal Distilling in the United States, 1946-** . Washington, D.C.: Distilled Spirits Council of the United States. Free.
This is an annual compilation of official statistical data on illegal moonshining
operations in America. It deals with the medical, social, and economic effects of
these operations on the nation.

543.   **Bonded Wineries and Bonded Wine Cellars Authorized to Operate.** Washington, D.C.: Government Printing Office (Internal Revenue Service,
Bureau of Alcohol, Tobacco, and Firearms). Free.

544.   **Breweries Authorized to Operate.** Washington, D.C.: Government Printing
Office (Internal Revenue Service, Bureau of Alcohol, Tobacco, and Firearms). Free.
Both of these annual lists include the names and addresses of every single license
issued for wine making and/or beer making in the United States, on a commercial
basis.

545.   **Brewers Almanac, 1938-** . Washington, D.C.: United States Brewers
Association. $15.
An annual containing statistics on production, withdrawal, taxes, exports, labor,
consumption, retail outlets, Repeal, and the local options in the states, derived
mainly from the latest available U.S. Census of Manufacturers data. Information is
historical, with the retrospective data being given by region or state.

546.   **Brewers Almanack, 1888-** . London, England: $25.
An annual with much of the same useful materials as for the United States, but of
course pertaining to the United Kingdom and to Eire.

547.   **Brewery Manual and Who's Who in British Brewing, 1963-** . Northwood
Publications. Elm House, 10 - 16 Elm Street, London WC1X OBP,
England. £ 5.
This is an annual, comprehensive directory of the British brewing industry, listing
all brewing companies, personnel, and financial information. The "who's who"
section gives detailed background information on all individuals of importance in
the industry: directors, head brewers, and bottling managers.

548. Canada. Statistics Canada. **Breweries, 1972-** . Ottawa: Supply and Services Canada. cat. no. 32-205. $10.

549. Canada. Statistics Canada. **Control and Sale of Alcoholic Beverages in Canada, 1928-** . Ottawa: Supply and Services Canada. cat. no. 63-202. $10.

550. Canada. Statistics Canada. **Distilleries, 1918-** . Ottawa: Supply and Services Canada. cat. no. 32-206. $10.

551. Canada. Statistics Canada. **Wineries, 1919-** . Ottawa: Supply and Services Canada. cat. no. 32-207. $10.

These annual collections of statistics provide the necessary data for retrieval of information about alcoholic beverages in Canada.

552. Commerce Clearinghouse. **Liquor Control Law Reports, 1934-** . Chicago: CCH. $175.

This monthly reports on the current developments and changes in the construction and implementation of laws concerning the importing, distributing, manufacturing, and selling of liquor and liquor-products.

553. Distilled Spirits Council of the United States. **Annual Statistical Review, 1951-** . Washington, D.C.: DISCUS. Free.

This annual provides an analysis of the beverage distilling industry, with highlights of the local option elections each year. There is a tabulation of the "wet" and "dry" population of all states as of December 31 of each year. Comparative and historical data go back only to Repeal. Other tables include public revenues, tax rates, import duties, stock, bottled output and foreign trade.

554. Distilled Spirits Council of the United States. **Public Revenues from Alcoholic Beverages, 1937-** . Washington, D.C.: DISCUS. Free.

A straightforward annual accounting, with the appropriate tables, of the tax money derived from the sales of alcoholic beverages, operation of state liquor stores, and license fees, with comparative data and type of beverage sold. Compilation is by both federal and state data. Reports show the method of controlling local collections, and allocation of state taxes, where available.

555. Distilled Spirits Council of the United States. **Summary of State Laws and Regulations Relating to Distilled Spirits, 1935-** . Washington, D.C.: DISCUS. $8.50 paper.

Each biennial edition covers a great deal of material, all of it compiled from state statutes, administrative regulations, interpretative rulings, and replies to questionnaires. Part One concerns the control (monopoly) states, with tabular data and explanatory notes. Part Two is about the licensed states, and contains similar data. Miscellaneous tables are in Part Three, and comprise fees (by state), commodities other than distilled spirits that may be sold (e.g., potato chips, tobacco), and a complete list of federal excise tax rates on distilled spirits since 1791, when it was nine cents per gallon (it is now over ten dollars).

556.   **European Spirits, 1970-** . Stamex, B.P. 505, Hilversum, Pays-Bas, Belgium. 1,000 Belgian francs.

Covered in this triennial are European distillers of whiskey, gin, eaux-de-vie, vodka, Cognac, schanpps, and liqueurs. The directory part of it covers 1,100 businesses in 25 countries with details on names and addresses, telephone and telex and/or telegraph numbers, year founded, number of employees, names of directors and export heads, affiliated groups, and production programs. There is also a register of over 1,900 trademarked products.

557.   **European Wine World, 1984-** . Bologna, Italy: Edizioni Annuari D'Italia, 1984- . Various paginations. $150.

This extremely useful annual publication covers all of the wines of the world, and some beers and spirits as well. It is a listing of European wine exporters for eighteen European countries and sixteen non-European countries such as Canada and the United States. The remaining half of the space lists world wine importers and agents in sixty-three countries. For both categories (importers and exporters) there are names, addresses, phone numbers, and telex numbers (if applicable). Within each country there is a regional or state arrangement for the importer or exporter if they are not national groups.

558.   **From the State Capitols: Alcoholic Beverage Control, 1946-** . New Haven, Conn.: Wakeman-Walworth, Inc. $145.

This weekly covers state and local regulations throughout the United States that affect the production and marketing of alcoholic beverages.

559.   **Harper's Directory and Manual of the Wine and Spirit Trade, 1888-** . Harling House, London: Harper's Trade Journals. £ 5.

Section 1 of this annual is a directory of the wine and spirit trade in the United Kingdom and Eire (alphabetically); section 2 is a geographic arrangement of section 1; section 3 is a directory of wine and spirit trade overseas (alphabetically by country); section 4 is a list of wines and spirits, shippers and agents, brand names, and ancillary trades (worldwide, arranged by beverage); section 5, a list of trade associations and bonded warehouses in the United Kingdom and Eire. There is an index.

560.   **The Impact American Wine Market Review and Forecast, 1983.** New York: M. Shanken Communications, 1983. $150 paper.

Also available are *The Impact American Distilled Spirits Market Review and Forecast,* and *The Impact American Beer Market Review and Forecast.* These first came out in 1974; they are market research reports. In each, there is brand data and expenditures, media expenditures, marketing achievements, category and market trends, new products, maps, tables, charts, and projections to 1991 and beyond. For instance, the review on wines shows the shifts in drinking patterns and the areas in which wine consumption is up. The spirits review shows a negative (or, at best, flat) market, the impact of white spirits, and some conclusions that new brands and images are needed. The beer review shows a declining market, one that is segmenting into specialized brews and audiences.

561.   **Liquor Marketing Handbook, 1954- .** New York: Gavin-Jobson. $25.
This annual compendium provides market trend information and statistics that provide the basis for marketing and advertising decisions of distillers, vintners, and importers of alcoholic beverages. Each annual has around 350 pages of tables, maps and projections, and ads. The four sections cover: 1) the National Liquor Market (consumption, sales, regional breakdowns, distribution maps, projections, retail licenses, taxation, bootlegging, and retail sales prices); 2) Distilling Operations (production, storage and aging, usage and bottling); 3) The Market for Major Distilled Spirits Types (by type, including prepared cocktails, with maps and fifteen-year projections); 4) Advertising and Promotion (expenditures, directory of media personnel, the black market, outdoor advertising, and packaging).

562.   **Memento de l'O.I.V.** Paris: L'Office International de la Vigne et du Vin. approx. 1200p. 125 French francs.
This guide, in French, cuts a clear path through the voluminous documents issued by government sources in Europe. There are five main chapters, with the largest— about 900 pages—concerned with legislation from about 40 countries (wine codes, texts of laws, new laws) as well as legislation from the E.E.C. generally. Next come tables of statistics on cultivation, production, imports, exports, and consumption of all grape products (wine, table grapes, raisins, grape juice) for 70 countries, along with historical figures; followed by a section on wine origins that lists wines and principal growths for 20 countries, along with the area determination laws; a wine periodicals list that furnishes the names and addresses of 140 periodicals in 27 countries; and a list of national associations of wine and grape growing in 40 countries. Produced at irregular intervals, the last in 1979.

563.   **Modern Brewery Age Blue Book, 1941- .** Norwalk, Conn.: Business Journals Inc. Annual. $50.
This publication covers the brewing and malt beverage distribution industries, with lists of breweries and names of management and supervisory personnel.

564.   **Shaws Wine Guide, 1952- .** London: Shaws Price Guides. £ 10.
This is one of Shaws' many industrial guides published three times a year. Listed here are wines, beers, and spirits, plus ciders, by their names, with the current list or retail prices. This gives an idea of the range available, and of the "recommended prices." This strictly factual presentation does not mention selection or quality.

565.   **Sunbelt/Frostbelt: Past, Present and Future.** New York: Impact Research, 1983. 96p. $100 paper.
This report, with 40 graphs and charts, analyzes on a state-by-state basis where wine, liquor, and beer consumption will increase or decrease, and why, to 1991. The contents: population review, alcoholic beverage consumption, demographics of the market, trends and projections. Highly useful for market locations.

566.   **Wine and Spirit Trade International Yearbook, 1971- .** London: Haymarket Publishing. £ 15.

There are four main sections in this annual: agents, shippers, opening prices of Scotch whisky, distilleries (alphabetically by product), blenders, and vintage summaries are in part One; part Two lists merchants in the United Kingdom and Eire; part Three lists whisky blends and brands; and part Four has materials about the trade (customs, legislation, trade association lists).

567.   **Wine Marketing Handbook, 1971- .** New York: Gavin-Jobson. $17.

This short annual publication (about 160 pages) does for wine what the *Liquor Marketing Handbook* does for spirits. Its set up is very similar: part One covers the National Wine Market; part Two deals with production and inventories; part Three is called "Market for Major Wine Types" (table, dessert, vermouth, Champagne, and sparkling), and part Four is "Wine and Advertising." Using this tool, one will be able to find sales and advertising figures, marketing data, the distribution of American and imported wines, consumer characteristics, taxes imposed, production, and the depletion rates.

568.   **Wineries and Wine Industry Suppliers of North America, 1939- .** San Rafael, Calif.: Hiaring Co.

This annual is the December issue of *Wines and Vines*, and is not available separately. It contains copious amounts of data on all American wineries and wine bottlers: size, officers, products, brands, distribution, and buyers' guide. It presents a resumé of laws and regulations affecting wine in each of the fifty states. Some coverage is also given to Canada and to Mexico. Trade associations and grower groups are also covered.

569.   **World Drink Directory, 1982- .** London: Wine Warehouses Pub. Co. £ 40.

With over 800 pages, this annual directory gives details on about 12,000 companies in 135 countries that produce or sell wines, beers, and spirits (as well as soft drinks and ciders). For example, about 5,000 European wine growers are listed. Directory-type data include: names, addresses, telex, cable, telephone numbers, the main channels of trading, parent company, brands owned, sales agencies represented, directors' names, and senior management. The products and brands have been classified by generic type and country of origin.

9 *Magazines about Wines, Beers, and Spirits*

Magazines, newsletters, newspapers, journals, trade organs—all form part of what we call "periodicals," and all are extremely valuable to their respective audiences for news and views, short articles on specific products, and currency of information. Not all periodicals will appeal to everybody. Each has a specific audience. People who read do so for a variety of reasons—they may be consumers who need guidance on purchases, tasters who need to know drinkability odds, retailers and agents who need the latest marketing figures, industrial brew masters or wine tasters who need to know the latest techniques (or even amateur home brewers who need new recipes). Readers may be members of a particular association, or followers of a particular country's wines, or even readers who shun the "bought" goods for the purity and low cost of "make-your-own."

There are, obviously, magazines for everybody. Most of the ones found in this section are ones that are relatively easy to obtain by subscription, and they will satisfy a wide range of tastes. These titles are arranged alphabetically, but there is also a "quick index" to their major substance, just prior to the major listing. Also, the best magazines—in my opinion—have been noted with an asterisk, and listed below as "best magazines." They should cover all of the basics and the essentials, and even a wider territory of subjects. Only the die-hard specialists need delve any further for more data.

Magazines dealing with *beer:*

All about Beer.

Magazines dealing with *wine:*

The Connoisseurs' Guide to California Wines

Decanter

Food and Wine

The Friends of Wine

The International Wine and Food Society Journal

Revue du Vin de France

Robert Finigan's Private Guide to Wines

Vintage

Wine Spectator

Wines and Vines

Their annotations will reveal why they are the better magazines. Some trade and technical materials are listed only in Chapter 8, while virtually all of the magazines that deal with homemade products are in Chapter 10. Additional tasting indexes and newsletters to guide consumers can be found in Chapter 5. There is also a wealth of specialized trade, professional, societal and association periodicals that are *only* available through membership; these will be located in Chapter 11.

There are also great quantities of *free* newsletters that are sent to club members or to clients of firms. In order to get these you need to belong or to buy on a regular basis. The major retail stores such as Sherry-Lehmann in New York City have a chit-chat newsletter indicating what to buy, when to buy, certain wine futures, etc. This is all part of the information flow that you get when you hang around any retail outlet. Certain wine importers and exporters such as H. Sichel und Sohne, Torres, or Chateau Mau will have a newsletter about their products and their current vintages. Promotional literature in the form of newsletters also come from American wineries, principally California, such as *Bottles and Bins* (Charles Krug Winery), *Inglenook News, Mirassou Latest Press,* or *The Warner Way* (from Michigan). These are usually monthly, with up-to-date information on the climatic conditions surrounding their vineyards, progress reports on the wines (both in the cask and in sales), technical processes such as pruning techniques, personal notes, sales information, and recipes. Certainly, if you are buying from any winery, then you should get on their free mailing list!

Most of the periodicals that follow are indexed somewhere, although many are not to be found in such general indexes as the *Readers' Guide* or *The Magazine Index.* There are, though, two specialized indexes that will arrange for proper access to the tasting notes of many periodicals and consumer guide newsletters. One is the *Consumer Index to Product Evaluations and Information Sources,* which since 1973 has provided access to reviews and tasting notes of wines as found in *Vintage, The Friends of Wine, Gourmet, Bon Appetit, Wine World, Robert Lawrence Balzer's Private Guide,* and both general magazines (*House and Garden, Vogue, Esquire,* etc.) and consumer testing magazines (*Consumer Reports, Consumer's Digest, Consumers' Research, Canadian Consumer,* and *Which?*). About 3,200 wines are indexed annually. The other index is *The Wine Tasting Index,* which since 1978 has facilitated retrieval of some 11,000 wines each year (sorted by region, variety, vintage and producer); these have been taken from seventeen or so wine guides and newsletters of the previous year. Further details can be found under the consumer guides in Chapter 5.

Magazines dealing with *American* wines, which may include California wines, include:

The Cook's Magazine

Eastern Grape Grower and Winery News

International Wine Review
Oregon Wine Review
Vineyard View
Wine East
Wine Spectator
Wines and Vines
See also the section below on California wines treated separately.

Magazines dealing with *Australian wines:*

Australian Wine, Brewing and Spirit Review.

Magazines dealing with *beer:*

All about Beer
Brewer's Digest
Brewers Guardian
What's Brewing?

Magazines dealing with *California wines:*

California Grapevine
California Wineletter
Connoisseurs' Guide to California Wine
Just Released
Robert Finigan's Private Guide to Wines
Robert Lawrence Balzer's Private Guide to Food and Wine
Society of Medical Friends of Wine Bulletin
Wine Country
Wine World
Wineletter
Wines and Vines
Winestate

Magazines dealing with *Canadian wines:*

Bar
Beverage Canada
Canadian Wine Notes
Wine Tidings

Magazines dealing with *collecting and collectibles:*

> All about Beer
> Vineyard View
> Wine Tidings
> Wines and Vines

Useful *consumer guides:*

> Andrew Delaplane's Personal Guide to Wines of the World
> California Grapevine
> Connoisseurs' Guide to California Wine
> Consumer Wineletter
> Decanter
> International Wine Review
> Just Released
> Robert Finigan's Private Guide to Wines
> Robert Lawrence Balzer's Private Guide to Food and Wine
> The Underground Wine Letter
> Which ? Wine Monthly
> Wine Spectator

Magazines dealing with *food, cookery, and recipes:*

> All about Beer
> Bon Appetit
> The Cook's Magazine
> Decanter
> Food and Wine
> The Friends of Wine
> Gourmet
> House and Garden (London)
> International Wine and Food Society Journal
> Italian Wines and Spirits
> Revue du Vin de France
> Wine Country
> Wine Tidings

Wine World

Wines and Vines

Magazines dealing with the *English market and trade:*

Brewers Guardian

Decanter

Drinks International

Harper's Wine and Spirit Gazette

Which ? Wine Monthly

Wine and Spirit

Wining and Dining

Magazines dealing with *French wines:*

Bacchus International

Decanter

I. N. A. O. Bulletin

Journal de France des Appeallations d'Origine

Médoc Bordeaux

Revue du Vin de France

Revue Vinicole Internationale

Magazines dealing with *German wines:*

The German Wine Review

Magazines dealing with *Italian wines:*

Italian Wines and Spirits

Magazines dealing with wines of *New Zealand:*

New Zealand Wineglass

Magazines dealing with wines of *South Africa:*

South African Wine and Beverage

Wynboer

Magazines dealing with *spirits* (note that almost all glossy magazines will say something about spirits):

> Decanter
>
> Drinks International
>
> The Friends of Wine

Trade magazines that give market figures and statistics will be found in the chapter dealing with trade (Chapter 8), but the following are also useful:

> Bacchus International
>
> Bar
>
> Beverage Canada
>
> Brewer's Digest
>
> Brewers Guardian
>
> California Wineletter
>
> Decanter
>
> Drinks International
>
> Harper's Wine and Spirit Gazette
>
> Impact Newsletter
>
> Market Watch
>
> O. I. V. Bulletin
>
> Wine and Spirit
>
> Wine Spectator
>
> Wines and Vines

570.* **All about Beer,** 1980- . bimonthly. $16.97 for 12 issues. McMullen Publishing Co., 2145 W. LaPalma, Anaheim, CA 92801.

Topics in this magazine, which became a glossy after sixteen tabloid issues, include: cooking with beer (using beer as an ingredient or as an accompaniment), such as in chili recipes; history and lore, such as stories about early American breweries, bars, pubs, and taverns; material about ales; data on home-brewing (techniques, recipes, tips, even some technical information, such as about different hops); news and views; "pub of the month"; useful classified ads with names and addresses of suppliers for accessories or home-brew materials; blind tastings, but with regular beer drinkers and not just educated palates; representative bars from different parts of the world; and collecting memorabilia (also called "breweriana"). There is some attempt at humor and nonbeer articles that fit a jock image, especially about beer-sponsored events. A pretty good magazine, extremely useful for the contacts and the historical matter.

571. **Andrew Delaplane's Personal Guide to Wines of the World**, 1978- .
monthly. $24. P.O.B. 3470, Fort Pierce, FL 33448.
This newsletter is eight pages long, and it is basically a consumer guide to the
wines of the world (not just to American wines). Included with the tasting comments and evaluations are cooking tips, a question-and-answer section, some
travel notes, and book reviews.

572. **Australian Wine, Brewing and Spirit Review**, 1882- . Monthly. $20. 13-31
Barrett Street, Kensington, Victoria, Australia.
Gives good coverage of the "down under" wine industry, with charts and marketing
patterns, plus profiles of the wine merchants and wine proprietors. Articles are on
wineries, consumer consumption, equipment, markets, microbiology, and grapes.
And it appeals to both the consumer and to the trade.

573. **Bacchus International: La Revue de la Sommellerie**, 1973- . bimonthly.
150 French francs. Editions CAMS, 23 Boulevard de Bonne, Nouvelle,
Paris, France.
An interesting little magazine, highly useful to the trade and to the wine steward in
particular. The text is in both French and English, and there are book reviews
and classified advertisements for its circulation of about 10,000. This magazine is
of some value in Britain and on the continent, but is perhaps of limited interest in
North America.

574. **BAR: Beverage Alcohol Reporter**, 1949- . monthly. $20 for 10 issues.
Vincent-Clarke Publications, 258 Sheppard Avenue East, Suite 2B, North
York, Canada M2N 3B1.
An industry publication, full of news and views for the Canadian trade (restaurants
and hotels and liquor merchants). It has articles on wines tasted, interviews with
executives, material on new hotels and restaurants that have opened, and book
reviews. Useful for operators and bartenders.

575. **Beverage Canada**, 1975- . $10 for 10 issues. Arthurs Publications, Suite
204, 5200 Dixie Road, Mississauga, Ontario L4W 1E4.
Very similar to *BAR* magazine, appealing to the same audience and featuring the
same kind of news; but editorial matter varies. Where *BAR* is a continual survey
of the scene; *Beverage Canada* concerns itself with thematic issues as *Wines and
Vines* sometimes does. Topics include annual wrap ups of white wine, red wine,
brandies (Cognac, Armagnac, etc.), white spirits, Scotches, Ryes, etc. There are
interviews with wine makers and brew masters, as well as research directors.

576. **Bon Appetit**, 1956- . monthly. $18. 5900 Wilshire Blvd., Los Angeles,
CA 90036.
This is mainly a food magazine, with many advertisements and some wine content.
In addition to recipes and themes, cooking schools and some travel articles, there
may be some editorial matter on wines. Recent articles have covered Alsace, Cham-
pagne, parties, and general news, as well as lots of liquor and wine ads. There are,

as of 1984, two regular columnists: Anthony Dias Blue's "Wines and Spirits" column, which is a basic consumer guide on some type or category of wine each month, and Hank Rubin's question and answer column, in which consumers try to find out more data about what's behind a particular wine label, or get their wine collection appraised as to value or drinkability times. Useful for the food material, much more so than for wine.

577. **Brewer's Digest**, 1926- . monthly. $14. Anmark Publications, 4049 West Peterson Avenue, Chicago, IL 60646.

This is a technical publication, dealing with brewing, fermentation, and malt and hops, with statistics and trade news. It is very useful for announcements of new products, trends, history, book reviews, and so on. The *Annual Buyer's Guide and Directory List of Personnel* is published as part of the January issue and is available separately at eight dollars.

578. **Brewers Guardian**, 1871- . monthly. $12.50. Northwood Publications, Ltd., Elm House, 10 - 16 Elm Street, London SC1X OBP, England.

This British equivalent to *Brewer's Digest* is a trade publication, covering much the same area as the latter, but with additional information on the European scene and some material on wine and spirits.

579. **California Grapevine**, 1975- . bimonthly. $18. P.O.B. 22152, San Diego, CA 92122.

This evaluative newsletter has about 16 pages in each issue. It attempts comparative reviews and assessments of California cabernet sauvignon, chardonnay, and zinfandels, with periodic surveys of other varietals (and jug wines and selected imports). Occasionally it will deal with the status and drinkability of older wines. The detailed tasting notes are derived from weekly double-blind tastings, with a panel of writers, merchants and amateurs. Regular features also include "Grapevine Recommendations" for previously assessed wines and "Forthcoming Releases" as an indication of newly issued wines from the various wineries.

580. **California Wineletter**, 1948- . semi-monthly. $40 for 23 issues. Phyllis Van Kriedt, P.O.B. 70, Mill Valley, CA 94942.

This is a trade newsletter, with news and views for the industry. It has statistics and book reviews, with the occasional article by Robert Jay Misch, and of course it has a strong history of data interpretation (it is almost forty years old). Some of the material is also used in the newsletter *Wineletter*, also produced by Van Kriedt, but for consumers (see entry 624).

581. **Canadian Wine Notes**, 1983- . monthly. $12. Cangro Associates, Suite 2-1511, 300 Regina Street N., Waterloo, Ontario Canada N2J 4H2.

This one is subtitled "The newsletter that brings you into touch with the Canadian wine industry." Currently developed topics include histories of the wineries, an introduction to new products, news and views, technical studies and vintage reports from the various regions, tasting notes, food notes, prizes, and awards. Stress, of course, is on Canada, particularly on Ontario vineyards and wines. In September 1984 it became a 24-page glossy magazine.

582.* **Connoisseurs' Guide to California Wine**, 1978- . bimonthly. $20. P.O.B. 11120, San Francisco, CA 94101.

This is one of the granddaddies of California wine evaluations. Many wine tastings are reviewed and wines are rated, some rather harshly, but then there is always an eye to value. A great wine is not great if it costs too much. The editors use numerous symbols to indicate the concise data about the wines. Food topics are also covered. Their information and ratings have resulted in a book, *The Connoisseurs' Handbook of California Wine* (3d ed., Knopf, 1984), which contains all the collated information at their press time.

583. **The Consumer Wineletter**, 1974- . monthly. $20. P. O. B. 135, Irvington, NY 10533.

Edited by the renowned Henri Fluchère, this newsletter covers the basics of wines. Regular columns include "Wine of the Month," "Buys of the Month," and a large article on one particular region in the world. This article is illustrated with maps and drawings. Other topics deal with tips and advice (how to serve, how to store, decant, etc.) and news of wine releases around the world, as well as material on wine tastings.

584. **The Cook's Magazine**, 1981- . bimonthly. $18. 1698 Post Road East, Westport, CT 06880.

With a circulation of over 100,000 and heavily devoted to cooking, this magazine presents about 30 articles every issue on cookware testing, the science of cooking, interviews with top food personalities, regional cooking styles, and many useful recipes. There is unusually good stress on American wines.

585. **Decanter Magazine**, 1975- . monthly. $38. St. John's Chambers, 2 - 10 St. John's Road, London SW11 1PN, England.

This is the leading wine magazine in the English-speaking world, primarily because it is interesting and informative, it reports on older vintages (so that you can see how well your cellar is holding up), it comments on future releases (so that you can buy more wine), and it appeals to both the trade and the consumer. There is lots here of value to Americans, although the stress is on the British market. Writers include Michael Broadbent's "Taster's Diary," Edmund Penning-Rowsell, Burton Anderson, Pamela Vandyke Price, and many others. It seems that all the British M. W.s have written for *Decanter* at some time or another. There is a lively letters column, with the typical British nastiness and arguments and correction notices. Features include a consumer's column, tasting notes, spirits, "worst wine label of the month," cooking with wine, "Decanter's Dinner Party Menu" (with recipes), wine merchants' biographies, monthly lists of wine auctions and exhibits, restaurant reports, acerbic book reviews, extremely useful and informative advertisements, and a worthwhile "diary" of events (tastings, dinners, wine courses, wine tours, wine festivals). Recent articles have concerned Alsatian wines, individual Bordeaux châteaux and their wine masters, Châteauneuf du Pape, Champagne, Australia, California, Cape wines (South Africa), New Zealand, and reports on wine fairs. A bargain at the price, given the quantity of wine data.

586.   **Drinks International,** 1967- . bimonthly. £ 6. I. P. C. Business Press, Surrey House, 1 Throwley Way, Suttom, Surrey SM1 4QQ, England.
A trade publication for the hotel and restaurant business, and the public houses too, stressing alcoholic beverages such as spirits and cocktails. Recipes are given, as well as informative ads, news and views, and profiles of leading hotels, lounges, restaurants, bartenders, sommeliers, and so forth.

587.   **Eastern Grape Grower and Winery News,** 1975- . bimonthly. $11. P.O.B. 329, Watkins Glen, NY 14891.
This informative magazine appeals principally to the user of East coast wines (mainly New York style), and is geared to the trade. There are regular columns on wine making and wine production, technical news, and useful data about grapes and vines.

588.*   **Food and Wine,** 1978- . monthly. $15. The International Review of Food and Wine Association, 1120 Avenue of the Americas, New York, NY 10036.
This is basically a food publication, with the emphasis on American cooking and wine. It has a circulation of over 350,000, and was formerly known as the *International Review of Food and Wine.* It is now owned by American Express. The wine and spirits editors (Eliza McCoy and John Walker) produce a monthly column under the name of "Peter Quimme"; it is from this column that they originate their Signet paperbacks on wines and spirits. Vinous material here concerns California Zinfandels, a Bordeaux buying guide, the Finger Lakes district of New York, dining at wineries, Virginia wines, British beers, use of wine in cooking, Vermouths, wines and spicy foods, California cabernet sauvignons, Rioja wines, Cognac, wine lists in restaurants, and so forth. The rest of the magazine has general articles on food, news of new products, entertainment features, recipes, book reviews, and so forth.

589.*   **The Friends of Wine,** 1964- . bimonthly. $20. Les Amis du Vin, 2302 Perkins Place, Silver Springs, MD 20910.
Beginning as a 1-page newsletter for a Washington, D. C. wine club in 1964, this glossy magazine has since evolved into an all-purpose periodical that suits the requirements of Les Amis Du Vin (a commercial wine-buying club that operates through retail stores). It includes wine reviews, wine news, opinions, letters, wine and food matchups, recipes, book reviews, consumer guides, articles on spirits, tasting notes—all the usual material in a general wine magazine. Recent articles have included features on Italian sparkling wines, the chardonnay grape in other parts of the world, restaurants in New York City, wine bars in New York City, Champagnes, other sparkling wines, and an evaluation of Burgundy growers who also bottle (Domaine-bottled wines).

590.   **The German Wine Review,** 1980- . semi-annually. $7.50. Deutscher Wein-wirtschaftsverlag, Meininger GmbH & Co., Maximilianstrasse 7 - 17, D6730 Neustadt an der Weinstrasse, West Germany.
Die Weinwirtschaft is a German-language weekly meant for the wine trade, as it is concerned with machinery and technology as well as tasting wines and marketing

(it costs $150 annually in the U.S.). Twice a year the publisher translates the better articles, the ones that are aimed more at consumers and North Americans, and puts them out as an "export" edition, *The German Wine Review.* Nothing here, of course, is critical nor evaluative, but there is trade data, advertising, marketing news, and articles, and notes about the state of technology and wine and food matching. Recent topics have included interviews with wine masters and executives, vintage harvests, wine history and wine lore, foods, wine laws, notes about various regions, wine festivals, wine seminars, and collecting.

591.   **Gourmet: The Magazine of Good Living,** 1941- . monthly. $18. 560 Lexington Avenue, New York, NY 10022.

This colorful magazine, with stress on travel articles that can give prominence to wine, contains many articles on foods that involve the use of wine or spirits. There is often an occasional article on wine, but very rarely one on spirits alone. Restaurants of New York, London, Paris, San Francisco, and Los Angeles are regularly reviewed, and there are also survey articles on restaurants in different cities around the world. One recent issue's articles covered New York, London, California, West Germany, France, North Dakota, Italy, Switzerland, Guatemala, and the American Southwest. The wine editor is Gerald Asher, an eclectic wine writer and merchant.

592.   **Harpers Wine and Spirit Gazette,** 1879- . weekly. £ 42. Harper Trade Journals, Harling House, 47 - 51 Great Suffolk Street, London SE1 OBS, England.

This is the major trade publication for the British wine trade. It contains articles on merchandising, equipment, trade figures of imports and exports, book reviews, market statistics, trade news and views, and general information. All of it is valuable, especially because of its weekly frequency; the news is current. The subscription also includes a valuable annual directory listing all the people and companies in the British trade.

593.   **House and Garden,** 1934- . monthly. $41. Condé Nast Pub. Ltd., Vogue House, Hanover Square, London W1R OAD, England.

The stress here is British and European, for this is the overseas and separate edition of the U.S. *House and Garden.* It incorporates *Wine and Food* magazine, which was founded by André Simon in 1934, as a separate section (about 30 to 50 pages each month). About one-third is wine and two-thirds is food. Recent articles have included after-dinner drinks, Portuguese wines, buying wines for Christmas, wine-in-a-box, Cape wines from South Africa, cooperage in Cognac, cider, English wine. There are excellent color photographs, wine reviews, and book reviews, and addresses for suppliers.

594.   **Impact Newsletter,** 1971- . semi-monthly. $120. M. Shanken Communications, 400 East 51st Street, New York, NY 10022.

This calls itself "marketing, financial and economic news and research for the wines and spirits executive." It covers companies, brands, advertising, personnel changes, promotional news, and so forth. With facts and figures, it is a highly useful publication for the trade and also for the interested consumer who is buying into wine futures.

595.   **Institut National des Appellations D'origine des Vins et Eaux-de-vie Bulletin,** 1938- . quarterly. $14. 138 Avenue des Champs Elysees, 75008 Paris, France.

The I.N.A.O. is the government body that checks into the proper application of the A.O.C. and V.D.Q.S. standards and limitations as they apply to wines and spirits in France. This Bulletin, while in French, is highly useful for those who follow the French wine scene, either whether one in the trade, the technical side or is just a very interested consumer. There is much technical and legal documentation here, as well as the updated changes and corrections to the A.O.C. laws and regulations.

596.*   **International Wine and Food Society Journal,** 1974- . $30. 32 - 36 Fleet Lane, London EC4M 4YA, England.

This publication originally began in 1934, founded by André Simon, as *Wine and Food*, a gastronomic quarterly. It died with no. 149 in 1970, became subsumed into *House and Garden* (London), where it is still a feature, and at the same time became resurrected in 1974 as the *Journal.* One-third of the book deals with Society news, views, business, advertisements, and so forth, such as dinners and proceedings held around the world (thus, it is a good collection of menus). The balance are long, academic-type articles on a variety of wine and food themes such as changing patterns of wine drinking, dining out, Hungarian cuisine, the "second" wines of the châteaux of Bordeaux, cuisine of Cognac, Australian vintages, food in Nice, the history of mustard, American foods at holiday time, Madeiras, Indian tea, American wines, and so forth. The material is scholarly in tone, and well researched, and there are book reviews. The quarterly publication schedule became annual in 1984, due to a policy of fiscal restraint, but it is anticipated that the quarterly format will return. News of the society will still be published quarterly, but only on a regional basis. It is also available with membership.

597.   **International Wine Review,** 1984- . bimonthly. $25. Beverage Testing Institute, Inc. P.O.B. 285, Ithaca, NY 14851.

This new publication promises no advertising since it is going to rely entirely on subscriptions and will be a buying guide and will stress product evaluation. Articles include stories behind the wine competitions and the medals, commentaries on the University of California (Davis) wine scoring system (20/20), the drinkability odds chart, descriptions of all of the newly designated wine regions of America (as promulgated by the B.A.T.F.), Champagne and Bordeaux competitions, a consumer price index for wines, and material about rare wines and collectors' items.

598.   **Italian Wines and Spirits,** 1977- . quarterly. $15. (North American Edition) P.O.B. 1130, Long Island County, NY 11101.

This is an elegant and classy magazine, with excellent photography and superb use of color and graphics. Its covers (reproductions of Italian still lifes emphasizing food and wine) are stunning. The articles center on foods, restaurants, wines, the regions of Italy (with maps of the D.O.C. zones), the character of the wines and foods, and so forth with individual features on specific wines and their American reception. This is not a critical magazine; it is sponsored by *Civiltà de bere,* the Italian wine trade magazine in Italy. With a circulation of some 55,000 and lots of full-page ads for Italian wines, the magazine also has big-name contributors: Burton Anderson, Emanuel and Madeline Greenberg, Hugh Johnson, Robert Jay Misch, Hank Rubin, Sheldon Wasserman, and various Italian writers.

599. **Journal de France des Appellations D'origine: Vignobles et Vins,** 1943- . monthly. 30 French francs. Societe d'editions et d'Information Viti-vinivoles, Rue de l'Ecole-des-Tambours, Macon, France.
In a tabloid format, this trade publication deals with French wines. There are charts, market statistics, import and export figures, interesting advertisements, and so forth. Highly useful for the futures buyer, even if it is available only in French (circulates about 25,000 copies).

600. **Just Released,** 1983- . monthly. $18. P.O.B. 708, Calistoga, CA 94515.
An interesting idea for a newsletter: a review of all the new California wines that have just been released. Informative, and useful since it is sent by first-class mail.

601. **Market Watch,** 1981- . monthly. $60 for 11 issues. M. Shanken Communi-cations, 400 East 51st Street, New York, NY 10022.
This one describes itself thus: "forecasts and insights into the wine and spirits industry." Actually, it is a more slick version of *Impact Newsletter* (see entry 594), but with essentially the same data in a more glossy and graphic form (color, larger print, opinions) that can be digested easily. It has some articles, such as on sparkling wines and on Armagnac, that stress how to sell them (this *is* a trade publication). These are needed by the retail stores who tend to sell only regular spirits and jug wines. Other items: news, tracking of popular brands (how well or how poorly they are selling), tracking of ad campaigns and special promotions and even selected retail operations. Useful for those consumers who like to see what goes on behind the scenes, but have it presented in a palatable format.

602. **Médoc Bordeaux: Bulletin d'information du G.I.E. des Vins du Médoc,** 1977- . quarterly. 50 French francs. 1, cours du XXX Juillet, Bordeaux, France.
This is a bilingual publication: French and English. Recent theme issues have been about Listrac, St. Estèphe, Moulis, and other communes. Each area is examined in turn, and for each issue there is material on the types of wine pro-duced, the history and customs of the area, food, labels, aerial maps, types of grapes, marketing, etc. The price is to U.S. addresses. A highly useful publication for the Bordeaux specialist.

603. **New Zealand Wineglass,** 1975- . quarterly. Price not available. Wineglass Publishing Co., P.O.B. 9527, Auckland, New Zealand.
A publication that deals with everything in the New Zealand wine industry: news and views, tasting notes, evaluations, marketing figures, and so forth.

604.　　**O.I.V. Bulletin,** 1928- . Monthly. $13. Office International de la Vigne et
　　　　du Vin, 11 rue Roquépine, 75008 Paris, France.

This is the leading wine organization of the world. Neither the United States nor
Canada have ever joined, but in 1984 their application was being considered. The
O.I.V. represents about 90 percent of the wine produced in thirty-one countries.
This French-language economic publication gives worldwide coverage on viticulture,
wine making, and wine economies. It details technological developments and also
carries some general articles such as "tourist influence on wine consumption."
Special sections include notes from the world press, new legislation (worldwide),
statistics, and abstracts from the major wine journals, as well as book reviews and
charts. A highly useful periodical, especially since the United States will be a member. The price is to U.S. addresses.

605.　　**Oregon Wine Review,** 1983- . quarterly. $10. P.O.B.　10001, Portland,
　　　　OR 97210.

A specialized publication concerned with the wines of Oregon and the wineries
that produce them. There are tasting notes of evaluation and comparative
comments. Good details here relate to marketing skills and to climate.

606.　　**Revue du Vin de France,** 1927- . $25 for 5 issues (foreign, English-
　　　　language edition). Societe Francaise d'editions Vinicoles, 6 rue d'Uzes,
　　　　75081 Paris, France.

This technical and topical information, available here in an English translation,
devotes all of its space to French wines and French food. Each issue has quality
documentation and between 60 and 80 pages of text that is well-illustrated. Type
of material covered includes histories of wines and glasses, labels, the value of the
harvests, tasting notes (not too critical), wine lists in restaurants, legislation, food
and wine matchups, amateur wine makers, and book reviews. Recipes are taken
from its sister publication *Cuisine et Vins de France* (only available in French)
and stress regional characteristics, always complemented by the appropriate
regional wine. Studies on wines and the vine, as well as restaurant ratings, are
reported. Technical information of value include data on wine disorders (causes,
symptoms, and remedies). Of late there has been a special tear-out section with a
glossary of terms for the whole wine-making spectrum, from vine cultivation
through to testing and aging. This may pose a problem for libraries with patrons
who pinch.

607.　　**Revue Vinicole Internationale/International Wine Review: Revue des
　　　　Vins, Vins de Liqueur et Aperitifs, Eaux-de-vie de Liqueurs, Jus de Fruits,
　　　　Cidres, et Boissons de Qualité,** 1880- . monthly. 250 French francs
　　　　(foreign rate) for 10 issues. Leader International Press, 18 rue Godot-
　　　　de-Mauroy, 75009 Paris, France.

With text in both French and English (plus appropriate translated summaries),
this periodical covers technical, trade, and regional studies of French alcoholic
beverages. There are a food section, news and statistics, bibliographies, and book
reviews.

608.* **Robert Finigan's Private Guide to Wines,** 1972- . monthly. $36. Walnuts and Wine Inc., 724 Pine Street, San Francisco, CA 94108.

This consumer newsletter, by an industry consultant to the wine business, reviews the current vintages and recommends wines on a worldwide basis. It is not restricted to California wines. Two editions are published: one for California, and one for the rest of the world. The international edition presents a consumer-evaluative section on California wines. This is followed by a section examining wines from a particular region in the world and its vintage years, and by a section commenting on new releases. The California edition also includes material about various California restaurants and their wine lists. This information may or may not be useful to a library or to a collector, and thus if ordered, the newsletter's scope should be carefully considered and requested appropriately.

609. **Robert Lawrence Balzer's Private Guide to Food and Wine,** 1969- . monthly. $22.50 for 11 issues. The Wine Press Limited, 12791 Newport Avenue, Tustin, CA 92680.

This newsletter, put together by another wine consultant in California, reviews and rates all kinds of wines, but predominantly California ones. Tastings are conducted, the reader is led through the steps, and the wines are comparatively evaluated. All of the material here is balanced and informed, written by an experienced hand who has long been respected in the California wine industry.

610. **Society of Medical Friends of Wine Bulletin,** 1956- . semi-annually. Free (to members, who must be physicians or surgeons). P.O.B. 218, Sausalito, CA 94965.

While this society is a local one, usually restricted to the Bay Area, it does have a subscription mailing list of over 2,000. The nation-wide subscribers to this newsletter get a chance to read about the latest developments in the area of medical interests in wine and nutrition, and there are book reviews and bibliographic notices for other writings about medicine and wine.

611. **South African Wine and Beverage,** 1981- . bimonthly. 24 Rand Royal Publications (Pty) Ltd., 100 First Avenue, Box 1157, Edenvale 1610, South Africa.

A nicely put together periodical that presents the essential information about the South African wine industry: facts and figures, consumption, export-imports, retail stores, technical and trade materials, and tasting notes, along with some book reviews.

612. **The Underground Wineletter,** 1981- . bimonthly. $20. P.O.B. 663, Seal Beach, CA 90740.

Editor John Tilson here concentrates on esoteric and expensive wines, both domestic and imported, with a series of wine tastings and evaluations and critical notes.

613. **Vineyard View,** 1970- . quarterly. $5. Greyton H. Taylor Wine Museum, R. D. 2, Bully Hill Road, Hammondsport, NY 14840.

This periodical covers the New York state wine and grape industry, both historical and contemporary. Along with book reviews, there is also a food page dealing with wine cookery. An eclectic publication produced by one of the more colorful and eclectic personalities in the wine business.

614.*   **Vintage,** 1970- . monthly. $35. P.O.B. 2224, New York, NY 10163.
Editor Phil Seldon presents detailed tasting notes and specific buying recommendations for both domestic and imported wines. The range of the notes is from "Outstanding" to "Unacceptable." New releases are also reviewed, albeit not as critically as the formal tastings. About two to three hundred wines are covered in each issue. Articles seem to deal with exposures and investigations, certainly with "controversial" issues. But at the time *Vintage* was supported by its subscribers alone. Now that it is once again accepting advertising, its advocacy articles may not continue. Recent articles have been on the Beaufolais nouveau, cabernet sauvignon (236 wines rated and evaluated), sparkling wines (180 bottles here), and Hank Rubin's material on a cross-referenced listing of all important American wine competition winners (from 14 wine judgings).

615.   **What's Brewing?** 1972- . monthly. £ 7. Campaign for Real Ale, 34 Alma
        Road, St. Albans, Herts. AL1 3BW, England.
This is the superb newsletter compiled by the number one consumer advocacy group in the world: CAMRA. This group completely turned around the mighty giants of the British ale industry, an industry that was quickly becoming one of conglomerates and distributors of watery chemical beer. By withholding their services, many thousands of beer drinkers in Britain brought the industry to its knees. Sales declined so drastically, home-brew concentrates became so widely available that the industry had to respond with some real ale for a change. Support was given to the smaller independents, and the larger brewers gave in. Each now produces some kind of real ale. This newsletter continues to document the effort, by pointing out news and views from the independents, what the larger corporations are up to, where to go for the best ales in the land, and so forth. Twenty-five thousand subscribers cannot be wrong!

616.   **Which ? Wine Monthly,** 1983- . Price not reported. Consumers Association
        of Britain, 14 Buckingham Street, WC2N GDS England.
This new publication, now edited by Kathryn McWhirter (and with consultants Steven Spurrier and Edmund Penning-Rowsell), is a pocket-sized independent guide to wine buying. The tasting panel is identified, and the ratings are produced. For example, the April 1984 issue had ratings on forty dry sparkling wines for under £ 6 a bottle (under $9 U.S.), and this included two French Champagnes. Useful, even if it is meant for the British market.

617.   **Wine and Spirit,** 1974- . monthly. $60. 38 - 42 Hampton Road, Tedding-
        ton, Middlesex TW11 OJE, England.
This is a British trade publication, useful for its marketing data. There are reports from correspondents in various vineyards around the world, technical details, market figures and price movements, auction prices and bargains, new product information, and comparative tasting notes for merchants.

618.   **Wine Country: The Magazine from California's Winelands,** 1981- .
         monthly. $19. Napa Valley Magazine Inc., 4253 Park Road, Suite 4,
         Benicia, CA 94510.
Formerly entitled *Napa Valley Magazine's Wine Country,* this slick glossy covers
both California and imports from other countries. Recent articles have stressed
the California wine harvests, personalities such as Parducci and Joseph Phelps,
the wine cellars at Hart Castle, items on Inglenook and the Franciscan winery,
German beer, the Merlots of Bordeaux (and a comparison with the Merlots of
California), and the Rieslings of Germany (and a comparison with the Rieslings of
California). Regular columns feature wine with food, wine finds (bargain prices),
cooking with wine, wine showcase (new releases of California wines), notices of
wine classes and wine tastings, and news and views.

619.   **Wine East: News of Grapes and Wine in Eastern North America,** 1982- .
         bimonthly. $10. 620 North Pine Street, Lancaster, PA 17603.
This magazine is fast becoming the best magazine about non-California North
American wines. It covers the latest developments in the East, and its regular
articles always include an in-depth profile of a winery, features on grapes and
wines used in the East, and people. Excellent photography and design.

620.*   **Wine Spectator,** 1976- . semi-monthly. $30. M. Shanken Communications,
         400 East 51st Street, New York, NY 10022.
This is in tabloid format, with a circulation of around 21,000, and it is consumer-
oriented (unlike the other publications from Shanken Communications). But there
is also trade news here that might be of interest to retailers and consumers alike.
A regular feature "Special Report" presents ratings of categories of wines, including
"best buys," and there are new release recommendations as well. Other news items
that are covered include auction price results, a calendar of upcoming international
events, and anything that might be useful for last-minute insertion (since the
magazine does come out twice a month). Articles concentrate on food and wine.
There is a section on California wines, restaurants, wine and health, and so forth.
The only real drawback is in the "journalese" style of the articles: many items
are presented as news when they really are not.

621.   **Wine Tidings,** 1973- . $20 for 8 issues. Kylix International, Suite 414,
         5165 Sherbrooke Street West, Montreal PQ H4A 1T6, Canada.
Formerly known as *Tidings* and as the communicating newsletter for the wine-
buying club The Opimium Society, this glossy magazine has evolved in much the
same way as *The Friends of Wine* has. It is the only general, all-purpose magazine
for the Canadian wine reader in Canada, with recent articles on Madeira, zinfandel,
collecting wine memorabilia, Hawaii, Port, Bordeaux wine houses, Carmel wines
from Israel, Australia, and doctors and wine. Regular material includes news of
interest to Canadians, food and recipes, travel items, book reviews, vintage notes,
collectibles, tastings and ratings, and (with 1984) a regular column from Pamela
Vandyke Price.

622.   **Wine Value Reports,** 1983- . bimonthly. $24. Omnivent International,
         P. O. B. 1295, Barrington, IL 60010.

This periodical stresses value. The typeface is basically a computer print-out's with many abbreviations that the reader has to learn. The book presents its own ratings scheme, prices and a special values index. All of the wines evaluated are sorted by alphabet, price, and value. Each issue has special features, such as "The Best of Bordeaux," "Wonderful White Wines of California," "Matchup Food and Bordeaux," "How to Read a Label," and "California Chardonnays"—the latter indicating the hundred best values available at their press time.

623. **Wine World**, 1971- . bimonthly. $15. 6308 Woodman Avenue, Suite 115, Van Nuys, CA 91401.

This glossy publication has broadened its scope over the past decade, The "Taster's Guide" of ten wines has now become a "Buyer's Guide" of twenty-five wines; the critical writing has lessened in this feature, but the prices are now nationally available prices. The wines are reviewed rather than rated, but the notes do include some indication of whether the wine is ready for drinking now or needs more time in the cellar, as well as what temperature to serve it at, and what food to eat with it. All of this is extremely useful for the novice who just wants to be told the answer to the question: "What wine should I buy now and what do I do with it when I get home?" There are occasional recipes and food columns, some classified ads, and some book reviews. Opinion notes are given about bottles in a "letters to the editor" column. In 1983 *Wine World* embarked on a series of articles by Frank E. Johnson on individual Bordeaux château estates such as Château Pichon Longueville in Pauillac, with tasting notes, a description of the style of the wine, the label, and a history of the vineyards, etc. A California winery is profiled in each issue, and there are occasional articles on wine lore (literature, music, humor, art). Recently they have started a wine-buying club in conjunction with selected retail stores, almost like Les Amis du Vin, called the "20/20 Wine Club." Members are supposed to buy some of the twenty-five wines evaluated.

624. **Wineletter**, 1967- . monthly. $12. Phyllis Van Kriedt, P.O.B. 70, Mill Valley, CA 94941.

This is very similar to *California Wineletter*, with its news and views, but it is meant for the consumer and not for the trade.

625.* **Wines and Vines: The Authoritative Voice of the Grape and Wine Industry**, 1919- . monthly. $22. Hiaring Co., 1800 Lincoln Avenue, San Rafael, CA 94901.

This is the American wine trade industry magazine, with comprehensive coverage of the U.S. production of wine through marketing statistics, charts, and news. Articles deal with proprietors and grapes. Foreign coverage is excellent, but most of the material is in the form of short news releases and relates directly to the agent or importer of the products. There is an annual directory issue in December, one that lists every single winery that has a B.A.T.F. license and bond. For 1983, there were 1,037 of these. The directory issue is available separately for an extra payment of $20. Recent articles were about the German wine laws of 1971, London wine bars, a history of wine packaging (amphorae, corks, pitchers, etc.: this is evolving into a regular column), grape diseases, wines of New Mexico, and wines of British

Columbia. The ads stress new equipment and manufacturers, but there is also news of people, supplies and suppliers, markets, government actions, a calendar of events, notes about changing ownerships, statistics about anything and everything, a food column for menus and recipes that either use wine or call for wine as accompaniment. A good publication, highly useful for the California wine producer and other North American wine producers as well.

626.   **Winestate,** 1983- . Monthly. $20. 900 Santa Fe Avenue, Albany, CA 94706.
This colorful glossy, just getting established, reviews, wines, foods, and spirits, with a concentration on California.

627.   **Wining & Dining: Eating Out and Entertaining In,** 1980- . Monthly. £ 9.50. H. S. Publishing, 16 Ennismore Avenue, London W4 1SF, England.
A glossy publication, stressing the characteristics of menu preparations and wine selections, whether one eats out or dines at home. Good, gracious, elegant living.

628.   **Wynboer,** 1970- . monthly. 24 Rand. K.W.V., P.O.B. 528, Suider-Paarl 7624, South Africa.
A useful publication from the vast K.W.V. cooperative, stressing the materials available through the K.W.V. It is a self-help periodical for the wine producers, grape growers, and estates of the Paarl area in South Africa, with technical material and trade news.

10 Brewing Beer and Wine Making at Home

As of 1985, any adult may make wine and beer for personal family use and not for sale, in the United States, and no registration is necessary in the United States. A one-person household may make 100 gallons of wine and 100 gallons of beer per year, and a household with more than one member may make 200 gallons of wine and 200 gallons of beer in a calendar year. The limits are the same for Canada, but the Canadian beer maker is "supposed" to get a free license from Revenue Canada's Customs and Excise Branch before he or she can make beer at home. In effect, this is registering. But the regulation is not enforced, and application forms are not normally available at wine and beer supplier outlets.

The rising cost of commercial wines has encouraged wine making at home, even more so in Canada and Great Britain, where the taxes on alcoholic beverages are punitive. In many cases, homemade beverages are the only category choices available: there may be no commercially available fruit or vegetable wines, nor ales, bitters, and stouts in the region. If you want it, you have to make it yourself. Handbooks, easy-to-use equipment, plastics, and good concentrates have all contributed in no small measure to the increased interest of the hobbyist. Unfortunately, some of the books present problems: the British and Canadian texts use Imperial measurements and tend to produce a semidry wine or beer, and all texts use exact measures and exact recipes that do not take into account the balance of the final product as the drinker might appreciate it. While this chapter concerns beer and wine making at home (and "gentleman" vineyardists) and deals with "amateur" manuals, there are certainly useful materials available in chapter 8 that deal with technical literature, and in chapter 11, which covers the professional associations of commercial wine makers and brew masters.

629.*   Acton, Bryan and Peter M. Duncan. **Making Wines Like Those You Buy.** 2d ed. Andover, Hants., England: Amateur Winemaker Press, 1968. 160p. illus. £ 1.50 paper.

This team of amateurs has also written other books on home wine making, including materials on making wines from concentrates. This particular book has a strong component on finishing off the wines, such as the addition of glycerol to create a better body. Other, additional material covers sparkling wines, Madeira, Port, sherry, and vermouth. Amateur Winemaker Society is the leading British group, quite similar to the American Wine Society; their materials, of course, have a strong British orientation.

630.　Adams, John F. **An Essay on Brewing, Vintage and Distillation, Together with Selected Remedies for Hangover Melancholia; or, How to Make Booze.** Garden City, N.Y.: Doubleday, 1970. 108p. illus. out of print.

The author's purpose is a simple one: "to write a book about wine making and brewing based on the thesis that the person reading the book could actually do it." Adams tells it all: what equipment is necessary, what ingredients to use, the fallacies of famous rumors about making booze, and finally, what to do about the hangovers that result from reading this book. Included are some hard-to-find recipes such as bathtub gin and white lightning.

631.　Adkins, Jan. **The Craft of Making Wine.** New York: Walker, 1983. 91p. illus. index. $4.95 paper.

Originally issued in 1972, this guide takes the reader on a tour of the families of wine, discusses the tools of making it, provides a step-by-step guide to red wine and white wine, talks of country and flower wines, and discusses concentrates, sparkling wines, and a host of related topics. Reading a wine maker's manual is one thing, but actually being able to turn the pages and visualize each operation in pleasant and instructive drawings is another.

632.　Anderson, Stanley F. and Raymond Hull. **The Advanced Winemaker's Practical Guide.** Toronto, Canada: Longmans Canada, 1975. 120p. illus. index. $4.95 paper.

This oversized book is more for the experienced hand, but is listed ahead of Anderson's other books because of alphabetical order. Part One contains a high amount of technical jargon, with data on how to judge wines, using a 20-point score. Part Two has seventy recipes for more advanced work, including sherries and other fortified wines.

633.　Anderson, Stanley F. and Raymond Hull. **The Art of Making Beer.** New York: E. P. Dutton/Hawthorn, 1971. 119p. illus. index. $3.95 paper.

This is a clear, concise, step-by-step manual for the beginning beer maker. It lays down explicitly the principles that govern the quality of the home brew. The importance of sugar control, often overlooked in other guides, is thoroughly explored, as well as all other operations (such as brewing, bottling, storage, and use of the hydrometer). The illustrations are clear and instructive, and the explanation of equipment eliminates the mysteries that many other manuals don't dispell. Several dozen types of beers and ales are explained, as well as basic instructions for making cider and perry.

634.*　Anderson, Stanley F. and Raymond Hull. **The Art of Making Wine.** New York: Dutton/Hawthorn, 1971. 181p. illus. $3.50 paper.

Anderson is the operator (founder) of the famous Wine Art chain of stores which sell wine- and beer-making supplies, materials, and equipment. His name has become synonymous with home brewing and home vinification. This exceptionally clear guide is a simple explanation of the principles of wine making. Most of the common problems of the beginner are thoroughly discussed, and directions for adjusting and adapting procedures to meet local conditions are welcome additions. The book is clear, simple, and instructive.

635.   Beadle, Leigh P. **Making Fine Wines and Liqueurs.** New York: Farrar Straus Giroux, 1972. 110p. $4.95.
Beadle presents modern-day recipes for wines, and some delightful hints for the manufacture of infusions and liqueurs (using both bought and homemade syrups). A very practical book.

636.*   Beadle, Leigh P. **The New Brew It Yourself: A Complete Guide to the Brewing of Beer, Ale, Stout and Mead.** 3d ed. New York: Farrar Straus Giroux, 1981. 109p. illus. $5.95.
This is one of the more useful home-brewing books, especially for beginners. It is all here: specific gravities, hops, campden tablets, primary fermentation, use of enzymes and yeast, beer recipes, and illustrations. This is basically a beer book, with some other material on mead. The most important consideration here is the stress on "what can go wrong" and the cures for bad beer-making habits.

637.   Berry, Cyril J. J. **Amateur Winemaker Recipes.** Andover, Hants., England: Amateur Winemaker Press, 1971. 124p. illus. £ 1 paper.
Another recipe-packed home wine book from *The Amateur Winemaker*. The dozens of wines included range from the common dandelion to the exotic woodruff, from parsnip-fig to celery-apple. This book is included because of its wide variety of ingredients from which a palatable wine can be made. Non-British oenologists, though, may wish to cut the sugar recommendations in half, but only after finishing off the wine.

638.   Berry, Cyril J. J. **First Steps in Winemaking: A Complete Month-by-Month Guide.** 9th ed. Andover, Hants., England: Amateur Winemaker Press, 1970. 149p. illus. £ 1.25 paper.

639.   Berry, Cyril J. J. **Home Brewed Beers and Stouts: A Handbook to the Brewing of Ales, Beers and Stouts at Home, from Barley, Malt Extract and Dried Malt Extract.** 3d ed. Andover, Hants., England: Amateur Winemaker Press, 1970. 132p. illus. £ 1.50 paper.

640.   Berry, Cyril J. J. **130 New Winemaking Recipes.** 2d ed. Andover, Hants., England: Amateur Winemaker Press, 1968. 132p. illus. £ 1.20 paper.

641.   Berry, Cyril J. J. **Wine Making with Canned and Dried Fruit.** Andover, Hants., England: Amateur Winemaker Press, 1968. 96p. illus. £ 0.75 paper.
Since its beginning in 1957, the British monthly magazine *The Amateur Winemaker* has become one of the world's most important publications for the home wine maker. A spinoff of the magazine has been the series of guides, manuals, cookbooks, and hobby books for the home vintner and brewer. Berry, as editor of

the magazine, has had a string of interesting books. These four concern wines, beers, and fruit wines, as well as cider, perry, and mead. The directions are all there, as well as about 130 recipes per book. There are also tips for judging and exhibiting. Most of the wines finish off sweet; the British like them that way. The best method for cutting down is to work backwards and produce a dry wine (use a hydrometer), and then add a sugar syrup to make up the sweetness that *you* like.

642. Bravery, H. E. **Home Brewing without Failures: How to Make Your Own Beer, Ale, Stout and Cider.** New York: Arco Books, 1966. 159p. illus. index. $5.95.

643. Bravery, H. E. **Successful Winemaking at Home.** rev. ed. New York: Arco Books, 1968. 112p. illus. $2.50 paper.

Bravery has produced a couple of complete books, for both beginners and experienced hands. For the beginner he explains simple methods, using readily prepared malt extracts and dried hops, or processed grape juice and concentrates; for the more advanced brewer, grain malts, mashing and mixing grain malts, and extracts are discussed, while the advanced wine maker gets a peek at the techniques involved in grape crushing and sulphiting. There is also information here about commercial beer making and wine making; and there are ruminations on cider and mead, and a few recipes that are hard to find elsewhere, such as treacle beer, rose-petal mead, and brown ale.

644. Brown, John Hull. **Early American Beverages.** Rutland, Vt.: C. E. Tuttle, 1966. 171p. illus. bibliog. index. $5 paper.

This manual contains scads of great old-time beverage recipes—some potent, some not. All types of colonial drinks and the methods of preparing them are included. Items here include posset, sassafras mead, flummery causle, spruce beer, and absinthe ratafia—all handled in the "traditional way." Interspersed with the recipes are bits of historical lore on American drinking habits.

645. Brown, Sanborn C. **Wines and Beers of Old New England: A How-to-Do-It History.** Hanover, N.H.: Univ. Press of New England, 1978. 187p. illus. index. $12.50; $5.95 paper.

This interesting and readable little book gives the history and early techniques of wine and beer making in colonial times of the New England states. The recipes here include material on how to make present-day wines, cider, and birch beer based on traditional methods.

646. Burch, Byron. **Quality Brewing: A Guide Book for the Home Production of Fine Beers.** San Rafael, Calif.: Joby Books-Clear Fermentations, 1983. 48p. illus. bibliog. index. $2.50 paper.

An interesting little book with a few modern, up-to-date recipes for making lagers at home. The photographs make good illustrations for techniques and what the final product should look like.

647.   Carey, Mary. **Step-By-Step Winemaking.** New York: Golden Press, 1973. 64p. illus. $3.95 paper.

This is a very practical "how-to" book, with many colorful illustrations, meant especially for the beginning wine maker. Material covers preparing and crushing the must, adjusting the sugar content, yeast nutrients, primary and secondary fermentation, clarifying, acid tests, bottling, and aging. There is a special section on "what to do if"—on when fermentation seizes and stops; chlorinated water; over-acidity; yeastiness; cloudiness; and so forth. Reds, whites, and rosés are covered, as well as wine making all year round (using concentrates, fruit wines, and flower wines).

648.   Delmon. P. J. and B. C. A. Turner. **Quick and Easy Winemaking from Concentrates and Fruit Juices.** New York: Hippocrene, 1973. 107p. illus. index. $6.95.

The process of making wines from juices and concentrates is a relatively easy one, considering the problems involved in pressing and racking raw fruit. Various recipes are offered here to avoid the pitfalls that could exist. However, there are other difficulties here to watch for: British measurements and product availability (Polish bilberries, Australian apricots).

649.   Duncan, Peter M. **Wine Making with Concentrates.** rev. ed. Andover, Hants., England: American Winemaker Press, 1974. 90p. illus. £ 0.90.

There is an incredible amount of business being done in England with grape concentrates, especially since there are so few native grapes (and those are usually reserved for commercial wines). This handy book has proved popular in the making of different kinds of grape and nongrape wines using grape juice as a basis.

650.*   Eckhardt, Fred. **A Treatise on Lager Beers: How to Make Good Beer at Home.** 7th ed. Portland, Ore.: F. Eckhardt Associates, 1983. 96p. $2.95 paper.

A modern, up-to-date book on making a particularly difficult type of home brew. Ales are so much easier to make at home, and the British, Canadians, and Australians do this with ales. But the American taste is for lagers. In 1977, Eckhardt wrote a book entitled *Beer Tasting and Evaluation for the Amateur.*

651.   Foster, Charles. **Winemaking, Brewing, and Other Drinks.** Charlotte, Vt.: Garden Way Publishing, 1983. 80p. illus. index. $8.95.

Garden Way specializes in publishing books about the natural life, with cooking from fruits and vegetables that you grow yourself. This book, first published in England, is no exception; it is a short manual on the preparation of materials for home wine making and home brewing. It is a good introduction for the novice, but of course it lacks the depth required to be of use to the more experienced beverage maker.

652.*   Geary, Don. **The Home Brewer's Handbook.** Blue Ridge Summit, Pa.: TAB Books Inc., 1983. 199p. illus. index. $15.95; $10.25 paper.

More than half of this book concerns the basics of beer making at home: the brewing process, additives, equipment, sterilizing, ingredients, how to make it from a can and how to make it from scratch, various mixtures for balance of the final product, storing and aging. He deals nicely with the issue of exploding bottles, although he is being too cautious, despite the danger. The book opens with the origins of beer and the distinction between ale and lager. He gives eleven recipes for canned extracts to be used in beer making, and thirty-two recipes for using ground whole grain malts. Near the end of the book, Geary also introduces alcoholic cordials (using vodka) and other alcoholic drinks such as root beer, applejack, spruce beer, and apple mead. There is a section on troubleshooting, on suppliers (along with a mail-order list of addresses), and a glossary of terms. A very good book for the American market.

653.   Gennery-Taylor, Mrs. (pseud). **Easy to Make Wine: With Additional Recipes for Cocktails, Cider, Beer, Fruit Syrups and Herb Teas.** 3d ed. Tadworth, Surrey, England: Elliot Rightway, 1980. 124p. illus. index. £ 0.75 paper.

The key to this slim guide, first published in 1957, is simplicity and economy. It is one of the few vintner aids that ignores fancy equipment and recommends wine making in saucepans, preserving pans, and earthenware bowls. The information is clear and direct; there is added material on remedies, Christmas drinks, the wine calendar, dandelion coffee recipes, and other products that clearly fall into the "peasant wine" category of clove and carrot, marigold and tomato, wheat and barley mixtures. There is also some "medicinal" advice, such as "cowslip wine will cure jaundice."

654.   Hardwick, Homer. **Winemaking at Home.** rev. ed. New York: Funk & Wagnalls, 1970. 258p. illus. index. $8.95.

One of the best all-purpose, good wine making books, especially for the North American home vintner. Its real strength lies in presenting data that will prevent the amateur from spoiling his wine through unsanitary conditions, microorganisms, or temperature fluctuations. It does not imply that wine making is simple enough for anyone to attempt, and in dealing with the possible problems, Hardwick shows the reader the way to fine wine. The book is well illustrated and capably written, with over two hundred recipes (originally written in 1954).

655.*   Hutchinson, Peggy. **Home Made Wine Secrets.** rev. ed. London: W. Foutsham, 1976. 129p. illus. $6.95.

An excellent amateur manual for winemakers, first written in the 1920s, which does not take into account the explosion of interest in oenology and the subsequent flood of available wine making products. It has a rather folksy approach, combined with simple instructions for a blend of enjoyable reading and understandable directions. It has a really good and clear explanation of how to unstick a stuck fermentation, but unfortunately it has no index for troubleshooting.

656.   Jagendorf, Moritz. **Folk Wines, Cordials and Brandies: Ways to Make Them Together with Some Lore, Reminiscences, and Wise Advice for Enjoying Them.** New York: Vanguard, 1963. 414p. illus. index. $15.

This sage approach to the folk art of creating one's own intoxicants is thought of as the best of the country wine manuals. Jagendorf intersperses his instructions with meandering memories, wisdom tempered with the humor of mistakes, and gentle advice on the use and abuse of what this book is about—the creation of excellent wines and other spirits. Buried in the absorbing narrative is much information on country wines, musts, aging, seasons for fermenting, flavors, and fruits. A thoroughly charming reading experience.

657.* Kurth, Heinz and Geneste Kurth. **Winemaking at Home**. Scarborough, Canada: Prentice-Hall Canada, 1983. 80p. illus. bibliog. index. $7.95 paper.

This is a clear and direct book that pulls no punches. For example, the authors state that for berry wines the minimum storage is four years (!), in order to develop the very complex flavors and nuances. Home wine makers are not used to books that tell them they have to wait virtually "forever." There are kits that can produce cheap wines after twenty-eight days, and these are obviously disdained by the true home vintner. Four years *is* a long time, and I am sure that the results are worth it; but meanwhile ...? This book deals with small or large quantities, expressed in both metric and imperial measurements. There are step-by-step illustrations and pictures of the equipment; both are exceptionally reproduced as drawings in full color. The method used here is direct from fruit must, and the topics discussed include bacteria, water, sugar, acid, tannin, and the final blending and finishing off of the fermentation. Types of wines include floral, berry, fruit, herbs, and vegetables. Most ingredients for the 46 recipes can be had from the supermarket.

658. Line, David. **Beer Kits and Brewing**. Andover, Hants., England: Amateur Winemaker Press, 1980. 160p. illus. index. £ 1.60 paper.

659. Line, David. **The Big Book of Brewing**. Andover, Hants., England: Amateur Winemaker Press, 1974. 256p. illus. index. £ 1.80 paper.

660. Line, David. **Brewing Beers Like Those You Buy**. Andover, Hants., England: Amateur Winemaker Press, 1978. 168p. illus. index. £ 1.40 paper.

These three heavily illustrated books convey just about all there is to know about making beers at home, usually from a can of extract but also from malted scratch. The first book deals with the concentrates, the second one covers some of the lore of beer making, and the third book is for the more than amateur beer maker who wants to finish off his beers with a premium taste and flavor. Accent is on ales, but lagers, cider, and perries are also here.

661.* Lundy, Desmond. **Leisure Winemaking**. Calgary, Canada: Detselig Enterprises, 1978. 823p. illus. bibliog. charts. $12.95.

Lundy's book lies midway between a do-it-yourself manual and a textbook for the professional. It is easy to read (despite some spelling and grammatical errors), and it has plenty of line drawings. Topics covered include sterilization with sulphites, equipment (crushers, presses, wooden barrels), conducting tests, and a discussion of wine ailments, pectic enzymes, racking and filtering, sugar types, acid control, yeasts, and nutrients. Basic recipes are given for table wines, fortified wines, fruit wines, and ciders (for both fruits and concentrates), with good detail on how to formulate your own recipes. This latter is a unique and useful feature in the sea of amateur books. There are lots of tables, charts, mathematical equations, and diagrams—all designed to keep the knowledgeable home wine maker happy. All *opinions* (to Lundy's mind) are sourced to a 4-page bibliography so that the reader knows what is fact and what is speculation, and can read further on the speculations and form his own judgment.

662.* Mares, William. **Making Beer.** New York: Knopf, 1984. 170p. illus. bibliog. index. $7.95 paper.
This book is more a story of how Mares became a proficient home brewer; it takes the reader through the steps that Mares himself took to complete the necessary processes and techniques. Along the way, then, topics such as these are discussed: types of malts and recipes, the importance of the water used, the varieties of the hops, the differences in yeasts, the equipment needed. Other material here includes a short history of beer, some profiles of American brewers and breweries, his travels, and a glossary.

663. Miller, Mark. **Wine: A Gentleman's Game.** New York: Harper & Row, 1984. 224p. illus. index. $19.95.
Miller is the founder of the Benmarl Vineyards, which overlook the Hudson River. This book is about "the adventures of an amateur winemaker turned professional." Miller bought the vineyard in the 1950s when he was still a commercial artist (he did the illustrations in this book), and later he decided to turn his hobby of wine making into a full-time career. It took him ten long years to produce award-winning red and white wines. To start from scratch would take almost as long, since the vines bear little usable fruit during their first four or five years, and red wines should be stored for another four years or so before drinking.

664. Mitchell, John R. **Improving Your Finished Wines.** Andover, Hants., England: Amateur Winemaker Press, 1978. 111p. illus. index. £1.20 paper.

665. Mitchell, John R. **Scientific Winemaking Made Easy.** Andover, Hants., England: Amateur Winemaker Press, 1975. 246p. illus. index. £1.50 paper.
These two books are designed for the more advanced amateur wine maker. They discuss both how to improve the efficiency of the winemaking operation and how to finish off the wine after secondary fermentation, in order to give it the *gout* necessary for a tasting.

666. Moore, William. **Home Beermaking.** 2d ed. Oakland, Calif.: Ferment Press, 1983. 72p. illus. index. $3.95 paper.
A useful little book, jam-packed with the usual beer recipes. New to this edition are chapters on beer design and steam beer (one of the great American beer creations).

667. Morse, Roger. **Making Mead.** New York: Scribner's, 1980. 128p. illus. index. $9.95.

A nifty single-purpose book, if all that you are interested in is the making of mead, or honey wine. Material here includes a history, some recipes for a basic wine plus variations (dry to sweet, light to heavy), and the different kinds of methods and obtaining of supplies, for the different kinds of honeys available.

668.   Novitski, Joseph. **A Vineyard Year**. Photographs by Nick Pavloff. San Francisco, Calif.: Chronicle Books, 1983. 120p. illus. $14.95 paper.
Novitski was a former correspondent for the New York *Times*; this book documents his first year as a viticulturist. This was in Dry Creek Valley, sixty miles northwest of San Francisco, and the vineyards grew zinfandel, gamay and carignane grape varieties. He bought the land in 1977 for $585,000 and sold it in 1982 and 1983 (two separate divisions of land) for a total of $1,200,000. This book, with its one hundred color and forty black-and-white pictures documents his 1980 growing year, one that had a long, cool summer that was a good year for wines. Beginning with the pruning in the winter, Novitski takes us through the year from flowering to harvesting. So much of what happens depends on the climate and the ability to do a lot of hard work fast. Throughout the book, the neighbors and farmhands are introduced. An enjoyable, unhurried account.

669.*   Nury, F. S. and K. C. Fugelsang. **The Winemaker's Guide: Essential Information for Wine Making from Grapes or Other Fruit**. 2d ed. Santa Cruz, Calif.: Western Tanager, 1982. 106p. illus. index. $5.95 paper.
This is a useful book for the home wine maker, although its primary audience is the professional. The material is arranged in *aide memoire* style. Useful for checking that elusive fact.

670.   Papazian, Charles. **Joy of Brewing**. rev. ed. Boulder, Colo.: Log Boom Brewing, 1980. 88p. illus. $4.50 paper.
One of the newest features of the amateur brewer is turning professional and operating a microbrewery (in Canada and in England, sometimes the microbrewery is attached to a tavern for the express purpose of dispensing draught beer only, with no take-out service). This is the story of one such firm, one that began making beer for fun and drinking and then expanding so that it could be sold to their friends and to others.

671.   Reese, M. R. **Better Beer and How to Brew It**. Charlotte, Vt.: Garden Way Publishing, 1981. 128p. illus. index. $6.95 paper.
A companion book to Foster's *Winemaking* (see entry 651), also published by Garden Way. It is a good introduction to the whole field for the novice, giving choices between extracts from a can and malting from scratch.

672.   Shales, Ken. **Brewing Better Beers**. Andover, Hants., England: Amateur Winemaker Press, 1970. 78p. illus. £ 1.25 paper.
This is a lively paperback with many recipes for all types of malt liquors, from light lagers to the blackest double stout. But it is really an addition to the advanced brewer's library, since many of the recipes are complicated.

673.   Tarr, Yvonne Young. **Super Easy Step-By-Step Winemaking**. New York:
        Vintage Books, 1975. 108p. illus. index. $6.95 paper.
This is a useful little book by a commercial food writer. It is basic, it is American,
and it is in large print (which means that you can see it at a distance if you are
following along with the production, or at least you will not be mistaken about
anything). Covered are fruit and flower wines, ingredients to use, and equipment.
Recipes appear for dandelion, violet, rose-petal, strawberry, date, peach, and apple
wine (among others). Concluding material deals with how to bottle and how to
store the wine, as well as a section on troubleshooting and sources of supply.

674.*   Tayleur, W. H. T. **The Penguin Book of Home Brewing and Wine Making**.
        Baltimore, Md.: Penguin Books, 1973. 336p. illus. index. $4.95 paper.
Tayleur, author of many brewing histories, ran a professional advisory service for
amateurs. The entire book is very technical and is recommended for the serious
student. Copious explanatory notes cover, in detail, fermentation, yeast, basic
ingredients, equipment, and processes. He goes into the re-use of yeast (a topic other
books ignore), filtering, and clarifying (always tricky). Section 2 covers brewing:
history, uses of hops and malt, kits, and the formulation of recipes (which include
the rare Brapple and Rowan Ale). Section 3 (the largest) covers wines: history,
kits, concentrates versus grapes, wines of fruit and flower (dried, berries, herbs,
cereal, root, vegetables, leaves, tree saps), and sparkling wines. There is an important discussion on blending. Section 4 covers fortified wines and liqueurs, including
port and the Pearson Square. Section 5 is for cider and perry; section 6 is honey
and mead. There are conversion tables and a well-developed index for each section
so that there is no confusion as to what is being looked up and where. The
glossary has at the beginning of each definition an identification pertaining to
whether the term is used in brewing or in wine making.

675.   Taylor, Walter S. and Richard P. Vine. **Home Winemaker's Handbook**.
        New York: Harper and Row, 1973. 195p. $9.95.
For the eastern wine drinker, the name Taylor is quite familiar. This Taylor is the
son of the New York State wine family that grows all of those grapes in the western
part of the state. Taylor, who now operates his own experimental winery, covers
much the same ground as do other well-known wine making manuals. However,
the fascinating section on growing grapes for personal uses is well worth reading.

676.   Tritton, S. M. **Tritton's Guide to Better Wine and Beer Making for
        Beginners**. New York: Dover, 1970. 153p. illus. index. $2.95 paper.
Originally published by Faber and Faber in 1965, this Dover reprint is a gift to
vintners wherever they practice their art. The complete wine- and beer-making
book, it contains a great deal of information packed into a few pages. The chapter
on racking, stabilization, clarification, and fining of wine is intelligent and time
saving. Particularly interesting is the introductory chapter for beginners, in which
the author recommends starting out making three simple wines (orange, apricot,
and apple)—a sensible approach, since grapes can prove difficult for novices to
handle. Also included is material on aperitifs, liqueurs, showing and judging of
wines, and wine faults, with preventions and cures.

677.*   Turner, Ben C. A. **The Compleat Home Winemaker and Brewer.** rev. ed.
         London: Emblem, 1982. 160p. illus. index. $19.95 paper.

Turner is a prolific writer in the area of home wine making and brewing. In this
oversized, colorful book he sums up a great deal of his knowledge. Originally
published in 1976, this revised edition contains some 55 pages directly on wine
making (history, processes, ingredients) and 30 pages on brewing (plus mead,
cider, and perry). The balance of the book is a year planner and calendar that is
highly useful, for Turner tells you when to make wines for the coming months
ahead, as the fruits and vegetables go into season, and how to have wines available
for seasonal holidays (and so that you don't run short). The recipes are arranged by
month, with about 12-15 per month, covering fruit (canned, fresh, dried), flowers
and leaves, grains and vegetables, and herbs and spices. For example, for January
Turner states that you need parsnips, oranges, lager, and barley wine, for "they all
need long storage and should be nicely matured by next Christmas." In March,
Turner directs you to make sap wine and wines from grains. The recipes are for a
minimum of six bottles (one Imperial gallon); they can, of course, be scaled
upwards. The range of data is from beginner to advanced, with chapters on technological reasons, ingredients and equipment, problems and solutions, bottling, racking, and serving. Also, there is information on exhibiting beers and wines, much
more important now that the American federal government has legalized home-
vinted wine exhibitions. Recipes are also employed for punches and mulled wines.

678.   Turner, Ben C. A. **Wines from the Countryside.** London: B. T. Batsford,
         1984; distr. by David & Charles. 120p. illus. index. $16.95.

Here is more common sense about making nongrape alcoholic beverages. Turner
opens with a short history of *home* wine making, tracing it from the seventeenth
century up through the modern times in the United Kingdom. He details some
modern equipment and kits that would be needed, and then proceeds to list the
various types of wines that can be made from surplus agricultural products. Many
of these need not be bought, for they can come from a garden or an open field.
He gives material about apricots, berries of different styles, cherries, currants,
plums, and oranges, as well as ciders from apple and pears (and wines from apples
and pears). He proceeds with data about wines from flowers, leaves, roots
parsnips, carrots, potatoes), and stems (celery) as well as herbs in general. Other
beverages discussed include beer and mead (made from nectar) and some kinds
of liqueurs that need either extracts or grain alcohol for the base. Some of the
rewarding appendices include material on troubleshooting and some notes on the
acid levels of popular fruits with notes on the plants to avoid (they are poisonous)
such as ivy, orchids, lilac, honeysuckle, and so forth. The many line drawings are
useful, graceful illustrations. Turner gives us about one hundred recipes that are
fairly easy to follow, and for small quantities such as for a gallon or so.

679.*   Turner, Ben C. A. and C. J. J. Berry. **The Winemaker's Companion: A
         Handbook for Those Who Make Wine at Home.** Toronto: Mills and Boon,
         1972. 208p. illus. index. $9.95.

This perennial best-seller was first issued in 1960; this is its first North American
issue, with some special editing for the North American market. All quantities
are in Imperial, U.S., and metric measurements. At the time, Turner was President

of the National Association of Amateur Winemakers (U.K.), while Berry was editor of *The Amateur Winemaker* magazine. Seventy-one different kinds of fruit and vegetable wine recipes appear at the back; these are actually secondary to the scope of the book, which is a detailed explanation of home fermentations. Material also includes items about troubleshooting, maintaining a cellar, keeping records, entering competitions and exhibitions, and the various wine-making associations. Other material covered: beers, mead, cider, and perry (along with appropriate recipes).

680.* Wagner, Philip. **Grapes into Wine: The Art of Wine Making in America.** New York: Vantage Press, 1982. 302p. illus. index. $6.95 paper.

This is a classic, practical manual for the small producer and home wine maker. It was first published in 1933 as *American Wines and How to Make Them*, in order to help the amateur during Prohibition, and was revised over the years (last in 1976). Wagner emphasizes the principles of wine making and believes that America can produce wines of great quality, as shown by the chapters on the history of American viticulture. Chapters on French, New York, and California wines and wine growing all contribute to his practical use of wines. Exact detail is presented on equipment and layout design for wine making, supplemented by charts and excellent illustrations. All of this is held together by a superb introduction, to the background of what wines are all about. There is little here on other forms of nongrape wines, but the book is extremely useful for anyone contemplating a "boutique" winery.

681.* Wagner, Philip M. **A Wine-Grower's Guide.** 3d ed. New York: Knopf, 1980. 224p. illus. index. $10.95.

Wagner, former newspaper man and former owner of Boordy Vineyards in Maryland, here emphasizes grape growing rather than wine making. He presents a detailed description of the many varieties available for growth in North America (*lambrusco* and *vinifera* strains, among others), their common and uncommon hybrids, and their methods of cultivation. A good book for the grape grower, for the viticulturalist who likes to grow a few acres of grapes and make his own wine.

682. **Wine Art Winemaking Recipe Booklet.** rev. ed. Vancouver, Canada: Wine Art, 1983. 64p. illus. $1.39 paper.

683. **Wine Art Beermaking Recipe Booklet.** rev. ed. Vancouver, Canada: Wine Art, 1983. 64p. illus. $1.39 paper.

Wine Art is a series of franchised stores, founded by Stanley Anderson, that sell wine and beer concentrates. The directions and recipes here are keyed to the tins of concentrates and packages of acid blends sold by the store. There are also some recipes for wines from natural juices. These books are regularly revised in order to keep abreast of changes.

It would be a poor wine maker or brewer, professional or amateur, who relied entirely on "book" sources for information about beers and wines. Informative data is conveyed through other types of communication channels (and this is what this book is all about). In common, then, with the rest of this book (which deals basically with the armchair drinker, the spectator rather than the doer), what remains in this chapter on the amateur vintner is an explanation of further sources of data that must be checked out if you are to stay abreast of changes and developments in the technology of wine production. It is simply not enough to just read a book and follow recipes; you must join groups (or form one), get in touch with government agencies who are looking out for the vineyardist, take courses from people more knowledgeable than yourself, peruse catalogs, and read magazines for the home vintner.

Government Documents

Government documents are primary documents, written by experts and available at a low cost, expressly for the encouragement of home wine making. They are available from most state departments of agriculture as well as from the federal government. Two good examples of the latter are:

684.   D. R. MacGregor's **Home Preparation of Juices, Wines, and Ciders** (available as Publication No. 1460, Department of Agriculture, Ottawa, Canada) and

685.   **Growing American Bunch Grapes** (available as Farmers' Bulletin No. 2123, Government Printing Office, Washington, D.C.).

Extension Courses

Many universities and colleges, particularly the state-run schools, offer extension courses in home wine making. In many of the agricultural states there are courses in home grape growing as well. All of these courses are supported by a publications program that probably is based on regional experiments with regard to grape growing. These publications are normally available free, or at modest cost to out-of-state residents. Some examples are:

686.   Carroll, D. E. **Making Muscadine Table Wine.** (Dept. of Food Science, North Carolina State Univ., Raleigh, NC: this pamphlet concerns the strong-tasting Scuppernong wine).

687.   Eakin, J. H., Jr. **Winemaking as a Hobby** (Pennsylvania State Univ.), Box 6000, University Park, PA 16802).

688.   Fessler, J. H. **Guidelines to Practical Winemaking.** (Rockridge Laboratories, Elmwood Station, Berkeley, CA 94705).

689.   Gallander, J. F. **Wine Making for the Amateur.** (Ohio Extension Bulletin No. 549, Co-operative Extension Service, Ohio State Univ., Columbus, OH).

690.   Robinson, W. C. **Experimental Wine Production.** (New York State Agricultural Experimental Station, Geneva, NY).

691.   Robinson, W. C. **Homemade Wine** (Cornell Extension Bulletin IB 84, Cornell University, Ithaca, NY).

692.   Vine, R. P. **Making Wine at Home** (Co-operative Extension Service, Mississippi State Univ., Mississippi State, MS).

Manuals

There are many manuals and self-help texts available from the various associations and periodicals that deal with home wine making. The National Association of Amateur Winemakers (U.K.) sponsors *The Amateur Winemaker* magazine and has a publishing arm of books by a single author that are available in British bookstores. Many are annotated above as commercial books. The American Wine Society is a similarly constituted association, but its publication program is restricted to orders through the association. For example, it has many manuals at $2.50 each, such as: *Elements of Wine Tasting; Sensory Identification of Wine Constitutents; Still Wines from Grapes; Wine Blending; A New Method of Making Sparkling Wine at Home; Wine Analysis; The Use of Sulfur in the Preservation of Wines,* and so forth. There are also reprints from the *AMS Journal* (about two dozen or so articles) at $2.50 each; these are highly useful but specialized.

Associations

There are three interesting national associations. On a regional basis there are many clubs and activities for fun, but all three national groupings are also for serious workers.

692a.   **American Homebrewers Association,** P.O.B. 287, Boulder, CO 80306.
This group publishes the quarterly journal *Zymurgy* ($8 a year) and sponsors the National Homebrew and Microbrewery Conference (the fifth one was held in 1983), always in Boulder, Colo.

692b.   **American Wine Society,** 3006 Latta Road, Rochester, NY 14612.
With 5,000 members (founded in 1967), this group publishes the quarterly *AWS Journal,* manuals and various bulletins and essays on an irregular basis. Membership is $20 a year, and there are ninety regional chapters, all of whom seem to be exceptionally active. Members are drawn from all aspects of the industry (suppliers, grape producers, home wine makers, armchair connoisseurs, and wine merchants), and the society sponsors educational programs, wine tastings, trips to vineyards and wineries, and gourmet dinners. Each year they publish "Home Wine and Beer Makers Information," a guide that lists suppliers of equipment and services for beer and wine making, as well as suppliers of grapes or juice for home wine makers, or even vines for sale. Since the legalization of exhibitions of homemade wines, the AWS has been preparing standards for wine shows.

692c. **National Association of Amateur Winemakers,** Andover, Hants., England.
Founded in 1951, this British group actively promotes the exhibition of homemade
wines and beers. It has developed standards and prizes for such wine shows. It also
publishes *The Amateur Winemaker,* which has the highest circulation of any such
similar publication (over 25,000 subscribers from around the world). The association also has an active publication arm (Amateur Winemaker Press), which presents
a series of instructional manuals for the home wine maker; all of its publications
are available through British bookstores and by mail order throughout the world.
This is one of the premier wine groups of the world.

Magazines, Periodicals, Newsletters

The best, cheapest, easiest and fastest way of keeping up with news and
views, technological changes, and so forth, is through the serially issued magazine/
newsletter format. The following deal exclusively with the amateur; other wine and
beer magazines, for the armchair critic or the trade, will be found annotated in
Chapter 9. In the periodicals that follow, perhaps one of the best sections is the
classified ads, a section useful to any collector or hobbyist.

693. **The Amateur Winemaker,** 1957- . monthly. $20. South Street, Andover,
       Hants., England.
This is the leading British publication; it includes recipes, articles, a queries column,
and the occasional book review. The publisher also issues paperback reprints or
books culled from previous issues, such as *First Steps in Winemaking, 130 New
Winemaking Recipes,* and *Making Wines Like Those You Buy,* through its pub-
lisher, The Amateur Winemaker Press. As with all British publications, sugar and
Imperial measurements must be watched carefully. This is the official organ of the
National Association of Amateur Winemakers; its circulation is a gigantic 25,000.

693a. **American Journal of Enology and Viticulture,** 1954- . quarterly. $45.
        American Society of Enologists, P.O.B. 1855, Davis, CA 95617.
This is the leading professional journal for the commercial wine maker, but of
course it has a wider application for the home amateur as well. It contains reports
and reviews of original research on the grape vine and its products, with special
emphasis on wine and brandy. Each issue has many technical and scholarly articles
dealing with specific problems that confront the wine maker. Added features are
bibliographic notes, book reviews, and abstracts, as well as news of research in
progress. Highly useful for the serious student.

694. **American Wine Society Journal,** 1969- . quarterly. $20. 3006 Latta Road,
       Rochester, NY 14612.
The Society was founded by Dr. Konstantin Frank, and it concerns oenology,
viticulture, brewing, medical and wine education, and data on American wineries.
Some recent articles have been on themes such as the vitis vinifera in the East,
yeasts, fining, aging, acidity, filtering, unusual food and wine affinities, wine and
nutrition, a tasting and evaluation of sparkling wines, plus some household hints
(e.g., barrel cleanliness), food recipes, book reviews, a report on AWS meetings
(the journal is free to members), and a directory of Ohio wineries (along with maps

and directions). Some of the ads are very important to follow up on, as they are sources of further information and assistance for the home wine maker.

695.   **Beverage Communicator**, 1981- . quarterly. $8. P.O.B. 43, Hartsdale, NY 10530.
This is the house organ of the Home Wine and Beer Trade Association, a group of equipment and ingredient suppliers. It has many articles on wine making and beer making, and it is especially useful for spotting trends that alert the members to the provision of new equipment and new ingredients.

696.   **Home Fermenter's Digest**, 1982- . monthly. $12. P.O.B. 602, San Leandro, CA 94577.
A relatively new publication, with stress on homemade wines and homemade beers. Some of these newer magazines may appeal to the amateur who cannot read through the technical material found in the *AWS Journal.*

697.   **Homebrew Supplier**, 1977- . monthly. $20. South Street, Andover, Hants., England.
This publication, edited by C. J. J. Berry, who also handled *The Amateur Wine-maker*, is devoted exclusively to beer production. This means that the beer-and-wine home producer must subscribe to both sets of British magazines if he wishes comprehensive coverage. But beer for the British is mainly bitters (an ale), or the brown ale or the stout; rarely is it a lager, which is the American taste.

698.   **Practical Winery: The Winemaking Review**, 1981- . bimonthly. $20. 15 Grande Paseo, San Rafael, CA 94903.
This periodical has been written for the professional, but it is still a good technical source for the serious amateur wine maker, or for the wine maker who makes wines from grapes. The emphasis on some of the articles is directed to wine making and wine consumers, with reports on how wine is made.

699.   **Zymurgy**, 1979- . quarterly $8. P.O.B. 287, Boulder, CO 80306.
This is the "house organ" of the American Homebrewers Association. It contains articles on how to make beer from malted scratch, from a can, how to modify recipes, how to apply finishing hops, how to bottle, and so forth. There is also advice on microbreweries (which are tiny regional breweries, selling bottled unpasteurized beer on the lees, i.e., dead yeast).

Catalogs

Less than a decade ago there were few suppliers of wine concentrates, or of such wine- and beer-making supplies as dried hops, wine yeast, or prepackaged and premeasured chemicals (acid blends, pectic enzymes, or grape tannins, stabilizers and sterilizing sulphites). Home brewing and vinification drew upon the imagination of the individual brewer or vintner. Crocks, pans, natural fruits and yeasts, home grape presses, and the magical raisin were used instead of today's readily available specialist supplies. Often, the source of these supplies is now a corner drugstore (as in England), whose back corner shelf may display a selected number of concentrates, hydrometers, syphons, and yeasts. Hardware stores will also have these, as will some well-stocked department stores; and of course there is the franchised Wine-Art Store chain.

But all of these only operate in the larger city, and of course they only cover concentrates for wines and beers. There is still a healthy market for wine juice fans, or for those who prefer to crush their own grapes (and even grow them first). The mails will bring all the backup materials that any amateur or professional oenologist or brewer could desire. It is beyond the scope of this book to identify each and every supplier, for there are hundreds. But we can indicate where such lists will be. There are three leading sources for lists of suppliers and equipment.

For beer and wine concentrates, try the Wine-Art chain. Pick out a telephone book for a large city and look under its name in the white pages or under "Winemaking Supplies" in the yellow, classified section. They have mail order services. For technical materials and lists of evaluated, recommended suppliers of grapes, extracts, musts, juices, and so forth, write to the American Wine Society for its "Home Wine and Beer Makers Information" guide (see entry 692b). For just about everything else, try "Catalog of Supplies for the Amateur Wine Maker and Beer Maker" from SEMPLEX of USA, P.O.B. 12276, Camden Station, Minneapolis, MN 55412. Edited by Fred Schafer, it has been available as an annual since 1962, free of charge. It lists supplies of equipment and books, including British books, on the art of wine making, grape growing, and beer making.

11 *Associations, Societies, and Clubs*

TRADE ASSOCIATIONS

Associations and trade groups are mainly promotional. They are useful for requesting information about a particular service or product, so long as you bear in mind that they are one-sided and deal first with their own members' wishes. Many that deal with a service are happy to give out data and information on request. Associations are always useful for the libraries and contacts that they contain. Certain promotional activities for tourists may be centered in a trade consulate or embassy.

International

700.   **Office International de la Vigne et du Vin**. Paris, France.
This group was formed in 1924, and represents 90 percent of the world's wine and table grape production in thirty-one member countries. It is usually known simply as the O.I.V., and it serves as a clearinghouse for new legislation and relations with governments. Despite it being a government support group, only in 1984 did the O.I.V. get applications for membership from Canada and the United States.

United States

701.   **American Bottled Water Association**. 1010 Vermont Ave, N.W., Washing-
        ton, DC 20005.
Founded in 1959 with a current membership of about 250, this group provides a focal point for the common meeting ground between owners and operators of bottled-water plants, dealers and distributors, with the prime purpose of "advancing knowledge and promoting improved" practices. It publishes a newsletter and *Bottled Water Reporter* (bimonthly), a good source for up-to-date information, facts, and figures. This is a useful association for delving into beverage matters.

702.   **American Society of Barmasters**. P.O.B. 1080, Louisville, KY 40201.
"To stimulate increased public acceptance of our nation's fine bars and taverns," this group encourages the creation of original mixed-drink recipes through its

biennial Early Times National Mixed Drink Competition. The association is a good source for cocktail recipes and new things to do with alcoholic spirits.

703.   **Association of American Vintners.** P.O.B. 84, Watkins Glen, NY 14891.
Founded in 1978 with a current membership of ninety-six, this group is restricted to wine producers and suppliers *east* of the Rocky Mountains. The group provides legislative and consumer information, as well as maintaining lists of new and old wineries—whether members or not—for other non-West Coast wineries. For the consumer, it is a good source for maps of the growing areas, special events, touring notes, and routes.

704.   **Association of Tequila Producers.** P.O.B. 58083, World Trade Center, Suite 147, Dallas, TX 75258.
This group was founded in 1979 to promote tequila. It sponsors seminars, and publishes histories and free literature on the production and lore of tequila, along with food and drink recipes.

705.   **Brewers Association of America.** 541 W. Randolph Street, Chicago, IL 60606.
Founded in 1942, this group is devoted to the smaller and regional brewers of beer. There are about thirty current members, and they receive a semi-monthly *Bulletin* with news and views, facts, and figures. The group used to be known as the Small Brewers Association.

706.   **Distilled Spirits Council of the United States.** 1300 Pennsylvania Building, Washington, DC 20004.
Also known as DISCUS, this association was founded in 1973 as a merger between the Distilled Spirits Institute (founded in 1933), the Licensed Beverage Industries (formed by a merger in 1946 of several other groupings), and the Bourbon Institute (formed in 1958). It has thirty current members as the national trade association of producers of domestic beverage distilled spirits and distillers' dried feeds. Through its publications program (some resources have been noted in chapter 8, dealing with Trade and Technical materials) it provides statistical and legal data for both the industry and the media. Through its 2,000-volume library and occasional consumer relations sheets, it provides a dialog with the public. A good group for all kinds of domestic distilled spirits data.

707.   **National Association of Beverage Importers.** 1025 Vermont Ave., N.W., Suite 1205, Washington, DC 20005.
Founded in 1934 with a current membership of about seventy-five, this group represents importers of alcoholic beverages. Through its many publications such as *Import Report* (monthly), *Statistical Reports* (monthly), and its annual *Statistical Review*, it compiles and reports statistics from various sources, including the Bureau of the Census and the Internal Revenue Service. Before 1978 it was known as the National Association of Alcoholic Beverage Importers. Its main concerns are promotion of specific types of wines and spirits, and to this end it has special committees that deal with beer, Champagne and sparkling wines, Cognac, fortified wines, German wines, Italian wines, Rioja wine (from Spain) and Scotch

whiskey. As the major umbrella group dealing with "imported" wines, it also sponsors talks and lectures by visiting producers from other parts of the world.

708.   **National Licensed Beverage Association.** 309 N. Washington St., Alexandria, VA 22314.
Founded in 1950 with a current membership of over 40,000 (and local regional groupings), this trade association represents bars, taverns, restaurants, cocktail lounges, and hotels selling alcoholic beverages for on-premises consumption. Through its publications such as the *Brief News Update* (monthly), the bimonthly *News,* and various annual directories and compendia of statistics, it keeps its membership alert to impending legislative changes and also provides forums for discussion of new techniques.

709.   **National Liquor Stores Association.** 1025 Vermont Ave., N.W., Suite 1004, Washington, DC 20005.
Founded in 1933 with a current membership of some 10,000 stores and various regional groups, this association serves as the trade group looking after the concerns of the package liquor store. It has a quarterly publication (*News and Views*) and an annual, *Directory.*

710.   **National Wine Distributors Association.** 101 E. Ontario Street, Room 760, Chicago, IL 60611.
Founded in 1978 with a current membership of 205, this is a grouping of independent wine distributors and "provides information, guidance, and programs designed to assist members in achieving their potential in the wine business." It sponsors seminars and lectures, provides educational materials, and compiles statistics for its monthly *Wine Marketing Perspectives.* It also publishes special reports and a listing of wine distribution opportunities.

711.   **Sommelier Society of America.** 435 Fifth Avenue, New York, NY 10016.
Founded in 1954 with a current membership of six hundred, this group "seeks to impart greater knowledge of wines and spirits among those who serve and sell these products." Wine stewards, members of the food trade, wine importers and distributors, and wine connoisseurs form the bulk of the members. It certainly tries to provide enlightenment to all of its members, through operating a correspondence school on all areas of wines and alcoholic beverages, conducting Wine Captains Seminars in New York (as well as holding monthly tastings), and by sponsoring tours of the world's wine areas. Its commitment to information dispersal is seen by its maintenance of a library and a monthly *Newsletter.*

712.   **United States Brewers Association.** 1750 K Street, N.W., Washington, DC 20006.
Founded in 1862, this group represents manufacturers responsible for about 86 percent of industry sales in the brewing business. It maintains a library of over 5,000 volumes on the beer and brewing industry. It publishes the *Brewers Almanac* (annually) and various pamphlets such as *The Story of Beer: The Beverage of Moderation; Barley, Hops and History;* and materials for parties and cooking with beer.

713.   **Wine and Spirits Guild of America.** 1766 Dupont Avenue South, Minneapolis, MN 55403.
Founded in 1948 with a current membership of about forty, this group represents liquor firms dealing with over five hundred retail wine and spirits outlets. With its library of books and pamphlets and data collection on wines and spirits, it promotes an exchange of information on merchandising, marketing, and buying of wines and spirits.

714.   **Wine and Spirits Shippers Association.** 11800 Sunrise Valley Drive, Suite 410, Reston, VA 22091.
Founded in 1976 with a membership of 235, this group is concerned with importing and distributing alcoholic beverages. It is mainly involved with efficient and economical—but safe—distribution of beverages, through effective packaging. It deals with many foreign countries to ensure that packaging standards are up to American strengths. A useful group, particularly if you have to move a wine cellar to another country. They won't do it for you, but they can provide good advice.

715.   **Wine Institute.** 165 Post Street, San Francisco, CA 94108.
Founded in 1934 to upgrade the industry after Repeal, this association represents some 370 California winegrowers. It conducts research and market surveys, directs public relations, sponsors wine technology studies, compiles statistics, and researches the wine history of California. For all this it maintains a 3,500-volume library. Its *Monthly Bulletin* contains appropriate statistics, and the Institute usually provides free technical review service on checking the accuracy of any wine writer's manuscript, so long as it is on California wine. One useful publication is its *California Wine Wonderland,* an annual short tour guide, available free.

Canada

716.   **Association of Canadian Distillers.** 350 Sparks Street, Suite 506, Ottawa K1R 7S8.
Founded in 1947, this group represents all the manufacturers of spirits in Canada, and serves as a united front against the burden of taxation as applied by the provincial monopoly stores. It is very active in promoting an awareness of the social benefits and social ills of alcohol, as well as the actual pricing of a bottle of spirits.

717.   **Brewers Association of Canada.** 151 Sparks Street, Suite 805, Ottawa K1P 5E3.
This is the national trade association for Canada's brewing industry, founded in 1943. It collects and distributes industry statistics on sales and materials, performs research work, and maintains a library. It also publishes many pamphlets and other promotional items, most of which deal with cooking and beer.

718.   **Canadian Wine Institute/Wine Council of Ontario.** 89 The Queensway West, Suite 404, Mississauga, Ontario L5B 2V2.
This group represents the interests of the wine industry in Canada, particularly the interests of the Ontario area (which is mainly the Niagara peninsula, but also

includes the north shore of Lake Erie). It maintains a library and publishes various pamphlets concerning recipes, tastings and parties.

United Kingdom

719. **Campaign for Real Ale (CAMRA).** 34 Alma Road, St. Albans, Herts., A11 3BW, England.
This group actively promotes the concept of drinking unpasteurized, freshly-made ale with no preservatives and of a strong flavor. It has been instrumental in bringing back the good-quality ales to England. It publishes the *Good Beer Guide* (a listing of pubs and the beers that they serve) and a newsletter, *What's Brewing?* A good group for information about British beers, and ales in general.

720. **English Vineyards Association.** York House, 199 Westminster Bridge Road, London SE 1, England.
This group is devoted to maintaining grape vineyards in England. It publishes a quarterly *Journal* for the dissemination of information. More and more "English wine" is being made, with grapes suited to a colder climate, such as those of the Germanic style or of the type produced in the American Pacific Northwest.

721. **Scotch Whisky Association.** 17 Half Moon Street, London W1Y FR8.
Designed "to promote and protect the interests of the Scotch Whisky trade at home and abroad." Produces movies and a Scotch Whisky Distillery map, statistical reports, and brochures such as *Scotch Whisky* (well-illustrated with historical photographs), which describes the process of making Scotch. Materials are available in six languages.

PROFESSIONAL AND SCIENTIFIC SOCIETIES

722. **American Society of Brewing Chemists.** 3340 Pilot Knob Road, St. Paul, MN 55121.
This group produces a *Journal* (1940-) and a *Newsletter* for up-to-date information on the matter of brewing. The association does original research and publishes lab reports focussing on technological improvements.

723. **American Society of Enologists.** P.O.B. 1855, Davis, CA 95616.
Founded in 1950, this group seeks "to promote technical advancement of enology and viticulture through integrated research by science and industry; to provide a medium of exchange of technical information; [and] to improve wine and grape quality." It publishes the quarterly *American Journal of Enology and Viticulture.*

724. **Independent Wine Education Guild.** P.O.B. 883, Station Q, Toronto M4T 2N7, Canada.
The only such group in North America affiliated with the British Wine and Spirit Education Trust (the group that awards the Master of Wine appellation upon the successful completion of three layers of courses). The Canadian group seeks to

improve the appreciation and wise use of beverage alcohol, and to establish a high level of professionalism within the industry and among the public. To this end, it has adapted—for correspondence—the first two layers of the M.W. designation courses (the third layer is only applicable to the British wine trade, since it is all about legislation and regulations that only apply to that country).

725.   **Master Brewers Association of the Americas.** 4513 Vernon Boulevard, Madison, WI 53705.

This professional association, founded in 1887, is open to brewers only It publishes the informative *MBAA Technical Quarterly* (since 1964) and the *MBAA Communications* (for news, since 1975).

725a.   **Society of Wine Educators.** 1048 Oak Hills Way, Salt Lake City, UT 84108.

Founded in 1977 with a current membership of five hundred, this group is open to individuals who have taught wine appreciation, wine making or other wine related courses in the past three years to a "well-defined or professional audience." It has a quarterly newsletter—*SWE Chronicle*—with book reviews, it publishes a guide to wine courses, and recently it has encouraged and improved wine writing by offering a *Resources Catalog* to the members.

726.   **Vinifera Wine Growers Association.** The Plains, VA 22171.

Founded in 1973, this group is comprised of grape growers and wine makers united to expand technology in the premium wine-growing field, such as those produced from the vinifera family (cabernet sauvignon, chardonnay, riesling, pinot noir, etc.). It collects, analyses, and disseminates information as a clearinghouse, always concentrating on the latest in the area of techniques. Its scope embraces the commercial, state, and federal agencies, as well as foreign countries. It conducts seminars, sponsors awards, publishes books (and the *Vinifera Wine Growers Journal,* a quarterly), and holds wine festivals, and it is a resource for speakers.

727.   **Wine Masters Guild of California.** 500 Sansome Street, San Francisco, CA 94111.

This group of professional wine masters in the California industry serves as a clearinghouse for the latest developments in the state and abroad. Through its *News* (a monthly), it reports on statistics, updates, and new techniques, along with book reviews.

PROMOTIONAL ASSOCIATIONS

Australia

728.   **Australian Wine and Brandy Corporation.** 55 Handmarsh Square, Adelaide SA 5000, Australia.

This group conducts correspondence courses (one such is called Wine Appreciation Course) based on Australian wines; it also produces maps, brochures, and booklets as well as films.

France

729.   **Food From France, Inc.** Food and Wine Information Center, 1350 Avenue of the Americas, New York, NY 10019.
This group represents various trade and promotional groups dealing in French wines, foods, and tours. It is a one-stop place of inquiry for the novice. The West Coast office is at 400 Montgomery Street, San Francisco, CA 94104.

The French wine trade is very well organized in its approach to promotion. Each wine-producing area has either a promotion board or a consortium that regulates production and engages in promotion. Various "comités de vin" are coordinated by the Comité National des Vins de France, and all have colored maps of "Routes du Vin," usually 24" by 36", with French, English, and sometimes German texts. These notes summarize the characteristics of the local wines. Highway maps are sometimes provided for tours, and these are detailed as to locations of vineyards. Cooperatives, especially in the non-A.O.C. areas, carry out wide promotional and tourist activities, with statistics, brochures, more maps and histories, lists of restaurants and hotels, lists of exporters and importers, and so forth. All of this material is vital for the traveller, and certainly useful for the armchair connoisseur who is attempting to build up a library of resources. No matter what quality of wines are produced in an area, there will be these semipublic bodies (delegates of the producers and negociants) for marketing; they will be able to supply the traveller with almost anything, especially if they are contacted far in advance of actual site visits. The list that follows is fairly complete, and it serves as an example of the various promotional groups available in Europe. Certainly, there are an equal number of similar bodies serving Germany, Italy, and—to some extent—Spain.

General

730.   Comité interprofessionel des vins doux naturels, 19 avenue de la Grand-Bretagne, 66000 Perpignan.

731.   Comité national des vins de France, 43 rue de Naples, 75008 Paris.

732.   Confédération nationale des industries et commerces en gros des vins, cidres, sirops, spiriteux et liqueurs de France (C.N.V.S.), 103 blvd. Haussmann, 75008 Paris.

733.   Bureau national interprofessionnel de l'Armagnac, Place de la liberté, 32800 Eauze.

734.   Bureau national interprofessionnel de Cognac, 3 rue Georges-Briand, 16100 Cognac.

Alsace

735. Comité interprofessionnel des vins d'Alsace, 8 place de Lattre-de-Tassigny, 68003 Colmar (Haut-Rhin).

Bordeaux

736. Conseil interprofessionnel du vin de Bordeaux, 1 cours du XXX Juillet, 33000 Bordeaux.

737. Maison du Vin, Barsac.

737a. Conseil interprofessionnel des vins de la region de Bergerac, 2 place du Docteur-Cayla, 24100 Bergerac.

738. Maison du Vin, Blaye.

739. Maison du Vin, Cadillac.

740. Syndicat viticole des Graves et Graves supérieures.

741. Maison des Vins de Graves, 33720 Podsenac.

742. Syndicat des crus bourgeois du Médoc, 24 cours de Verdun, 33000 Bordeaux.

743. Maison du Vin. St.-Emilion.

Burgundy

744. Comité interprofessionnel de la Côte-d'Or et de l'Yonne pour les vins d'appellation d'origine controllée de Bourgogne, rue Henri-Dunant, 21200 Beaune.

745. Union interprofessionnelle des vins du Beaujolais, 24 blvd. Vermorel, 69400 Villefranche-sur-Saône (Rhône).

746. Comité interprofessionnel des vins de Bourgogne-Mâcon, 3 bis, avenue Gambetta, B.P. 113, 71000 Mâcon.

Champagne

747. Comité interprofessionnel du vin de Champagne, 5 rue Henri-Martin, 51200 Epernay.

Côtes de Provence

748.   Comité interprofessionnel des vins des Côtes de Provence, 3 avenue Jean-Jaurès, 83460 Les Arcs-sur-Argens (Var).

Côtes du Rhône

749.   Comité interprofessionnel des vins des Côtes du Rhône, Maison du Vin. 41 cours Jean Jaurès, 84000 Avignon.

Loire Valley

750.   Conseil interprofessionnel des vins d'Anjou et de Saumur, 21 blvd. Foch, 49000 Angers.

751.   Comité interprofessionnel des vins d'origine du pays Nantais, 17 rue des Etats, 44000 Nantes.

752.   Union viticole Sancerroise, Comité de propagande des vins de Sancerre, Mairie, 18000 Sancerre.

753.   Comité interprofessionnel des vins de Touraine, 19 square Prosper Merimée, 37000 Tours. [also look after Vouvray, Chinon, Bourgueil, and Montlouis wines].

Other Regions

754.   Groupement de développement viticole, Maison de l'agriculture, 46 avenue Jean-Jaurès, 18000 Bourges.

755.   Groupement interprofessionnel des vins de Corse, 6 rue Gabriel-Pèri, 2000 Bastra.

755a. Syndicat interprofessionnel du vin de Cahors, Chambre d'agriculture du Lot, Avenue Jean-Jaurès, 46001 Cahors.

756.   Comité interprofessionnel des vins de Fitou, Corbières, et Minervois, Route nationale 113, 11200 Lézignan-Corbières.

757.   Comité interprofessionnel des vins de Gaillac, 8 rue de Pere-Gibrat, 81600 Gaillac.

758.   Société de viticulture du Jura, Maison de l'agriculture, 39000 Louis-le-Saunier.

759.   Syndicat des producteurs des vins à appellation controllée Jurançon, 5 place de la République, 64000 Pau.

760.   Syndicat de défense des vins de Madiran et du Pacherenc, Château de Crouseilles, 64000 Crouseilles.

760a.   Confédération générale des vignerons du Midi, 1 rue Marcelin-Coural, 11000 Narbonne.

761.   Comité national du Pineau des Charentes, 31 avenue Victor-Hugo, 16000 Cognac.

762.   Syndicat régional des vins de Savoie, 11 rue Métropole, 73000 Chambéry.

763.   Fédération régionale des V.D.Q.S. Savoie-Bugey-Dauphine, 2 place du Château, 73000 Chambéry.

Germany

764.   **German Wine Information Bureau**, 3rd Floor, 99 Park Avenue, New York, NY 10016 (in Canada: 20 Eglinton Avenue East, Toronto M4P 1A9).
The Bureau offers a correspondence course, along with appropriate booklets and brochures, maps, charts, and posters. Audio-visual materials include slides, films, and tapes. It administers the German Wine Society and distributes German wine periodicals in the United States. Throughout Germany, as in France, there are many wine museums, wine fairs, and tourist sources of vinous information—all of these can be collated through the German Wine Information Bureau. In Germany itself there is the German Wine Institute (Deutsche Weininstitut, Gutenbergplatz 3 - 5, 6500 Mainz, West Germany), which runs intermediate and advanced residential courses on German wines. The Institute will prepare about 150 different wines for sampling, as well as trips to local festivals and vineyards, guest speakers, meals, and so forth—all conducted in English, for a week at a time, several times throughout the year (the advanced course is only given in October). Through the German Wine Institute, should you choose not to go, you can still get many audio-visual devices (slides, tapes, films, maps, posters) at reasonable cost.

Italy

765.   **Italian Wine Center**, 499 Park Avenue, New York, NY 10022 (in Canada: 1801 McGill College Avenue, Suite 750, Montreal H3A 2N4).
Operated out of the Italian Trade Commission offices (these are located in several cities: Houston, Chicago, Los Angeles, San Francisco, Washington, D.C., and Atlanta). The Wine Center produces the *Infovino* newsletter and gives some industry support; it also arranges for educational tours, trade programs for retail stores, and a variety of free materials. In New York, the Center has "The Enoteca," a tasting area for the trade and the press that is operated every Wednesday afternoon. The rest of the space and time is given over to a display of some 2,000 D.O.C. wines and bottles to admire. There is also a graphics library with materials

that can be loaned or rented: these are photographs (color, black and white), slides, and 16mm films. Scattered throughout Italy, and usually affiliated with the local consortium of wine producers and tourist assistance, are the *enoteche*. These are one-stop research, tasting, and purchasing establishments that are located in all the wine-producing areas of Italy. In some respects they are an advancement on the French ideal of the tourist support, since here in Italy the traveller can actually buy the wine he has been tasting or looking at.

Portugal

766.   **Portuguese Information Bureau,** 727 Park Avenue, New York, NY 10021.
As an office for potential tourists to Portugal, this center provides a wealth of information from a variety of sources. In addition, it can provide wine posters, charts, vineyard maps, and wine-bottle labels.

Spain

767.   **Sherry Institute of Spain,** 220 East 42nd Street, New York, NY 10017.
Booklets and maps can be obtained from this group, although it is mostly geared to trade support rather than to tourism.

768.   **Rioja Wine Information Bureau,** 770 Lexington Avenue, New York, NY
        10021.
More booklets and maps for this fine red wine area. Many of these functions—the Rioja and the Sherry information—may be replaced by the emerging Viña España group, which is the Spanish Wine Society that has been forming up in other countries. This group was established in Canada in 1984, and in England in 1983. It is due to arrive in the United States in 1985, as a club that can offer information to the consumer about Spanish alcoholic products, as well as take case orders and conduct tastings.

United States

769.   **Kosher Wine Institute of America,** 175 Fifth Avenue, New York, NY
        10010.
The Institute tries to promote kosher wine products throughout the world, along with wine-associated kosher products such as cheese and crackers. By disseminating this information it wants to tell people that the new grape cultivars being developed will facilitate *dry* table wines as well as sweet. It conducts lectures and tastings in the New York area.

770.   **Oregon Winegrowers Association,** 4640 S.W. Macadam, Suite 150, Port-
        land, OR 97201.
This group seeks to promote Oregon wines; it has the appropriate backup materials of brochures, maps, slides, posters, and so forth.

771.   **Washington Wine Institute,** 1717 136th Place, N.E., Bellevue, WA 98005.
This group seeks to promote Washington wines; it, too, has the appropriate backup
materials of brochures, maps, slides, and posters.

772.   **Wine Appreciation Guild,** 155 Conn Street, San Francisco, CA 94107.
The Guild acts on the behalf of the California wine producers. It offers a free
correspondence course called "Wine Study," and it has several pamphlets available
for national distribution. It has a component tasting kit (for the understanding of
how wines taste), additional wine courses for the restaurant and the retail store
trade, a library of materials about California and American wines, tour guides to
California and its wineries, calendars, photo posters of grape varieties or wine
scenes, map posters, miniposters of artwork, wine cellar records and blanks, art
prints and lithographs (mainly from Christian Brothers Wine Museum), European
wine maps, a wine selection wheel (matching wine with food), and a book-ordering
service. Its publications program extends to a series of cookbooks, usually around
128 pages and $7.95 in paper covers, and it also offeres for sale some wine-related
items as corkscrews, wine glasses, placemats to contain wine glasses with illustrations for tasting, and so forth.

Other Countries and Promotional Clubs

There are many other groupings of associations that have come together
for promotional purposes; all of these are subsidized to a greater or lesser degree,
and hence it is worthwhile to attend their tastings. They are scattered about in
other countries; some are in the United States as well. For example, there is (in
Canada) the Austrian Wine Society, the Viña España, the Amici dell'Enotria (Italian
wines), the German Wine Society with its thirteen chapters, Les Compagnons
des Vins de France with its nine branches, the Society for American Wines with its
seven branches, and the Australian Wine Society with its two branches.

CLUBS

Only national and international societies are listed here. Regional societies
are too numerous, too varied, and of an uneven quality (and many do not even
accept members outside a definite geographic area). The best source for obtaining
a list of these nearby clubs would be at the largest retail wine and liquor merchant
in town. In fact, he may even have a club of his own. Sometimes these stores will
publish a buying guide or newsletter. The local wine writers and wine educators
will also know of local clubs and groups. Most of these clubs publish a newsletter
for membership information. The International Wine and Food Society has a large
listing of regional branches that are affiliates, and this information may be obtained
from the Society's headquarters in London, England. Some commercial (i.e., profit-
making) clubs may flourish, and they may deal with importing wine cases in bulk
for resale to their membership. In effect, some of them are simply retail wine
importers doing business by mail. Other clubs exist that are promotional, that is,
they stress only one country's type of wine. Usually these clubs have been

subsidized somewhere along the way, and they do represent good value in that the tastings are cheap or free. But do recognize them for what they are: promotion. Some of these are listed in the previous section that deals with promotional associations.

Wine Clubs

773.   **Les Amis du Vin,** 2302 Perkins Place, Silver Spring, MD 20910.
Founded in 1965, this is a semicommercial operation for 40,000 members with 250 local groups. It is for "wine lovers devoted to the appreciation of fine wine and the art of leisurely dining." It has a "Wine-of-the-Month" plan, regular group wine tastings and dinners, wine area tours, and a speakers' bureau. It ties up with store owners in order to provide the wines, and it publishes a magazine.

774.   **Antique Bottle Collectors Association,** P.O.B. 467, Sacramento, CA 95802.
Founded in 1959, this group has about 1,700 members with 15 local clubs. Stress is on collecting old or antique bottles, such as historical flasks whiskey and liquor bottles, and wine bottles. Through a monthly publication, *The Pontil*, it promotes bottle collection and historical research into the methods of manufacture. Meets every June in Sacramento.

775.   **Commanderie de Bordeaux,** 99 Park Avenue, New York, NY 10016.
This group was founded in 1958; it currently has 600 members in 11 regional clubs. It seeks "to develop respect and appreciation for the wines of Bordeaux and encourages a temperate and understanding use; to foster the skillful preparation and appreciative consumption of haute cuisine." There are wine tastings and dinners within this gourmet society.

776.   **Confrérie des Chevaliers du Tastevin, Commanderie d'Amerique,** 22 East 60th Street, New York, NY 10022.
Founded in 1934 in France, this group has about 1,600 members in 30 local groups. Its headquarters are at the Château de Clos de Vougeot, Cote-d'Or, France. It is quite similar to the Commanderie de Bordeaux, except that the emphasis is on the use of Burgundian wines and cuisine.

777.   **The Enological Society of the Pacific Northwest,** 200 Second Avenue, Seattle, WA 98109.
This club sponsors festivals, lectures, seminars, and tours, as well as tastings and dinners. There is a newsletter, usually ten times a year.

778.   **The International Society of Wine Tasters,** 60 Sheridan Avenue, Williston Park, NY 11596.
Founded in 1964, this group currently has 1,800 members in four local groups. There are monthly wine tastings, seminars, and a library. It also provides speakers and a monthly newsletter, *Wine & Dine.*

779.   **International Wine and Food Society**, 32 - 36 Fleet Lane, London EC4M
        4YA, England.
Founded in 1934 by André Simon, this group has over 7,500 members affiliated
with about 30 branches in Great Britain and 100 overseas. It is dedicated to promoting the appreciation of wine and food, and it seeks improvement in the standards of cookery. Off and on, it used to publish a magazine or journal; now it has
an annual "book" and a quarterly newsletter produced on a regional basis. The
North American Committee seeks to coordinate all the activities of Canada, the
United States, and Mexico. The Society publishes many books, some of which are
available in North America from commercial publishers. In England it maintains
a library and it has weekly meetings in London (tastings, dinners, etc.) as well as
annual conventions around the world. Each chapter is free to set its own rules
on admission and on programs.

780.   **Napa Valley Wine Library Association**, P.O.B. 328, St. Helena, CA 94574.
This association has about 1,500 members; these are people interested in Napa
Valley wines, and they support and maintain a library of books, periodicals, and
ephemera about the Napa Valley wines. The library has 2,000 volumes. Other
services: there are conducted wine tastings, a quarterly newsletter, a published
bibliography of holdings, and oral histories.

781.   **Society of Medical Friends of Wine**, P.O.B. 218, Sausalito, CA 94965.
Founded in 1939 and restricted to those physicians and surgeons interested in the
nutritional and therapeutic values of wine. One of their purposes is to stimulate
scientific research on wine; another is to develop an understanding of its benefi-
cial effects, and a third is to encourage an "appreciation of the conviviality and
good fellowship that are part of the relaxed and deliberate manner of living that
follows its proper use." Quarterly dinners and annual vintage tours are the highlights for the more than 350 members who, not surprisingly, live in the Bay Area
for the most part. Their *Bulletin* has articles, quotations, book news, and tasting
notes; this is a good club for physicians to belong to.

782.   **Wine Label Circle**. 4 High Street, Tisbury, Salisbury, Wilts., England.
Founded in 1952, 160 collectors of wine-bottle labels meet in four branches
to discuss the "stimulation and encouragement of research, the interchange of
views between members, and the general study of decanter labels." A semi-annual
Journal is somewhat like the *Beer Mats Magazine*, and this club resembles the
Labologist Society (beer labels).

Beer Clubs

783.   **Beer Can Collectors of America**, P.O.B. 9104, St. Louis, MO 63117.
Founded in 1970, the approximately six hundred members who collect beer cans
(first produced in 1935) specialize in rare regional cans that are no longer produced.
Some members have over 5,000 cans. The prime purpose of the club is to provide
members with an opportunity to trade and buy beer cans, which is done at the
club's annual *can*vention. Individual members can apply for a mailing list of collectors so that contacts can be made on a person-to-person basis.

784.   **Beer Drinkers International, Inc.,** P.O.B. 8536, Calabasas, CA 91302.
This very loosely run club tries to foster appreciation of the art of brewing, and sometimes it awards letters of commendations to breweries. It gives out certificates, decals, discounts at some beer stores and restaurants, caps, T-shirts, aprons, badges, and so forth. There is a newsletter with chapter news; one of the aims of the club is to taste as many different beers as possible.

785.   **British Beer Mat Collectors' Society,** 142 Leicester Street, Wolverhampton WV6 0PS, England.
About five hundred members participate in the hobby of drip-mat collecting throughout the world, although the beer mat is largely a British phenomenon. Breweries have, since 1920 produced monthly offerings of new designs, and these are collected. *Beer Mat Magazine* is a monthly that lists items for trade and establishes the bid-ask price for rare, mint-condition mats.

786.   **La Confrérie du Houblon d'Or,** Hilton International Hotels, Quebec City, Quebec, Canada.
This club also celebrates the drinking of beer, albeit in a more refined style. It is known as the Brotherhood of the Golden Hops, and it is a North American affiliated section of the Chevaliers de la Bière (Knights of Beer), which is the club in France.

787.   **Labologists Society,** 335 Ditching Road, Brighton, BN1 6JJ, England.
Two hundred members collect beer labels and study the history of breweries, along with the social history connected with the brewing trade. Founded in 1958.

787a.   **National Association Breweriana Advertising,** c/o Brewers Digest, 4049 West Peterson Avenue, Chicago, IL 60646.
Composed of people from throughout the United States who specialize in collecting "breweriana." Founded in 1972 to support an annual trading convention.

788.   **Stein Collectors International,** P.O.B. 463, Kingston, NJ 08528.
Founded in 1965, now currently has a thousand members in about twelve regional groups. Steins are defined here as covered drinking mugs, usually used for beer. The society acts as a clearinghouse for member queries, sponsors seminars, distributes books, and presents awards. It meets once a year for purposes of trading; it publishes a quarterly, *Prosit.*

FAIRS, FESTIVALS, AND AUCTIONS

Fairs and Festivals

United States

There are some thirty-two wine-judging fairs in the United States, as of December 1983 (figure compiled by Hank Rubin, managing editor of *Vintage* magazine). Not all are important, for some are internal to the industry and hand out all sorts of prizes merely for entering. The best one is the Orange County

(California) Fair, held annually since 1977. It is the largest judging of premium varietal wines in the world (2,307 wines in 49 categories in 1984). It has a mandatory entry policy: all commercially available California varietal wines are judged. And the judging panel are all professional wine makers. Gold, silver, and bronze medals are awarded in 49 categories (there are numerous subdivisions based on price and sweetness levels). The "Awards Booklet," listing the winners, is available for $3.00 (P.O.B. 397, Garden Grove, CA 92642). Other interesting, large wine fairs include the American Wine Competition (held in September, in Hyde Park, New York), sponsored by the Beverage Tasting Institute. It is limited to four varietals: cabernet sauvignon, pinot noir, chardonnay, and riesling. There are about fifteen judges working their way through well over a hundred wines. Similar exhibits are the American Wine Exposition held every February in Dallas, Texas, and the San Francisco Fair and Exposition (annually since 1982; 1,862 wines, from 373 wineries).

Canada

There is an annual weeklong series of activities every September in St. Catharines, within the heart of the Niagara peninsula grape-growing area. This is all for fun. But there are three serious events, though with no prizes: The International Food and Wine Fair is held in October in Toronto. This is sponsored by the Escoffier Society and the wine importers' association, and was begun in 1980. There is an equal emphasis on both wines and foods, along with the related seminars and discussions. About one hundred wine merchants or distributors participate. The Salon International des Vins et Spiritueux/International Wine and Spirits Show, held every October in Montreal since 1979, is quite similar to the Toronto show, except there is more wine and not so much food. The United States Wine Fair is held each June in Toronto, Ottawa, Montreal, and other places. This is a promotional activity, reflecting on about fifty wine-making operations and about 150 wines. There are speakers, seminars, and so forth, covering wines from California, New York, Ohio, Michigan, and the Pacific Northwest. It was started in 1982.

England

There are three major wine festivals. The first is the Bristol World Wine Fair, held for ten days in mid-July. This has about three hundred exhibitors from thirty countries, including Australia, Austria, Belgium, Cyprus, France, Germany, Italy, Portugal, Spain, the United States, and Yugoslavia. In addition to displays and tastings there are seminars and prizes, and sales. It has been held since 1978. The second is the International Wine and Spirit Trade Fair, held every two years since 1970 at the Olympia Exhibition Centre, London, England, from May to June. There are about one thousand entrants from thirty-five or so wine-producing countries. This is run by the Club Oenologique. The last is London Kensington Fair, held annually since 1981 for the trade importers to show off their wines. No prizes; just a sales orientation.

France

The major wine fair in France is the VINEXPO, which began in 1981 as International Wine and Spirits Week, usually the second week of June at the Parc des Expositions in Bordeaux. The materials, though, are all French wines, notably from the Bordeaux area. There are seminars and prizes and tastings. At the same time there is VINITECH, an exhibition of wine-making materials and equipment. Since 1850, the Hospices de Beaune has been running a wine auction, usually the third Sunday in November, in support of the invalid hospital. This is an important auction because over the years the Hospices has had a number of vineyards donated to it, and the auction is of its own wines. The opening prices at the auction set the opening prices for all of the Burgundy wines, each November. These prices are for the current wine crop, still in the barrel (and in some cases still on the lees). At the same time there is a wine festival, with a formal charity dinner and opening of great vintages of the past. There is a general display of Burgundy wines and an exhibit of viticultural machinery.

The majority of wine festivals in France are lighthearted events, normally celebrating the current wine crop. There are no medals or serious tastings, just a lot of dinners and drinking. For a listing, the best idea is to contact the appropriate Maison du Vin or wine museum (as noted above). Just about all the festivals open on Friday or Saturday and close on Sunday night. For example, here is the annual schedule for the Loire valley-Touraine area: Amboise (Easter Day and Aug. 15), Azay-Le-Rideau (last Saturday in February), Bourgueil (first Saturday in February and Easter), Chinon (second Saturday in March), Cravant-Les-Coteaux (Ascension Day), Montlouis (third Saturday in February and August 15), Meusnes (Pentecost), Ouzain (third Saturday after Easter), Pauzoult (May 1), St. Georges-Sur-Cher (Easter), Thesée (First Sunday in July), Tours-Fondettes (second Saturday in February), and Vouvray (last Saturday in January and August 15).

Germany

The situation here is much as it is in France. The big trade fair is held every three years (it was in Stuttgart in 1983). About 60,000 persons attend this technical wine fair to see the offerings of 135 producers (over 1,000 wines), as well as some food products. Most of the wines were German. Local German wine festivals dot the countryside. Hundreds of towns and villages in the wine-growing regions have a Deutsche Winzerfeste, in which they celebrate the local wines and culture, select and crown a wine queen (who must be a daughter of a local grower, must have worked in a vineyard, and must know all about wines), and have a good time. There is a brochure listing the details of where and when, from May to November of each year, obtainable from the German Wine Information Service in New York or Toronto. Some individual technical tastings and machinery products are on view from time to time, as a sales promotion. These can be a trade fair, a wine fair, auctions, exhibitions and displays, or even wine estate sales. An annual program is available from Stabilisierungsfonds für Wein, Gutenbergplatz, 3 - 5, 6500 Mainz, West Germany—the German Wine Institute.

Italy

Italy has its local festivals as well; check with the nearest tourist help group for the listings. For the serious wine scholar, there are three big trade fairs a year: The BIBE Exposition, started in 1970, is held in Genoa every November. Here some 2,000 exhibitors gather from 20 foreign countries to promote their goods. About 500 exhibitors attend MEDIVINI, held in Palermo, Sicily, every October since 1979. Mediterranean and Sicilian wines are featured. VINITALY, begun in 1967, is held in Verona every April. About 1,400 exhibitors attend. Associated with each wine fair are lectures, conferences, materials on sales and distribution, visits to vineyards and cooperatives both before and afterward, and much scientific and technical discussion of wine-making processes—the newest and latest.

Auctions

Auctions are regularly held around the world, subject to legislation about alcoholic consumption. Sometimes tastings are allowed, sometimes they are not. The Heublein auction in the United States very nearly collapsed one year because the local merchants opposed the sale of wines apart from a retail store operation. There are superb advanced tastings that auction participants can engage in, usually upon payment of a very small additional sum of money. For the rest of us, the catalogs of these auctions are particularly enjoyable since they form a bid-ask list of prices, as well as giving us some entertainment through the illustrations and occasional text summaries.

789.   **Christie's Wine Review, 1972- .** $11. London: Christie's Wine Publications, 1973- .

This is an annual record of the actual prices paid at auction for rare wines and vintaged recent wines, with market reports and articles by such British writers as Edmund Penning-Rowsell, Cyril Ray, Harry Waugh, and Michael Broadbent. Recent editions of this annual have had articles on the Christie's wine sale archives of 50, 100, 150 and 200 years ago; a Cognac chronology with vintage notes; the development of British decanters; personal assessment of Bordeaux vintages; current wine markets and surging prices; a continuing history of Christie's; articles on collecting; fortified wines such as ports and their vintages; articles on individual Bordeaux châteaux; black-and-white and color photographs, and so forth. The heart of the catalog, though, is the 50-page "Price Index of Vintage Wines" for about 4,000 wines: Bordeaux, Burgundies, vintage Ports, and others. In 1984 there was a supplement to this index, a separately published 36-page title, "United States Wine Auction Prices," available for $6. Christie's has regular wine auctions in England; the *Review* is a record of the prices paid for the previous year.

790.   Mansell-Jones, Penelope, comp. **Christie's Price Index of Vintage Wines, 1984.** London: Christie's Wine Publications, 1984. 187p. index. $11.

This is a handy compilation of prices for wines sold at auction by Christie's. It has been extracted and summarized from previous *Christie's Wine Reviews.* References are to some 6,000 wines, listed in single columns by type, in vintage order, with the price obtained when last auctioned off (in pounds). There is an alphabetical index to the wines as well. And there is a U.S. section listing the most significant wines and prices (in dollars) at American auctions.

791.   **Heublein Premiere National Auction of Rare Wines, Catalog, 1969- .** P.O.B. 505, Farmington, CT 06032. $15.

Heublein, in addition to being a producer of wines and spirits, also has an annual sale every May of rare or unusual wines, usually some prestigious items from California's wine history, and some from the great vineyards of Europe. Heublein, of course, owns many California wineries such as Inglenook and Beaulieu Vineyards. This catalog has all the listings of the auction with some illustrations (such as wine labels) and tasting notes, a comparative review of wine prices in both Europe and the United States, and an index to previous Heublein selling prices (by types of wines). The price includes admission to the previews of tastings (held in different cities each year) and to the event itself. New to the 1984 edition is the series of comparative charts covering the period 1971-1983 of the most prestigious Bordeaux and ports.

12 *Additional Sources and Resources for Information*

Not everything you need to know about wines, beers, and spirits lies within the covers of a book or periodical, and even associations and societies can be one-sided. For in-depth research, you also need some "additional" sources of audio-visual information, educational courses, computer software, museums and archives, research libraries, and continuing bibliographies that attempt to impose some control over the burgeoning amount of alcoholic beverage information that is unleashed daily. The following twelve categories explore these auxiliary sources, and point the way for further research and resources.

REGIONAL GUIDES AND TOURIST INFORMATION

When searching for tours, restaurants, hotels, and even bed-and-breakfast places, the overall best source to begin with is an umbrella wine association such as the Wine Appreciation Guild in San Francisco (which can direct you to all manner of materials and more sources for information about California wines and wineries), or the Italian Wine Center for all kinds of data about travel in Italy connected with wines, the German Wine Information Bureau, SOPEXA (for France), and so on. Simply write or call any of the associations listed in Chapter 11 of this book. Occasionally there will be specialized tour agencies and regional groupings that will also provide good information. These include, for example in the case of California wines, such groups as the Santa Cruz Mountain Vintners (P.O.B. 2856, Saratoga, CA 95070), in the case of French wines any of the Maison des Vins, and for Italy the "enotecas." Again, see Chapter 11, on associations and societies.

WINE CHARTS AND RATINGS

These are useful as long as you use them with caution. They often contradict each other, but can be safe in determining the relative merits of one year against another if you are pressed for time or find yourself in a strange restaurant or wine store and feel that you must consult a chart. Most charts and ratings are in pocket format, perfect for the cheaters that flip them out surreptitiously from a wallet or purse. They are available just about everywhere. Almost every magazine in the wine business puts one out (usually as a premium for renewal), most wine stores and merchants will have them, most wholesalers and restaurants that pride themselves on wine lists will offer them, and almost all wine societies will put out a card or two. Associations for wines of a certain region or country will have lists, but these must be viewed with caution since they are not likely to disparage a bad year and indeed it will go overboard in promoting a good year. The best, safest charts are from the wine societies—the nonprofit ones, such as the International Wine and Food Society (which rates wines on a one-to-seven scale; its laminated card also serves as a membership card). Rating forms are also available from the Italian Wine Center (and this one is relatively honest), the American Wine Society, and even some wineries. The *Oregon Wine Review* (P.O.B. 10001, Portland, OR 97210) has a pretty good form that is useful for the newly emerging wines of the Pacific Northwest.

Another unusual wine chart is the "Drinkability Odds Chart" from the Beverage Testing Institute, P.O.B. 285, Ithaca, NY 14851. For one dollar you get a fold-out, pocket-sized card that indicates which wines are ready now, and which ones will improve with time. Included are ten French categories, ten California categories, five Italian ones, three from the Pacific Northwest, one for New York—Rioja (Spain), one for both sweet and dry German wines, and a section for Port. The Rioja and the New York columns are useful, particularly since this data is difficult to obtain on your own. But the two categories for German wines are too restrictive.

MAPS

A good source for maps is: Wine and Spirit Education Centers of America, P.O.B. 20450, Atlanta, GA 30325. This group, which sells primarily to wine educators, carries a wide range of maps and charts for all the wine-producing countries, almost always in stock. What follows are some of the better maps that are currently available:

World

792.   **Wine Map of the World.** 40" by 30". color. Bartholomew, 1977. £ 0.95.

Australia

793.   **The Wine Producing Areas of Australia.** 28" by 37". color. Australian Wine and Brandy Corp., 1983. $4.

England

There is very little wine produced in England, but there are maps of Scotch production and beer consumption.

794.   **Beer Map of Great Britain.** 40" by 30". color. Bartholomew, 1977. £ 0.95.

795.   **Harper's Distillery Map of the Scotch Distillers.** 3d ed. 48" by 48". color. Harper's Trade Journals, 1983. £ 1.50.

France

796.   **Decanter's Wine Map of France.** 830mm by 1035mm. three-color. *Decanter* Magazine, 1983. $11 (postage and packing included).

Germany

797.   **German Wine Growing Regions.** 36" by 48". color. Wine and Spirit Education Centers of America, 1982. $5.

Italy

798.   **Carta Enografica d'Italia.** 48" by 36". color. European Media Representatives (11-03 46th Avenue, Long Island City, NY 11101), 1982. $7 (postage and packing included).
This particular map divides the peninsula into five climatic zones, with all of the wine districts numbered and listed and the D.O.C. wines indicated. All the reds, whites, and rosés are grouped together and color coded.

United States

799.   **Wine Atlas of California.** 8½" by 11". color. Donald Holtgrieve (P.O.B. 4313, Hayward, CA 94540), 1978. $9.95.
This has been described by the publisher as "a set of twenty-two maps showing environmental conditions and grape distributions in the state. The maps include temperature, growing seasons, soil, precipitation, and other environmental influences on grape production, as well as several grape varietal distributions." This is for the technically-minded person.

800.   **California Wine Maps.** various sizes. no color. Sally Taylor and Friends (756 Kansas Street, San Francisco, CA 94107), 1981. $3.
Five hundred wineries are indicated, with 32 pages of maps and listings, with "Places to Eat" and "Places to Stay" as recommended by the wine makers. Separately published maps are now available from the periodical *The Wine Spectator* at $3 each. These cover Napa, Sonoma, Lake, Mendocino, Central Valley, Sierra Foothills, and the Coast.

801.   **The Wine Map of California.** 23" by 34". color. H. Shenson International, (650 5th Street, Suite 402, San Francisco, CA 94107), 1982. $6 (postage and packing included).
This map locates the wine-producing regions and about three hundred wineries, designed by Barbara Phillips.

802.   **Northern Sonoma County.** 36" by 48". color. Russian River Wine Road (P.O.B. 127, Geyserville, CA 95441), 1982. price not available.
This map covers forty wineries of three areas: Dry Creek, Alexander Valley, and the Russian River, plus some resorts, accommodation, and restaurants. This is a good example of a regional map.

Other maps can be obtained by perusing the various books dealing with wines (listed in the appropriate sections), such as Hugh Johnson's *The World Atlas of Wine* or the *Atlas of France,* and the *Wine Atlas of Germany.* Many local groupings may have available regional maps; always ask.

POSTERS

Posters make great decorations. They come in a variety of colors and sizes, and they may be new, current, or historical (either in the original or as reproductions). Many posters are free for the asking, if you are polite as you approach the wineries, breweries, or distilleries. Perhaps a wine merchant where you do your shopping may even set some aside. Travel and wine associations also have some posters. Others may be purchased from such groups as the Wine Poster Publishing Company, 1701A Octavia Street, San Francisco, CA 94109 or Vinformation, 1766 Union Street, San Francisco, CA 94123. Some of the more unusual California posters (which must be paid for) are listed below.

803.   **Vintage Wine Merchants Poster** (Box 15F, San Francisco, CA 94115) has a chart that covers the California North Coast. It is 18" by 24", and it evaluates the red wines (1974-1981) and the white wines (1978-1982) from the Napa, Sonoma, and Mendocino Counties. Price is $5. There is also a wallet-sized card available.

804.   **Wine Types Chart,** from the Wine Appreciation Guild, at 21" by 28", in color, is a guide to the use of different wines with different food types (designed by N. Kennedy), $2.50.

805.   **California Wine Poster,** from the Wine Institute in San Francisco, 36" by 48", in color, with a stylized depiction of a bottle of California wine. It explains the history, innovations, climate, and geography of California, and is a guide to the generic and varietal table wines. $3.75 includes postage and packing.

806.   **California Wineries Posters,** 20" by 30", in color, is published by Wine Poster Publishing Co. (1701 A Octavia Street, San Francisco, CA 94109). These are designed in art deco style, on heavy art stock, for six themes: Sterling Vineyards, Piper-Sonoma, Wente Brothers, Sonoma Vineyards, Cresta Blanca Winery, and the London Wine Bar (the latter operating in San Francisco). These are original commissions, at $17.50 each, postpaid.

806a.   **Wine Catalog Posters,** from abroad, is a good set of posters. These are from Christie's Wine Publications, published in 1983. The set is $18 for six posters that are 30" by 20" in dark sepia on antique laid, pure white paper. They are facsimiles of the title pages of interesting old Christie wine catalogs, dated February 1770, May 1777, July 1815, February 1822, February 1877 and June 1901.

VIDEO AND FILM, AUDIO, SLIDES, AND FILMSTRIPS

There are many, many films and video tapes available to the wine and food industry. Most have been put together in an educative mode for the schools of hospitality that dot the country; others have been created to meet the insatiable demands of the tourists. Most involve pretty girls, pretty grapes, pretty countryside, and the inevitable purple crushes done by some old geezer who is called a "wine-master." There is an equally old person who dispenses the wine and tastes it for you; he is called the "cellar master." If you've seen one of these films, you have seen them all. Only the language changes. It may be French one day, Italian the next, Spanish the next week, and it was Portuguese the month before. Every country has these. What follows are some of the more current and *interesting* films and video tapes.

807.   Balzer, Robert Lawrence. **Adventures in Wine.** Tustia, Calif.: Wine Press Ltd., 1982.
Two hours on three video cassettes. The story of wine as narrated by a master of the California wine scene.

808.   Brison, Fred R. and Eric Jones. **The Video Wine Guide.** Mill Valley, Calif.: Serendipity Productions, 1982.
Ninety minutes on one video cassette. Again, mainly California wines.

809.   Lembeck, Harriet. **A Wine Tasting Journey with Harriet Lembeck: An Adventure in Wine Education.** New York: Wine Wisdom Inc., 1983.
Six hours on four audio cassettes. Lembeck, who has a wine school in New York, here tells all about ins and outs of the wine trade. Particularly useful is the fact that the tapes are long and that the set does have correct pronunciation for the foreign-language wine names.

810.   Lichine, Alexis. **The Joy of Wine.** New York: David Geller Associates, 1982.
Eighty minutes on two audio cassettes or two records. This was previously available from MGM records as a commercial distribution in 1972. Lichine, one of the masters of wine (particularly French wines), gives his thoughts and ideas on how wines were made to be drunk. Good, but only available as sound.

811.   **The Video Wine Guide.** Houston, Texas: Video Wine Guide, 1983.
Ninety minutes on two video cassettes. Dick Cavett is the host, along with some names from the wineries in the United States and Europe. Here there is a tour of some of the great vineyards, cellars, and restaurants of the world, with basic data about wines.

812.   **The Wines of California.** Indianapolis, Ind.: Kartes Video Communications, 1982.
Four hours on four video cassettes. This series does a real first-rate job in that they restrict themselves to just one area (California) and they have four hours to do it: all you would want to know (and see) about California varietal red and white wines.

Filmstrips and slides are usually available to many groups and societies from the relevant travel and wine associations, such as the Wine Appreciation Guild, SOPEXA, Italian Wine Center, German Wine Information Bureau, and so forth. These can be rented at nominal cost (or free, with a deposit). Sometimes a speaker can also be provided by the association, one who takes a tour of several such wine appreciation groups throughout a state or region. Trade commissions are another good source, particularly if you are looking for deeper background, or food-related materials.

COURSES AND SEMINARS

These take several different forms. There are short courses available by correspondence through the California, French, Italian, and German wine associations; write to the appropriate association. But nothing beats a personal visit at this level—try to take a study tour, especially one that avoids the "first class" rates of travel, for these people are merely gourmands who only want to eat and drink without learning. Several of the wine clubs and societies sponsor study tours like these. For example, the Society for American Wines (operating in Canada) has an annual tour of California in which the travellers actually stay in the Napa and Sonoma Valleys at modest motels, preferring to spend all their money on the good-quality vintaged wines. Formal courses exist, for degrees in oenology such as the Ph.D. at the University of California at Davis. Then there are short courses offered through extension at universities, colleges, skills exchanges, even high schools. These can be quite useful, but they need to be evaluated and accredited. Certainly the most expensive of these are those offered in somebody's home, and not on a campus somewhere.

In North America, courses are summarized in the *Guide to Wine Courses,* available from the Society of Wine Educators (1048 Oak Hills Way, Salt Lake City, UT 84108). This is a directory of courses given by members of the society throughout North America. Listed are continuing education courses at colleges, in homes, and private courses at hotels and restaurants. The S.W.E. reports that there are thirty-three post-secondary schools in the United States offering credit courses, ranging from simply one course to a Ph.D. program (the one at the University of California at Davis).

For the industry, the Wine and Spirit Education Centers of America (P.O.B. 20450, Atlanta, GA 30325) offer certificate courses to members of the wine and spirit trade. There is a national curriculum, under license from the Wine and Spirit Trust of London (which, in England, leads on to the M.W. designation). In Canada, this course is available from the Independent Wine Educators Guild in Toronto. These are professional-level training programs, available through correspondence or at a regional center; and you don't have to be in the trade to take the course.

In Europe, for the trade of for the interested amateur, there are three good courses. France has the Institute International des Vins et Spiriteux (I.I.V.S.), 10 Place de la Bourse, 33076 Bordeaux, France, which runs four five-day courses per year, concentrating on Bordeaux wines. In Germany, the German Wine Academy (Kloster Eberbach, Mainz, West Gemany) has several courses a year, all in English. These are five-day seminars, with an advanced course each October, and they are available throughout the year. You get to taste and evaluate as well as learn about over 150 different German white wines. Most of the wine regions are visited by bus, and so are various wine cellars. Both the French and the German courses can be accessed through the relevant group (SOPEXA or the German Wine Information Bureau). For a longer length of time, there is the Université du Vin (Château de Suze-La-Rousse, 26130 Suze-La-Rousse), which opened in 1978, mainly for growers in France. The vignerons have the place from October through April, but the rest of the year it is open to *négoçiants,* restauranteurs, and amateurs. It is equipped with laboratories that have the latest in electronic gadgets for wine, vine, and soil analyses. There are also tasting rooms, a wine library, and a museum.

COMPUTER SOFTWARE

This is a newly emerging area. There are, as yet, no Computer-Assisted Instructional programs (CAI) on wines, but there is no reason why one could not be put together by any wine educator conversant with a computer. The software programs that do exist are of the inventory type, so that you can see at a glance what you have in storage. For instance, there are:

813.   **Cellar Master** ($55), from Vintage Information Systems, 1982 (Salem, Oregon), which also comes with the International Standard Wine Identification System (ISWIS).

814.   **Wine Record** ($35) and **Wine Steward** ($35), both from Vintage Information Systems, 1983.

815.   **Micro Barmate** ($40), from Virtual Combanatics, 1982 (Rockport, Me.).

816.   **Wine Cellar** ($40), from W. E. Software, 1982 (Chico, Calif.).

GAMES AND KITS

Some unusual materials here include bumper stickers (I Love Wine, I Love American Wine, Do It in the Vineyard, Statutory Grape, etc.), available from W.I.N.O., P.O.B. 7244, San Francisco, CA 94120. A catalog of wine accessories (collars, stands, glasses, and other doodads) can be had from The Wine Enthusiast, P.O.B. 63, Chappaqua, NY 10514. There is a game, entitled The Winery Game (P.O.B. 111, Vineburg, CA 95487), that was released in mid-1983. It simulates the wine business; players own wineries and buy grapes from different regions, bottle and store the wine, and then try to sell it on the open market. It is a game of matching wits: high-profit strategies versus high cash flow and turnover. It is packaged in a wooden box, with tiny barrels used as markers ($36).

Perhaps better is *Le Nez du Vin Encyclopedia of Aromas,* invented by Jean Lenoir of France. This package contains fifty-four bottles of fragrances representing scents commonly found in wines. With each scent there is a card analyzing it. Price: $250 plus tax (from Francis Mollet, 68 Lockwood Road, Riverside, CT 06978). The cheapest fun of all, though, is Carole Collier's book, *505 Wine Questions Your Friends Can't Answer* (New York: Walker, 1983. 174p.

$3.95 paper). Collier is an old hand at puzzles, since she creates a regular cross-world puzzle in *The Friends of Wine,* the magazine of Les Amis du Vin. There are many chapters here, covering wine making, wine geography, different countries, and different estates. There are about a dozen questions for each topic, such as the eight for Canada that check out as bona fide, and with the correct answers. There are even some questions that deal with themes such as wines in movies (e.g., What wine co-starred with Cary Grant and Ingrid Bergman in Hitchcock's *Notorious*? A 1934 Pommard that concealed some uranium. Or, when the Germans pay Rick's Café a visit in *Casablanca,* police chief Claude Rains recommends what Champagne? Veuve-Clicquot 1926). This book is of particular value for those into "trivia" games or for wine-school instructors who are always looking for questions to throw at their students in the form of a test.

MUSEUMS TO VISIT

The traveller, either in Europe or at home, has ample opportunity to visit wineries. There have been a number of important directories and associations indicated in the preceding chapters. But even without such a listing, most wineries will have a tasting room, which usually has a display of enchanting collections of materials from their past—perhaps an old bottle still containing its original wine, or tools or drinking vessels, even a cask or two. Most wine regions in Europe may put together a collection of equipment, artwork, original tools or other mechanical devices, stemware, and drinking vessels, as well as catalogs (which may be free). Some will even have a "wine library," a collection of old and new bottles for viewing purposes and label reading. Some will also have a library of books and magazines, which may be useful if you are doing research. For all of these, you have to ask, beginning with the local tourist association or group or "maison de vin." The following museums are acknowledged as leaders in their field; they have been arranged and categorized by geography and product.

United States

819.   Barton Museum of Whiskey History, Barton Road, Bardstown, KY 40004.
First opened in 1957, this museum concentrates on bourbon and on glassware, especially prior to 1919.

820.   Falstaff International Museum of Brewing, 1923 Shenandoah Avenue, St. Louis, MO 63104.
Founded in 1960, this museum concentrates on the history of the St. Louis brewing industry. Materials include nineteenth-century brewing equipment, advertising items, tavern furniture, and beer steins.

821.   Greyton H. Taylor Wine Museum, Bully Hill Road, R.D. 2, Hammondsport, NY 14840.
Open May 1 to October 31, this museum housed the original Taylor Wine Company from 1883 to 1920. Included among its exhibits are rare items from Prohibition to Repeal, a large area devoted to the making of Champagne in the nineteenth century, and many displays centering on ancient presses and other old equipment and

tools. In addition to a good wine and viticulture library (stressing hybrids and the Eastern climatic conditions), there is also a unique "Library of Grapes" from all over the world. These two hundred grape varieties are kept flourishing in a temperature- and humidity-controlled glass enclosure. The museum publishes a quarterly newsletter entitled *Vineyard View.*

Canada

822.   Seagram's Museum, 57 Erb Street West, Waterloo, Ontario.
Founded in 1984 by Joseph E. Seagram (one of the largest wine, spirit, and beer sources in the world), this museum was originally known as Barrel Warehouse No. 5 (since 1868). It has now been restored and renovated with a matching addition, at a price of $4.5 million. It is an industrial museum, dealing with the history of distilling and wines. Topics include: cork and cork production, cooperage and barrel making (there is a "living" small cooper's shed here in action), glass manufacture, wine presses, 5,000 bottles (empty), a bottling line from 1890, a wine library of books, antique prints and posters, a flavoring still, and associated modern items to enhance the collection such as audio-visual displays, films, slides, and posters (the latter for sale). Specialty wine and food shops are part of the building's structure. Most of the wine material here came up from the Wine Museum in San Francisco, which closed with the sale to Seagram's in the United States. Thus the wine themes to be continued include: the grape and the vine; the vintage and the harvest; wine making and the vintner; and wine in mythology. Almost 1,000 items were brought up; the corkscrew collection remained with Brother Timothy of Christian Brothers winery. Some books were also dispersed. Free admission.

Austria

823.   Vintners Museum, Krems, Austria.
Audio-visual displays enhance this collection of stemware, barrels, bottles, and other memorabilia associated with wine.

England

824.   The Ark, Tadcaster, Cambridgeshire, England.
This museum concentrates on brewing and pubs in England. There is a collection of handpumps and tall fonts, as well as barrels, glasses, and so forth. Open Tuesday, Wednesday, and Thursday only.

825.   Beer Mat Museum, 6 Brackley Road, Beckenham, Kent, England.
This museum is devoted exclusively to "beer mats," those blotter-like squares placed under glasses of beer to absorb moisture from spillage. Each brewery in the United Kingdom would release a different series every month, and regular patrons of pubs would collect them. At least one copy of each issue will end up in this museum.

826.   Harvey's Wine Museum, 12 Denmark Street, Bristol, England.
This is the only wine museum in the United Kingdom. It also has some travelling exhibits as well. Covered are such topics as the history of wine production, collections of antique glassware, silver items (glass, corkscrews, vessels), and corkscrews. The museum also maintains the Jack Harvey Memorial Library (open by appointment only).

827.   Museum of Cider, Ryelands Street, Hereford, England.
Opened in 1981 with funding by H. P. Bulmer's (the cider people), this museum tells the story of traditional cider making. Displays include a farm cider house with all of its equipment in working order and a complete set of travelling cider maker's tack. The resident cooper uses tools identical to those in use four hundred years ago, and there are remnants of both a 1905 and a 1927 distillery operation, which the museum uses to produce limited quantities of cider brandy (like Calvados).

France

828.   Château Mouton-Rothschild, Bordeaux, France.
The château has a wine museum, as described by Cyril Ray in his book *Mouton-Rothschild.* Other châteaux, perhaps not as prominent, also maintain some kind of wine museum or historical artifacts that deal with their own unique histories.

829.   Musée de vins de Beaune, Hospices de Beaune, Beaune, France.
Open all year, the Hospices de Beaune, which for five hundred years functioned as a hospital, is now also the site of an annual wine auction fund-raising drive to support its current medical activities. Throughout the grounds are scattered many reminders of the past; a wine museum shows traditional equipment and methods of vinification, plus the evolution of wines and vines. It is more of an industrial museum.

830.   Musée de vins de Touraine, Celliers Saint-Julien, 16 rue Nationale, 37000
        Tours, France.
Open every day except Tuesday and five national holidays, with admission set at four francs, this museum was founded in 1975. It is very typical of wine museums—there are hundreds scattered throughout France (not all are free nor are all very good; some are closed and associated with companies only). It concentrates on the activities of the region, in this case, "Jardin de la France"—the garden of France, the prime supplier of wines to Paris, from the Loire area. Special topics include mythology, legend, archaeology, wine and religion, wine and social rites (baptism, weddings, birth, celebrations, feasts), wine fraternities and groups, how wine is made, the good and bad effects of wine (medical aspects), types of wine cellars, and so forth.

Italy

831.   Enoteca Italica Permanente, Sienna, Tuscany, Italy.
Open all year and typical of the "wine libraries" established during the past ten years in Italy—those all-purpose information buildings that also have tourist data, tasting rooms, consumer information, and point-of-purchase units—the Sienna library displays the finest Italian wines available, both current and historical. All the wines may be tasted (except the old ones), either in the many tasting rooms or on the gazebo-like terraces where the vines are especially cultivated. Included in the tasting areas are artifacts, equipment, and drinking vessels, chosen for their historical worth and for interesting decorations.

832.   Museo del Vino, Cantine Lungarotti, Torgiano, Umbria, Italy.
The Lungarotti wine firm welcomes visitors, and like so many other Italian wine firms, it maintains a tasting room and a wine museum (as well as a library of both wines and books to look at and admire). All of it is in the name of promotion, but they are highly useful stopping points for the traveller to pause and refresh himself. Here there are four rooms plus an atrium. The first two rooms are arranged historically, while the last two deal with viticulture and viniculture. The library is in the atrium.

833.   Martini Museum, Martini & Rossi, Pessione, Turin, Italy.
This museum, in addition to dealing with the history of wine making, also presents items associated with the firm Martini and Rossi. Included here are vessels, glassware, jars, amphorae, and wine presses.

Netherlands

834.   Lucas Bols Museum, Rozengracht 103, Amsterdam, Netherlands.
Founded in 1924, this museum celebrates the corporate history of Erven Lucas Bols and Company, the Dutch spirits and liqueur firm. Included are bottles and other objects related to the distillation industry.

835.   Het Nederlands Wijnmuseum Arnhem, Arnha, Netherlands.
This independent foundation has, in addition to its museum, a rare and a current books library in various languages about wine, available for reference only.

836.   Likeurmuseum Verzameling B. J. De Jongh, Lange Haven 74, Schiedam, Netherlands.
Founded in 1950, this is a spirits museum devoted mainly to bottles. There are 6,000 here, all representative of gin and other strong alcoholic drinks, spirits, and liqueurs.

837.   National Gedistilleerdmuseum, Hoogstratt 12, Schiedam, Netherlands.
Founded in 1955 and located in the same town as the Likeurmuseum, this one contains items related to the history of the gin industry. It contains artifacts, bottles, stills, and paintings.

Spain

838.   Palace of Wine, Jerez de la Frontera, Spain.
Open all year, this building was restored in 1972 by the sherry producers who
now use it as their headquarters. The traditional style of the building nicely complements the displays related to the making and enjoyment of sherry. This is the place
to visit for information on the local *bodegas* and for maps, since it serves as an all-
purpose wine library, wine information, and wine-tasting distribution point.

839.   Museo Comarcal y del Vino, Villafranca del Panadès, Barcelona, Spain.
Located in the ancient palace of the former kings of Aragon, this museum contains
a collection devoted to the history of Spanish wine making. The castle itself was
built in 1285; it now stresses the cultural history of wine, especially of the nineteenth century. Open all year.

Switzerland

840.   Musée de la vigne et du vin, 2017 Boudry, Château d'Oex, Switzerland.
This museum, founded in 1957, covers the history of wine making in the Swiss
cantons (French).

841.   Weinmuseum, 1860 Aigle, Schloss, Switzerland.
This wine museum covers the history of wine making in the Germanic Swiss cantons.

West Germany

842.   Deutsches Weinbaumuseum, Oppenheim, Rhein, West Germany.
Founded in 1980 (closed during the winter through lack of funds to maintain the
heating bills), the industrial collections here cover tools, equipment, aids to wine
making (all back to the Roman times), wine presses (there is a giant one from 1790,
while there are others made of wood), vine-pruning knives and hoes, and a cooper's
workshop of 1900. Other areas stress more cultural matters such as drinking vessels,
bottles, corks, caps, labels, glasses, old vintaged wines, carved cask headings, a
history of German viticultural schools, and a typical wine cellar of the mid-
nineteenth century.

843.   German Wine Museum, History Museum of the Palatinate, Speyer, West
          Germany.
Founded in 1910, there are three basic rooms here: the Drinking Room, the Room
of Arms, and the Cup, Jug, and Pitcher Room. There are casks, glasses, bottles,
and corkscrews, with other artifacts that go back to Roman times.

844.   Das Weinbau Museum, Rathhausgasse No. 1, Bratislava, West Germany.
Open daily, this museum is on two floors, with eighteen exhibit halls. It produces
catalogs to its collection, and the materials here stress wood carvings for the cask
heads, pictures, artwork, and decorations.

LIBRARIES

In general, the libraries listed here will respond to requests for information; they may not all loan out books, but these should be requested from or through your local public library anyway. Libraries attached to a business or research firm may honor requests for information, but this is entirely dependent upon what time they have available and how much their work is considered public relations by the firm. Usually they are very cooperative, provided that they think you know what you are doing (i.e., there is nothing frivolous about you) and that you have a *bona fide* reason for using their collection. In addition, many of the associations or clubs listed in that chapter also have working collections of books. Quite often, though, these are not "libraries," and are usually stored in bookcases in people's offices.

None of this should be taken to mean that the libraries are actually open to your physical presence, or that the materials can circulate to you as actual physical borrowing. This is best left up to the well-established Interlibrary Loan Networks that have been put in place for the local library to extend its resources. Nevertheless, personal correspondence and a previously arranged personal visit can sometimes provide access to the materials; it does not hurt to try.

Large General Collections

845.   Hurty-Peck Library of Beverage Literature, 5600 W. Raymond Street, Indianapolis, IN.
Founded in 1959, all kinds of beverage material is collected through the written literature. Holdings include about 6,000 books; there are about 15 journal subscriptions. Their catalog was published as *Beverage Literature: A Bibliography* (Scarecrow, 1971: see the Bibliography section in this book).

846.   Library of Congress, Washington, DC.

847.   National Agricultural Library, Washington, DC.

848.   New York Public Library.

849.   University of California Library, Berkeley, CA.

850.   University of California Library, Los Angeles, CA.

Wines

United States

851.   Bancroft Library, University of California at Berkeley, CA.
This library contains the tapes and transcripts of an oral history series that documented early California history. The series began in 1969; there are twenty-one

interviews thus far, relating the insights and experiences of some of the leading figures in the California wine industry, such as the oenologists Maynard A. Amerine and Albert S. Winkler, the wine makers Louis M. Martini, Ernest Gallo, Ernest Wente, Louis Petri, Edmund Rossi, and the wine writer Leon D. Adams.

852.   University Libraries at the University of California, Davis, CA.
Since Davis is the home of the world's leading oenological education program, it has probably the world's largest collection of technical books. Their special collections include about 2,500 volumes on brewing and fermentation, about 13,000 volumes on oenology, viticulture, and wine (plus over 54,000 archival records and ephemera), and over 22,000 volumes on food sciences (along with some 4,200 archival records and ephemera).

853.   Roy Brady Collection, California State University, Fresno, CA.
Brady was the former editor of *Wine World;* the viticulture and enology collection here numbers almost 6,000 items. There is also a special card catalog to the enology collection.

854.   School of Hotel Administration Library, Cornell University, Statler Hall, Ithaca, NY.
Founded in 1950, this special-purpose library contains over 20,000 volumes and 400 journal subscriptions dealing with every aspect of the hospitality industry: food, wine, engineering, administration, accounting, advertising, sales, etc. It annually publishes *A Bibliography: Hotel and Restaurant Administration and Related Subjects.* Other academic institutions that have hotel or hospitality programs (or simply food courses) will also have library materials in support of the courses.

855.   New York State Agricultural Experiment Station Library, Cornell University, W. North Street, Geneva, NY.
Founded in 1882, this library of about 50,000 books and bound periodical volumes (over 1,000 journals are subscribed to) concentrates on grapes and wines.

856.   Gallo (E. & J.) Winery, Library, Box 1130, Modesto, CA.
Founded in 1969, this library concentrates on the subjects of wine technology, chemical and biological research, statistics and packaging. It has over 9,000 books, about 4,000 cataloged vertical file items, many drawers of trade literature, and 450 subscriptions to periodicals. It puts out occasional weekly and monthly catalogs and bibliographies.

857.   Michigan State Department of Agriculture Library, 1615 S. Harrison Road, East Lansing, MI.
Founded in 1957, this library has some material about wines in addition to other agricultural subjects. Very useful for local materials about Michigan wines. Many other state departments of agriculture maintain libraries that may also have book materials about wines.

858.   Napa Valley Wine Library Association Library, Box 328, St. Helena, CA.
This library is supported by a "Friends of the Library Group" and the St. Helena Public Library (where it is physically located). The subjects include brewing, cooking, drinks, gastronomy, grapes, wine, and wine making. There are over 3,000 books and 150 bound periodical volumes, plus over forty-five subscriptions to magazines. It has many special collections, such as an oral history program, photographs, over 1,500 wine labels, and over 100 reels of microfilm. This is an impressive resource, which also publishes a wine bibliography and *The Reporter*, a newsletter for wine professionals.

859.   Greyton H. Taylor Wine Museum, Bully Hill Road, R.D. 2, Hammondsport, NY.
Like many other museums, the Taylor Wine Museum also contains a library of both historical and current book materials. Museums are useful for their collection of rare printed materials (books, periodicals, posters, labels, etc.).

860.   Wine Institute Library, 165 Post Street, San Francisco, CA.
Founded in 1934, with such subjects as wine and wine making, plus viticulture, this library of over 3,100 books and periodicals specializes in clippings and brochures about the California wine industry.

Canada

861.   Canadian Wine Institute Library, Mississauga, Ontario, Canada.
Emphasis is on Canadian wines, principally of the Niagara peninsula.

862.   Ministry of Agriculture and Food, Horticultural Research Institute of Ontario Library, Vineland Station, Ontario, Canada.
This library deals with fruit, vegetables, food science, wine and wine making in a technical sense. It has many statistical publications, brochures, annual reports, and other documents and pamphlets (and 2,000 books and 1,500 bound periodical volumes and over 250 subscriptions to journals).

863.   Seagram's Museum, Waterloo, Ontario, Canada.
This library now has most of the Wine Museum of San Francisco's library.

England

These libraries (the latter founded by André Simon) serve to keep the members of the British wine trade up-to-date, especially those who have the decoration "M.W." after their names. But they are open to the public for reference use.

863a.   Jack Harvey Memorial Library, Harvey's Wine Merchants, 12 Denmark Street, Bristol, England.
This library forms a part of the Harvey Wine Museum.

864.   Institute of the Masters of Wine/Wine Trade Club Library, Guildhall Library, London, England.

865.   International Wine and Food Society, London, England.
An extensive library is maintained for the membership that is worldwide, although for practical reasons the heaviest use is made by the London and/or English members in general. All of the important books and journals are held here, including some rare items from André Simon, the Society's founder.

Italy

866.   Biblioteca Internazionale "La Vigna", Palazzo Contra porta Santa Croce, Vicenza, Italy.
This is Demetrio Zaccaria's private library, but is available for public consultation upon advance notice. It contains 15,000 books in various European languages, covering fifteenth-century incunabula up through to modern times. Subjects include wine, agriculture, and gastronomy.

Netherlands

867.   Het Nederlands Wijnmuseum Arnhem, Arnha, Netherlands.
This independent foundation has a rare and a current book library in various languages about wine for reference use only.

Beers

United States

868.   Anheuser-Busch Companies, Inc., Corporate Library, One Busch Plaza, St. Louis, MO.
Founded in 1933, and specializing in brewing chemistry and fermentation technology, yeasts, and the history of beer and the brewing industry, this library has over 9,000 books, 17,000 bound periodicals, hundreds of pamphlet boxes and files for clippings, pamphlets, patents, and 550 subscriptions to periodicals.

870.   Cincinnati Public Library.
This library maintains a collection of materials related to the Ohio brewing industry.

871.   Falstaff Brewing Corporation Library, St. Louis, MO.
A library is maintained as well as its museum.

872.   Fleischman Malting Company Library, Chicago, IL.

873.   Fleischman Research Laboratory Library, Stamford, CT.

874.   Jos. E. Schlitz Brewing Co. Library, Milwaukee, WI.

875.   Seibel Institute Library, Chicago, IL.

876.   U.S. Brewers Association Library, 1750 K Street, N.W., Washington, DC.

   Canada

877.   Brewers Association of Canada, 151 Sparks Street, Ottawa, Canada.

878.   Labatt Brewing Company Ltd., Central Research Library, 150 Simcoe Street, London, Ontario.
With holdings of 6,000 books, 3,000 bound periodical volumes, and subscriptions to 450 journals.

879.   Molson Breweries of Canada, Ltd. Information Centre, 1555 Notre Dame St. E., Montreal, PQ.
Founded in 1967, this library has about 1,000 books, a special collection of the history of brewing, 50 periodical subscriptions, and thousands of microfilm cards (as well as material in the form of clippings, patents, and pamphlets).

   Europe

880.   Institute of Brewing Library, London, England.

881.   Institute of Brewing Research Library, Nuffield, Surrey, England.

Spirits

882.   Barton Museum of Whiskey History Library, Bardstown, KY.
Founded in 1957, this library specializes in the history of whiskey prior to 1919. It contains books, catalogs, memorabilia, advertisements, and photographs.

883.   DISCUS: Distilled Spirits Council of the United States Library, 1132 Pennsylvania Building, Washington, DC.

884.   Filson Club Library, Louisville, KY.

885.   Schenley Distillers Library, New York, NY.

SECONDHAND BOOKSTORES

886.   Barbara L. Feret, Bookseller, 138 Crescent Street, Northhampton, MA 01060.
Catalog available.

887.   George's Bookshop, 89, 81 and 52 Park Street, Bristol BS1 5PW England.
This store has catalogs, and in addition to books on wine and food there are also wine maps available. George's Bookshop deals with worldwide mail.

888.   The Wine and Food Library, 1207 West Madison, Ann Arbor, MI 48103.
Mrs. Jan Longone has run this store for over ten years. Her catalogs (available
for $2) cover the topics of gastronomy, art and history of cuisines, wine lore and
vineyards, taverns and inns. She also has back issues of periodicals and pamphlets.

BIBLIOGRAPHIES (OTHER SOURCES OF DATA)

889.   Amerine, M. A. and L. B. Wheeler. **A Checklist of Books and Pamphlets
on Grapes and Wine Related Subjects, 1938-1948.** Berkeley, Calif.: Univ.
of California Press, 1951. 240p. out of print.
There are 1,789 items listed here; annotations are short or partial. This book has
been updated by two supplements: *A Short Checklist of Books and Pamphlets
in English on Grapes, Wines, and Related Subjects, 1949-1959,* 61p., and containing 600 references, and *A Checklist of Books and Pamphlets in English on Grapes,
Wines and Related Subjects, 1960-1968,* 84p., and containing about 900 references
(and it also includes some materials not covered by the earlier, 1949-1959 supplement). Both were published by the University of California at Davis.

890.   Amerine, M. A. and V. L. Singleton. **A List of Bibliographies and a
Selected List of Publications That Contain Bibliographies on Grapes,
Wines and Related Subjects.** Berkeley, Calif.: Univ. of California, Division
of Agricultural Sciences, 1971. 39p. $2.50 paper.
This "bibliography of bibliographies" contains references to about 375 items.

891.   **Catalog of Wine Education Materials.** rev. ed. Salt Lake City, Ut.: Society
of Wine Educators, 1983. various pagings. $25 looseleaf.
First issued in 1982, this catalog is "a listing of wine education aids and resources
available to assist the wine industry, the wine merchant and the wine educator."
It is a continuing project of the Society, and while the tool itself is a good idea,
it has an appalling series of inconsistent bibliographic styles that also makes some
of the book out of date (that is, the editor cannot find an earlier reference that
needs to be excised or revised). There are various chapters on the wine-producing
countries such as Australia, Canada, France, Germany, Italy, South Africa, Spain,
the United States, and so forth, and under each country the trade associations
are listed, educational courses noted, and maps and charts, booklets and films,
slides, newsletters, and wine-touring data are recorded. Other chapters cover a
listing of books (unannotated), magazines (unannotated), cassette tapes of lectures,
general clubs, educational institutions, and wine courses about the country, both in
Canada and the United States.

892.   **Consumers Index to Product Evaluations and Information Sources, 1973- .**
Ann Arbor, Mich.: Pierian Press, 1974- . quarterly (with annual cumula-
tions). $70.
This tool lists the various articles and books published throughout the years concerned, so long as the articles and the books are about the actual *evaluation* of
wines, beers, and spirits. The price is per year. It serves as an index to these books;
for further details about this index, see the note in the section on Consumer
Guides.

893.   Cornell University School of Hotel Administration. **Subject Catalog.**
         Boston, Mass.: G. K. Hall, 1981. 2 vol. $200.
This is a reproduction of the Hotel program's library's card catalog, which includes
the general subjects of hospitality, alcoholic beverages, tourism, and so forth.
A very useful listing of book materials.

894.   Dumbacher, Egon. **Internationale Weinbibliographie, 1955-1965 und
         Sachverzeichnis, 1956-1965 der Mitteilungen Rebe und Wein.** Wien,
         Austria: Bundesministerium für Land- und Forstwirtschaft, 1966. 334p.
         o.p.
About 7,400 references are listed here; now largely continued by *Wein-
Bibliographie* (see entry 904).

895.   **Food Science and Technology Abstracts, 1969-** . Slough, England: Inter-
         national Food Information Service, 1970; distr. by Unipub. monthly.
         index. $790.
This tool also contains abstracts on alcoholic and nonalcoholic beverages. The
annual author and subject indexes also include references to book reviews. Available online through various vendors.

896.   Lucia, Salvatore. **Wine and the Digestive System: The Effects of Wine and
         Its Constituents on the Organs and Functions of the Gastrointestinal
         Tracts: A Selected Annotated Bibliography.** San Francisco, Calif.: Fortune
         House, 1970. 157p. index. $9.95.
The 500 entries here are divided by subject (e.g., intestines, bladders, and so forth),
and within each subject the arrangement is chronological.

897.   Noling, A. W. **Beverage Literature: A Bibliography.** Metuchen, N.J.:
         Scarecrow Press, 1971. 865p. index. $50.
Covers 5,000 titles in total, about 1,200 of which are related to wine, wine making,
and grapes (mostly in English). Another 700 titles are concerned with beer, cocktails, cider, and perry. Most of the balance deals with nonalcoholic beverages.
The tool includes: author list, subject list, description of subject categories, short-
title list, appendices listing the reference sources consulted in this compilation, and
a list of major libraries specializing in the field. Some annotations.

898.   Schoene, R. **Bibliographie Zür Geschichte des Weines.** Mannheim. 1976.
         543p. $50.
There are 6,500 books on all aspects of grapes, wines, and related items, published
since 1471. Schoene cites library holdings for East and West Germany and Austria.
In all, the stress is on German-language works and German wines. There are
multiple indexes: author, title, subjects, and chronological. The overall arrangement
is in subject classified order.

899.   Simon, André L. **Bibliotecha Bacchia.** London, 1935; reprinted London:
         Holland Press, 1980. 2 vols. in one. $130.

A listing of works published before 1600, concerning viticulture, the art of wine making, table manners, drunkenness, decrees and regulations relating to the wine trade, rules of health, medical books, and treatises on agriculture. Volume One comprises incunabula, with 60 facsimile title pages among its 237 pages; Volume Two includes a description of 240 sixteenth-century books that are not mentioned in Vicaire's *Bibliographie gastronomique* (and thus Simon's book complements it).

900. Simon, André L. **Bibliotecha Vinaria.** London, 1913; reprinted London: Holland Press, 1980. 340p. (plus interleaves; over 600 pages total). $130.
This bibliography of 6,000 books and pamphlets deals with viticulture, wine making, distillation, and the management, sales, taxation, use, and abuse of wines and spirits. This is a facsimile of Simon's own copy, which he had annotated, adding hundreds of additional titles onto the interleaved blank pages.

901. Tudor, Dean. **Wine, Beer and Spirits.** Littleton, Colo.: Libraries Unlimited, 1975. 196p. out of print.
This tool listed about 550 references to print and nonprint sources of data about wines, beers, and spirits, as well as names of associations, clubs, trade groups, museums, contact names, sources of out-of-print books, sources of supply for wine- and beer-making equipment, and related materials. It was an annotated bibliography of the leading books of the time (1974), including historical works, literary and musical references, personal notes of contemplation, books about pubs and inns, and so forth—most of them now out of print.

902. Vicaire, Georges. **Bibliographie gastronomique.** London: Derek Verschagle, 1954. 972 columns. out of print.
First published in Paris in 1890, this reprinted bibliography of 2,500 books pertains to food and drink and related subjects, from the beginning of printing to about 1890. The reprint has appropriate indexes and an introduction by André Simon.

903. **VITIS: Berichte über Rebenforschung mit Dokumentation der Weinbauforschung, 1956-** . Siebeldingen, West Germany: Bundesforschungsanstalt für Rebenzuechtung Beilweilerhof, 1957- . quarterly. $9 per year.
Here are book reviews, abstracts, bibliographies, and charts along with summaries of technical research on wine. The text is in English, French, German, Italian, and Spanish.

904. **Wein-Bibliographie: Deutschsprachiges Schriftum in Auswahl und Nachträge aus früheven Jahren.** Traben-Trarbach, West Germany: Weinberg und Keller-Verlags, 1955- . 120 Dm.
This annual covers the years since 1953, listing all available book and periodical materials. Introductions and captions are in English, French, and German, with a stress on German wines and materials.

Index

Numbers in this author-title-association index refer to entry numbers in the text, and not to page numbers.